Girls Transforming

CRITICAL EXPLORATIONS IN SCIENCE FICTION AND FANTASY
(a series edited by Donald E. Palumbo and C.W. Sullivan III)

1 *Worlds Apart? Dualism and Transgression in Contemporary Female Dystopias* (Dunja M. Mohr, 2005)

2 *Tolkien and Shakespeare: Essays on Shared Themes and Language* (ed. Janet Brennan Croft, 2007)

3 *Culture, Identities and Technology in the* Star Wars *Films: Essays on the Two Trilogies* (ed. Carl Silvio, Tony M. Vinci, 2007)

4 *The Influence of* Star Trek *on Television, Film and Culture* (ed. Lincoln Geraghty, 2008)

5 *Hugo Gernsback and the Century of Science Fiction* (Gary Westfahl, 2007)

6 *One Earth, One People: The Mythopoeic Fantasy Series of Ursula K. Le Guin, Lloyd Alexander, Madeleine L'Engle and Orson Scott Card* (Marek Oziewicz, 2008)

7 *The Evolution of Tolkien's Mythology: A Study of the History of Middle-earth* (Elizabeth A. Whittingham, 2008)

8 *H. Beam Piper: A Biography* (John F. Carr, 2008)

9 *Dreams and Nightmares: Science and Technology in Myth and Fiction* (Mordecai Roshwald, 2008)

10 Lilith *in a New Light: Essays on the George MacDonald Fantasy Novel* (ed. Lucas H. Harriman, 2008)

11 *Feminist Narrative and the Supernatural: The Function of Fantastic Devices in Seven Recent Novels* (Katherine J. Weese, 2008)

12 *The Science of Fiction and the Fiction of Science: Collected Essays on SF Storytelling and the Gnostic Imagination* (Frank McConnell, ed. Gary Westfahl, 2009)

13 *Kim Stanley Robinson Maps the Unimaginable: Critical Essays* (ed. William J. Burling, 2009)

14 *The Inter-Galactic Playground: A Critical Study of Children's and Teens' Science Fiction* (Farah Mendlesohn, 2009)

15 *Science Fiction from Québec: A Postcolonial Study* (Amy J. Ransom, 2009)

16 *Science Fiction and the Two Cultures: Essays on Bridging the Gap Between the Sciences and the Humanities* (ed. Gary Westfahl, George Slusser, 2009)

17 *Stephen R. Donaldson and the Modern Epic Vision: A Critical Study of the "Chronicles of Thomas Covenant" Novels* (Christine Barkley, 2009)

18 *Ursula K. Le Guin's Journey to Post-Feminism* (Amy M. Clarke, 2010)

19 *Portals of Power: Magical Agency and Transformation in Literary Fantasy* (Lori M. Campbell, 2010)

20 *The Animal Fable in Science Fiction and Fantasy* (Bruce Shaw, 2010)

21 *Illuminating* Torchwood: *Essays on Narrative, Character and Sexuality in the BBC Series* (ed. Andrew Ireland, 2010)

22 *Comics as a Nexus of Cultures: Essays on the Interplay of Media, Disciplines and International Perspectives* (ed. Mark Berninger, Jochen Ecke, Gideon Haberkorn, 2010)

23 *The Anatomy of Utopia: Narration, Estrangement and Ambiguity in More, Wells, Huxley and Clarke* (Károly Pintér, 2010)

24 *The Anticipation Novelists of 1950s French Science Fiction: Stepchildren of Voltaire* (Bradford Lyau, 2010)

25 *The* Twilight *Mystique: Critical Essays on the Novels and Films* (ed. Amy M. Clarke, Marijane Osborn, 2010)

26 *The Mythic Fantasy of Robert Holdstock: Critical Essays on the Fiction* (ed. Donald E. Morse, Kálmán Matolcsy, 2011)

27 *Science Fiction and the Prediction of the Future: Essays on Foresight and Fallacy* (ed. Gary Westfahl, Wong Kin Yuen, Amy Kit-sze Chan, 2011)

28 *Apocalypse in Australian Fiction and Film: A Critical Study* (Roslyn Weaver, 2011)

29 *British Science Fiction Film and Television: Critical Essays* (ed. Tobias Hochscherf, James Leggott, 2011)

30 *Cult Telefantasy Series: A Critical Analysis of* The Prisoner, Twin Peaks, The X-Files, Buffy the Vampire Slayer, Lost, Heroes, Doctor Who *and* Star Trek (Sue Short, 2011)

31 *The Postnational Fantasy: Essays on Postcolonialism, Cosmopolitics and Science Fiction* (ed. Masood Ashraf Raja, Jason W. Ellis and Swaralipi Nandi, 2011)

32 *Heinlein's Juvenile Novels: A Cultural Dictionary* (C.W. Sullivan III, 2011)

33 *Welsh Mythology and Folklore in Popular Culture: Essays on Adaptations in Literature, Film, Television and Digital Media* (ed. Audrey L. Becker and Kristin Noone, 2011)

34 *I See You: The Shifting Paradigms of James Cameron's* Avatar (Ellen Grabiner, 2012)

35 *Of Bread, Blood and* The Hunger Games: *Critical Essays on the Suzanne Collins Trilogy* (ed. Mary F. Pharr and Leisa A. Clark, 2012)

36 *The Sex Is Out of This World: Essays on the Carnal Side of Science Fiction* (ed. Sherry Ginn and Michael G. Cornelius, 2012)

37 *Lois McMaster Bujold: Essays on a Modern Master of Science Fiction and Fantasy* (ed. Janet Brennan Croft, 2013)

38 *Girls Transforming: Invisibility and Age-Shifting in Children's Fantasy Fiction Since the 1970s* (Sanna Lehtonen, 2013)

39 Doctor Who *in Time and Space: Essays on Themes, Characters, History and Fandom, 1963–2012* (ed. Gillian I. Leitch, 2013)

Girls Transforming
Invisibility and Age-Shifting in Children's Fantasy Fiction Since the 1970s

SANNA LEHTONEN

CRITICAL EXPLORATIONS IN SCIENCE FICTION AND FANTASY, 38

McFarland & Company, Inc., Publishers
Jefferson, North Carolina, and London

LIBRARY OF CONGRESS CATALOGUING-IN-PUBLICATION DATA

Lehtonen, Sanna, 1979–
    Girls transforming : invisibility and age-shifting in children's fantasy fiction since the 1970s / Sanna Lehtonen.
        p.   cm. — (Critical explorations in Science Fiction and Fantasy ; 38)
    Includes bibliographical references and index.

    ISBN 978-0-7864-6136-3
    softcover : acid free paper ∞

    1. Children's stories — History and criticism.   2. Fantasy fiction — History and criticism.   3. Girls in literature.
    4. Magic in literature.   5. Self-realization in literature.
    6. Identity (Psychology) in literature.   7. Age groups in literature.   I. Title.
    PN3443.L44   2013
    809'.89282 — dc23   2013007857

BRITISH LIBRARY CATALOGUING DATA ARE AVAILABLE

© 2013 Sanna Lehtonen. All rights reserved

No part of this book may be reproduced or transmitted in any form or by any means, electronic or mechanical, including photocopying or recording, or by any information storage and retrieval system, without permission in writing from the publisher.

Cover illustration © 2013 Hemera/Thinkstock

Manufactured in the United States of America

McFarland & Company, Inc., Publishers
  Box 611, Jefferson, North Carolina 28640
    www.mcfarlandpub.com

For Minttu and Antti

Table of Contents

Preface	1
Introduction	7
1. Magic Cloaks and Potions: Motifs and Tropes of Invisibility and Age-Shifting	27
2. Witch Power: Invisibility, Age-Shifting and Empowerment	56
3. Deconstructing and Reconstructing Female Subjectivity: Magic Transformation and Girls' Coming of Age	99
4. Discourses of Gender, Power and Desire: Invisibility and Female Gaze	136
5. Crossing Borders: Queer Aging	164
Conclusion	191
Chapter Notes	197
Bibliography	208
Index	219

Preface

IMAGINE A GIRL OR A YOUNG WOMAN. What if she was able to turn invisible? Would she be free to do whatever she wishes? Would she, like H.G. Wells's invisible man, believe that she could rule the world? Or, is she like the Invisible Girl in Stan Lee's and Jack Kirby's *Fantastic Four* comic series where, in Nalo Hopkinson's interpretation, "The guys would be going *thwack* and *pow*, and she'd be invisible, whimpering, 'Oh, my. Oh, Reed, oh, oh.'"?[1] Has she turned into nothing and disappeared or, is she, as French psychoanalytic feminists might suggest, indefinable in her invisibility?

Imagine another girl or a young woman. What if she was able to turn magically younger or older, or resist the natural aging process? Would she be the superwoman of our age, the one that is properly empowered but always looks like a twenty-year-old? Or is she the Loathly Lady, the ugly hag who is really a beautiful young girl in disguise or under a curse? Is she a wise young woman? Or is she actually a wise old woman or the ugly hag in the disguise of a young girl? What would she do if she turned younger and forgot her real age? Would she be a happy girl without all the adult female worries? These questions and the representations of fantastically transforming girls and young women are the topic of this study — an exploration that focuses on children's and young adult books by contemporary English-language fantasists.

Why would someone who is interested in what it means to be a girl and a young woman in contemporary society want to study magic or supernatural bodily transformations in children's fantasy literature? To start with, bodily transformations are extremely interesting phenomena in regard to aged and gendered identities, both in real life and in fiction. Growing up does not necessarily take years. It may take only one significant moment. One significant transformation. And what proves this better than literary fiction? We are willing to believe that characters are changed by significant moments. Extraordinary events, rather than ordinary. No fiction tells the story of everyday life, year in, year out. No autobiography does that either, for that matter. Ordinary events mold us, slowly, but extraordinary events may transform us in a moment. In real life as well as in fiction, experiences and life narratives are not necessarily inscribed into one's bodily appearance; yet bodies affect the ways in which one's subjectivity is interpreted. Fantastic bodily transformations in literature often function as metaphors that address the ways in which one's changing body affects one identity and subjectivity.

Why, then, focus on tropes of invisibility and age-shifting? When I was doing research for this book, I was asked on several occasions whether I had ever wished that I could turn invisible or whether I had ever been an "invisible" girl. As regards the first question, the answer is yes, who would not desire invisibility, to be able to do whatever one wants without anyone seeing? When I learned during my research — quite accidentally, in fact — that my great-great-grandfather, the last sage in the family, supposedly knew how to make himself invisible, I regretted that he did not pass on his incantations to his son because my great-great-grandfather thought that his son was not good enough a person to become a sage. All that secret knowledge is now lost — although I am pretty convinced that most of it was based on good stories rather than actual facts. Moreover, if the tradition had been followed faithfully, the incantations would have never reached me since sageness was patrilineal. When it comes to the second question, I never was an invisible girl in the sense that I would not have had a sense of self and personality. I was quiet, shy, yes, but I always knew what I wanted to be and rarely made choices according to other people's preconceptions of me — for the better or worse. Instead, I have always felt too old or too young for my body — no one ever asked me about these experiences, though.

While invisibility seems exciting, aging is normal; and so are all kinds of conventional associations linked to how one should behave and what one should be at a certain age. I was amazed by the fact that few people were interested in the trope of age-shifting when at the same time people were obsessed with age and aging, reflected, for instance, in the views offered to me of how I should feel about my body and age at different points. As I saw it, (in)visibility, aging and gender were all related, in real world contexts as well as in imaginary realms.

There were also several reasons I wanted to focus on girls, rather than invisible and age-shifting children in general. First, personal experience of the fact visibility and age are assumed to matter to young female subjects in different ways than they matter to young male subjects. Second, there has been surprisingly little interest in representations of girlhood in children's fantasy literature. Try searching the words "girls" and "fantasy" on the Internet and what you will get is not girls' identity quests in fantastic fiction for children. Indeed, one of the most enlightening comments during my research came, quite unexpectedly, from a male dentist. His reaction to my explanation that I do research on the representation of girlhood in children's fantasy literature was laughter and an inquiry: "Would you be interested in middle-aged men's fantasies as well?" Well, isn't that just hilarious, but, no thank you, I would not — even though I cannot avoid them since middle-aged men's fantasies fill a lot of space in the popular culture. This was the answer that I wanted to give. I could not answer though, with a drill in my mouth. I never went back there. His comments told me, however, that still in the twenty-first century not everyone is eager to hear about girls and young women's experiences of this world or even understand why they would matter in the first place.

While doing research for this book, however, I found that middle-aged male dentists are not the only ones ignoring representation of girlhood in children's and young adult fantasy. From the perspective of gender studies and feminist theory, fantasy has not attracted as much attention as other "unrealist" (or fantastic) genres: science fiction, fairy tales, or horror and Gothic fiction.[2] I suspect that mainstream feminist criticism's lack of interest in fantasy literature might be partly due to the genre's assumed readership — since Henry James's famous remarks about realism as the serious form of literature, in contrast to frivolous fantasy literature, fantasy has been considered as suitable for less sophisticated readers, that is, children (and in James's times also women).[3] Even in many contemporary works, especially in comparison to science fiction and horror, it seems that fantasy is considered more clearly a genre for children and young adults.[4] Beverly Lyon Clark suggests in her introduction to a collection of studies of gender in children's fiction that major feminist theorists and literary critics have not been very interested in children's texts.[5] While Clark wrote her remarks over a decade ago, in 1999, after reviewing a good amount of feminist literary and narrative studies from the last decades, I agree with her. Feminist theory and criticism in general has been more interested in women, that is, adult females rather than girls. That said, there certainly has been plenty of feminist criticism of children's literature, including children's fantasy: as Clark and Lissa Paul note in their introductory texts, feminist criticism of children's fiction has existed since the beginning of the second-wave feminism.[6]

However, the criticism has been limited in two ways. First, it has mainly concentrated on fairy tales and Victorian children's literature — as Clark points out, much less work has been done with other genres or contemporary texts.[7] Second, the feminist criticism of contemporary children's literature has often taken the form of liberal-feminist sex-role or "images of women" theory — a fact recognized by both poststructuralist critics and liberal-feminist social theorists.[8] While these are important projects, instead of problematizing concepts such as "gender," "femininity," "girl," "woman" or "power," critics have often — for educational purposes — aimed at identifying stories with "empowered girls ... [who] may find strength by valuing positive feminine characteristics instead of striving to be as competitive, assertive, and powerful as boys,"[9] or "feminist" stories or books that are "truthful about the reality of being female."[10] These readings aim at finding essentially or "authentically" feminine or female-oriented characters in stories to serve as suitable role-models for young girls, thus relying on an identification theory which assumes that girls will only identify with their own gender (however that is defined) and that "empowered" characters will have positive effects on readers.

All of these notions reflect second-wave feminist views on gender in that they assume that there is something universal or essential about being a girl or a woman — an experience that is shared by all females and that is significantly different from the experience of being a boy or a man. Although generalizations about different phases of feminism are problematic and simplifying, I will here refer to the common, broad differentiation made between second-wave and third-wave feminisms. Whereas second-wave feminism, starting in the late 1960s and in the 1970s, has focused on the difference and inequality between two genders, male and female (whether denying the difference as in liberal and socialist feminisms or celebrating the difference as in radical feminism) and tended to talk about women as a homogenous group, third-wave feminism, influenced by poststructuralist, postcolonialist and queer theorizations from the 1980s onwards, has focused on the differences among women, questions notions of dualism and hierarchy, and views gender as a constructed, fluid category that intersects with other identity categories, such as age, ethnicity and social class.[11] To clarify, even though the concept of "postfeminism" has sometimes been used to refer to theorizations and types of analyses that are here termed third-wave feminist, I will differentiate between "postfeminism" and "third-wave feminism" because the former is commonly used to refer to an anti-feminist political backlash or to a situation where feminism is no longer relevant or needed.[12]

While feminist children's literature criticism has been heavily influenced by second-wave feminist theories, it has not, until recently, incorporated ideas from third-wave feminist theorizings, including poststructuralist feminism and queer theory. There certainly exist examples of poststructuralist readings of gender in children's fiction as well as adaptations of queer theory.[13] Because these kinds of readings are still rare, I suggest that the feminist approach to children's fantasy literature should continuously be rethought and reformulated. In this book, I will revisit several key concepts in feminist theory and apply different concepts in different chapters to address different issues, moving from the liberal-feminist concept of empowerment to notions of decentred subjectivities, female gaze and queer identities.

All of this, I suppose, led me to explore invisible and age-shifting girls in children's and young adult fantasy fiction; this is the first study on children's fantasy literature that considers the motifs and tropes of invisibility and age-shifting in length. This is not a book about girlhood in children's fantasy in general; yet, by looking at the tropes of invisibility and age-shifting it is possible to say a lot about how fantastic narrative devices can be applied to represent girlhood and how the fantastic narrative devices are, in fact, strongly connected with everyday discourses of gender circulating in the real world. This book will explore fantastic transformations as narrative devices that can be used to represent gendered experiences and to expose conventional gendered discourses: the transformations offer various perspectives on a girl's changing body and agency and provide links between real-life and fantastic discourses of gender, power, invisibility, growing up and aging.

The book focuses on selected works of contemporary fantasy published since the 1970s; these include works from critically acclaimed authors but also books by less well-known authors. A few minor examples come from books written in languages other than English. Even though I have tried to cover as much contemporary literature as possible, the selection is, admittedly, somewhat random, limited by accessibility as well as my own language skills. Yet, since the attempt here is not to provide an exhaustive study of the motifs of invisibility and age-shifting in general but, rather, to explore the ways in which these motifs are used in writing and rewriting representations of girlhood and young womanhood, I believe that the examples provide a wide spectrum of the various, often complex ways in which invisibility and age-shifting are employed to portray gendered experiences in contemporary English-language children's and young adult fantasy literature.

Finally, I would like to acknowledge the institutions who generously provided me the time and support needed to research and write this book: Tilburg University, University of Jyväskylä, Macquarie University, Ellen and Artturi Nyyssönen Foundation, Emil Aaltonen Foundation, and International Youth Library Munich. I also want to thank Finnish Concordia Fund, International Youth Library Munich, and Nordic Network for Children's Literature Research (funded by NordForsk) for providing me travel grants to attend international conferences and workshops where I have had the opportunity to discuss this project.

I would also like to acknowledge all the people who have helped me during various phases of completing this book and the research that went into it. I offer my sincerest gratitude to my doctoral supervisors, Professor Sirpa

Leppänen and Dr. Irma Hirsjärvi at the University of Jyväskylä and Professor John Stephens at Macquarie University, who generously shared their expertise and provided guidance, advice, and constructive criticism. I am most grateful to the three reviewers of my doctoral dissertation — an earlier, rather different version of this book — Professor Kimberley Reynolds, Dr. Alison Waller and Dr. Christine Wilkie-Stibbs, for their valuable suggestions for revising the text and developing it further. Several people at Tilburg University read different versions and parts of the manuscript, and I would like to offer my sincerest thanks to them all, and to Professor Odile Heynders in particular. Finally, I would like to thank the series editor, Professor Chip Sullivan.

Parts of this book draw on some of my previous publications, although here they appear in very different forms. These include: "Invisible Girls — Discourses of Femininity and Power in Children's Fantasy" in *International Research in Children's Literature* Vol. 1, No. 2 (2008) ed. by John Stephens and Pamela Knights, Edinburgh University Press, www.euppublishing.com, "Coal-Tinged Realism Meets Female Gothic: Gender, Class, and Desire in *The Ghost Wife* by Susan Price" in *The Journal of Children's Literature Studies* Vol. 7, No. 3 (2010), and "Shifting Back to and Away from Girlhood: Magic Changes in Age in Children's Fantasy Novels by Diana Wynne Jones" in *Papers: Explorations into Children's Literature* Vol. 21, No. 1 (2011).

My girlhood, in its beauty and its horridness, was shaped by the person with whom I shared a room until I left home at eighteen — my little sister Minttu. A room of my own has been necessary to complete this work, but I do not think that the initial inspiration would ever have occurred unless I had been forced to share a room in the past. What is more, this book would have never been finished without my partner Antti, who has been there throughout this project and has patiently listened to my musings, discussed my ideas and commented on my texts, but, more importantly, has offered love, support, encouragement, and has been washing all my clothes.

Introduction

FANTASTIC OR MAGIC BODILY TRANSFORMATIONS occur across human cultures and mythologies from prehistoric cave paintings to contemporary postmodern fictions. This is hardly surprising because metamorphoses are ubiquitous processes in nature and natural metamorphoses themselves may seem or be viewed as fantastic, magic or symbolic from mythological, religious or literary perspectives.

In mythologies and fictions, people turn into animals, trees, or inanimate objects; animals turn into people or other animals; inanimate objects become animate, and so forth. It is a common notion among critics who have examined representations of metamorphoses that bodily transformations address fundamental human concerns, such as the limits of self and identity, the process of aging and changing, the boundaries of life and death, and different kinds of power relations.[1]

While transformations can illustrate these types of general human concerns, they can also be used to explore more specific issues, such as gendered identities. What people turn into in stories is rarely coincidental, and their new bodily forms can reveal a great deal about their social identities and positions in social hierarchies and networks.

Invisibility and age-shifting are two popular types of bodily transformations in various kinds of fantastic stories, past and present. Invisibility is here understood as a state where characters' physical bodies are not seen by others — the physical bodies may be merely invisible but perceivable through hearing, touch or smell, or they may have completely disappeared (e.g., characters who exist as spirits or in spirit-bodies). Invisible dead people, or ghosts, are included in a few cases where they are among the main focalizers in the story; mostly the focus will be on living characters who turn invisible by supernatural means.

Age-shifting refers to any sudden transformation in a character's age, as well as to forms of "unnatural" aging, including rejuvenation and arrested or reversed aging. Immortality is a related concept and will be touched upon in relation to some texts; however, eternal life as such is not among the foci of this study.

Invisibility and age-shifting share some features with other types of fantastic bodily transformations: they can be linked to questions of identity, self and change as well as to discourses of power. However, although invisibility and age-shifting are supernatural or fantastic elements in stories, they also exist in certain forms in real-life contexts. While invisibility is a "real" condition to people who are culturally or socially ignored, it is also connected with non-existence and, ultimately, death. Age-shifting is connected both to the process of aging and to attempts to turn "magically" younger or older with the help of all kinds of technologies to shape the body, including clothing, make-up and cosmetic surgery. These transformations — whether fantastic representations or real experiences — can be associated with any gender, but they tend to acquire different meanings in relation to girls, boys, men and women.

Cultural invisibility and joys and worries of growing up and aging clearly also concern men, yet there are differences in what kinds of (in)visibility are associated with femininity, masculinity or transgender, and what kind of expectations are associated with young, middle-aged or old people of certain gender. For instance, in cultural stereotypes, a young woman's value is often determined by her looks (visibility), while old women become invisible and disregarded.[2] Given the importance of the issues of (in)visibility of women and women's coming of age and aging in feminist theory, exploring the connections of these theorizations in relation to young femininities in children's fantasy fiction is more than enough for the purposes of one study. I will here examine how invisibility and age-shifting contribute to representations of girlhood and young womanhood in children's and young adult fantasy by contemporary authors. Although my focus is on young femininities, I will, at points, also refer to works that feature invisible or age-shifting boys and young men, to draw some comparisons.

In terms of gender, I am interested in the ways in which gendered conventions and assumptions are negotiated and rewritten in texts, rather than in looking for suitable role models for anybody. Invisibility and age-shifting are examined as narrative, intertextual devices that can be used to represent gendered experiences and to expose, question, or rewrite conventional representations of girlhood and young womanhood: the transformations offer various perspectives on a girl's changing body and agency and provide links between real-life and fantastic discourses of gender, power, invisibility and aging. I will examine the intertextual connections of the fantastic transformations in terms of two main contexts. First, invisibility and age-shifting have frequently appeared in earlier stories and mythologies and therefore characters that turn invisible or magically younger or older function as recontextualized elements in the text. These transformations have often been gendered in earlier stories — particularly the different types of shape-shifting witches and goddesses — thus it is important to see how they are contextualized in the new stories and what effects this has on the representations of girls and young women in the texts.

Second, I will focus on resonances between the fantastic transformations and feminist theoretical and political discourses of gender, (in)visibility, aging and aged appearances and behaviors in real-world contexts. In fiction, fantastic bodily transformations address the limits and possibilities of gender both as performed and as material and embodied. (In)visible bodies and bodies of different ages limit the ways in which characters can act, behave and relate to others, yet the transformations may enable new forms of agency. Because gender and age as categories not only affect each other, but intersect with other identity categories including class and ethnicity, I will pursue some of these connections in the studied fiction.

Fantasy fiction offers writers a field where they can reimagine societal structures, norms and conventions related to gender. Yet, all children's fantasy is not particularly radical in terms of its treatment of gender. First, children's fantasy — as any type of literature — does not exist in a social vacuum; children's literature is an institutionally constrained form of socialization and is of massive importance educationally, intellectually, socially and financially.[3] Depending on the values and ideologies of the adult authors, editors and publishers, socialization can be about conservatism as well as about radicalism or encouraging critical thinking. While Kimberley Reynolds describes children's literature as a "paradoxical cultural space" that reflects both conservative values and subversive tendencies, other critics have emphasized either conservatism or subversive possibilities of children's texts.[4]

Similar discussions have concerned, of course, fantasy as a genre, critics often distinguishing between generic or genre fantasy (i.e., fantasy as a marketing category) and "fantasy proper" or "true fantasy," the latter being a subversive form of literature that aims at reimagining and questioning conventional representations as well as societal norms, beliefs and values.[5] This also has to do with the separation between (serious) mainstream literature and (popular) genre literatures — the first being a form of art and the latter forms of popular formula fiction. I mention these distinctions if only to discard them as criteria for selecting data for this study — the books that I discuss represent both awarded "quality" fantasy as well as popular "genre" fantasy.

While in some cases it does seem that quality fantasy equals critical treatment of gender and genre fantasy equals gender stereotypes, this is not always so.

Second, reimagining societies and gendered identities is not an easy task, and moving to the realm of fantasy does not automatically guarantee a radical shift from real-world gender ideologies. Moreover, fantasy as a genre relies extensively on the narrative patterns and motifs of its precedents: myth, legend, folktale and fairytale, and romance, all of which can be considered fairly conventional forms. As Brian Attebery suggests, "By making its conventional basis explicit and primary ... fantasy is empowered to reimagine both character and story.... But a willingness to return to the narrative structures of the past can entail as well an unquestioning acceptance of its social structures."[6]

The reliance on earlier storytelling forms and generic conventions can easily lead to depiction of past values and ideologies, unless the writers consciously aim at rewriting the ideological assumptions embedded in generic conventions. In relation to folktale rewritings, John Stephens and Robyn McCallum argue that "the conventionalized forms of folktales — for example, the formulaic beginnings and endings, the general recourse to character stereotypes, the recurrent patterns of action — tend to reinforce existing metanarratives and so make it difficult to reshape the stories without recourse to more drastic processes of revision, such as parody, metafiction, or frame-breaking."[7]

Because subgenres of fantasy also rely on fairly fixed conventions, similar processes of revision would be needed there. Generic conventions in fantasy are often gendered, such as the (male) quest narrative, and to rewrite conventional gendered discourses one would also have to challenge generic conventions.[8] Some of the texts that I will examine include irony, parody, word-play, disruptions in a linear narrative, intertextuality, metafiction, and narrative polyphony — I am interested in whether these kinds of postmodernist textual and narrative strategies are used in the construction of gender in the novels.[9] However, I do not assume that any of these "more drastic" textual and narrative devices automatically turn the novels into critical treatises of gender.

Feminist Discourse Analysis: Examining Gender in Narrative Fiction

Fictional narratives are ideological, that is, they are a way to represent and shape knowledge and thus they reflect certain worldviews and convey certain assumptions of gender. Judith Butler, among others, refers to the relationship between fictional identities and gendered discourses by noting that "literary narrative [is] a place where theory takes place."[10] The stories that people tell, whether fictional or real, do not merely reflect their pre-existing beliefs of gender, they are part of the process of shaping and forming those beliefs. This is obviously why the study of narratives is important in the first place and, furthermore, why I believe that subverting conventional gendered discourses in fiction might also have effects on readers and not merely on the characters in their fictional world. The focus in this study is on how gendered discourses that circulate in society can be referred to, reflected or created in fictional narrative texts; or, how gender is constructed in narratives.

The theoretical and methodological framework of the present study draws on what might be broadly termed as feminist discourse analysis or feminist stylistics.[11] The framework combines third-wave feminist theories with methodology drawn from narrative theory. Feminist criticism has explored gender ideologies in fiction for half a century, and while in the analytical chapters I will be using various concepts from different decades and by different feminist theorists, I will introduce some important starting points. These include the concepts of gender, discourse and multivoicedness. I will also say a few words about the problems of contextualization.

Gender and Discourse

My understanding of the concept of *gender* has been influenced by third-wave feminist theory, in particular by Judith Butler's notion of the performativity of gender, Rosi Braidotti's radical (poststructuralist) critique or embodied materialism, Judith Halberstam's queer theoretical work, and Adriana Cavarero's notion of the "narratable self." Gender is here understood as a fluid category that is constructed as a range of masculine and feminine identities — or femininities and masculinities — within and across individuals of the same biological sex; gender also interacts with other aspects of identity — such as ethnicity, age, class, and sexuality. Moreover, gendered subjectivity is a formation based on three main aspects: embodiment, discourse and narrativity.

As regards embodiment and discourse, subjectivity is based on a material, gendered and aged body, but social discourses regulate how material bodies are interpreted and what is appropriate, normal behavior for a person of certain gender and age. This understanding draws on a Foucauldian view of subjectivity. I will return to Foucault's notion of the "panoptic society" in relation to (in)visibility in Chapter 1, but will here describe what his analysis of subjectivity has meant to feminist theories of gender. In their adaptations of Foucault's theories of body, Braidotti and Butler emphasize the ways in which discourses regulate gendered subjects' bodies and behaviors.[12] For Braidotti, "Discursive practices, imaginary identifications or ideological beliefs are tattooed on bodies and thus are constitutive of embodied subjectivities." These practices, identifications and beliefs shape the notions of various ways of being a gendered subject.[13] Butler emphasizes a subject's role in "doing" identities and views gender as performatively constituted through the "stylized repetition of acts," albeit that a gendered subjectivity is always constructed in relation to normative and normalizing discourses of gender in biology, medicine, psychiatry, and law.[14] Although gender is always a doing, for Butler it is "not a doing by a subject who might be said to pre-exist the deed.... There is no gender identity behind the expressions of gender; that identity is performatively constituted by the very "expressions" that are said to be its results."[15]

Gender is, then, performed by repeating behaviors associated with versions of femininity and masculinity in social discourses about gender. Through repetition, the ways of doing gender become habitual, "tattooed on bodies" and inscribed in what Mieke Bal calls "habitual memory": habits are learned, internalized modes of behavior that are automatic and mostly unconscious, embedded in memory, even though originally enforced by discipline.[16] While subjects participate in the discursive production of gender by performing gendered "expressions," for Butler this does not mean that there are willful subjects who can decide on their gender.[17] Like Foucault, Butler emphasizes the restrictive aspects of power and (gendered) discourses, although she allows subjects a certain amount of agency in subverting gender through "a strategy of parodic repetition."[18] This is a view shared by Luce Irigaray, on whom Braidotti draws in her notion of parody, or the (exaggerated) "mimetic repetition of [the] imaginary and material institution of femininity" as critique of gendered practices.[19] While Butler is discussing drag queens as examples of parodic performance, Braidotti argues that it is also possible to parody one's own gender by performing an exaggerated, stereotypical form of femininity or masculinity.

The third aspect of subjectivity, narrativity, introduces continuity and coherence between the varying experiences of embodiment and different ways of doing gender at different ages. Narrativity explains how a person whose material body is in constant change and whose social position thus also repeatedly shifts (because young and old, feminine and masculine bodies are interpreted and treated differently in society) can still understand herself as the one and the same subject. Following Braidotti's notion of "nomadic subjectivity," I maintain that subjectivity consists of series of social locations that are negotiated in relation to other subjects and to discourses of gender and age. These locations are not disjointed but cohered by the experienced body and the sense of personal identity that is based on (embodied) memory.[20]

A similar understanding of subjectivity as both embodied and socially negotiated is found in Halberstam's queer theory, which offers "a model that locates sexual subjectivities within and between embodiment, place and practice."[21] Life narratives have a central role in how subjects understand their selfhood and personal identity — however, as Halberstam suggests, personal life narratives are also constructed in relation to societal norms about mainstream lives, or "heteronormative life trajectories."

The narrative aspect of subjectivity is also emphasized by the feminist philosopher Cavarero who — referring to identity or the *narratable self* rather than subjectivity — emphasizes each individual's desire for her own story, which again forms her identity.[22] For Cavarero, each person has a unique but not necessarily unified identity that lies in her story, her past and present: the self both consciously and through the uncontrollable "auto-narration" of memory constructs her own story and her identity. Although the idea of personal identity that is based on a narrative is hardly new, Cavarero's feminist input is to recognize the role of others in the construction of the personal narrative: because each individual is unable to tell one's story from birth to death, "The necessary other," in Cavarero's terms, is needed to fill in the gaps.[23] Moreover, in the process of shared storytelling, social discourses of age and gender are incorporated in personal identity narratives, stories of gendered individuals going through different phases in life. Thus, subjectivity and personal identity are always intersubjectively constructed, or, as Braidotti puts it, "subjectivity is a socially mediated process."[24]

What does this mean in relation to fictional characters that turn invisible or age-shift? I will analyze the ways in which the fictional girls' gendered subjectivities are constructed both in relation to others, to discourses of gender, to their own experiences of their bodies and to their personal identity narratives. The girl characters' bodily transformations are crucial in relation to subjectivity because in their different forms the girls also have different experiences of embodiment, they are able to enter different gendered subject positions and their personal identity narrative is affected by the transformations. Their transformations also raise questions about agency and empowerment. Focusing on gendered subjectivity not only as discursive but also as embodied and narratable makes it possible to think about representations of gendered bodies and gender in general in more complex ways. Yet, I do not suggest that by adopting a queer, third-wave feminist perspective all, or any, texts would begin to seem more complex or subversive in terms of gender representation.

While my main focus is on gender, it cannot be separated from other identity categories. Age is of particular interest here because I examine age-shifting as a narrative device in fiction that is aimed at readers of certain ages. Growing up and aging are inherent in the notion of identity as a narrative — we understand ourselves as beings that change as the time passes and the personal narrative (filled in by others) provides the connection between the newborn baby and all our later forms. My understanding of aged subjectivities is parallel to the definition of gender above: age is based on a material body but also a discursive construction.

Social, discursive construction of age refers to the meanings associated with aging and different ages and phases in life, such as childhood or old age.[25] As Margaret Cruikshank notes, "aging can be performed" because of a culturally determined idea that "'old' limits certain behavior or style choices."[26] While Cruikshank refers to old age, discourses of different phases of life also limit the choices at other ages (e.g., "suitable" behavior for a woman of ten or fifty). In regard to girlhood, there are several discourses in relation to which young females negotiate their subjectivities. Examples include the "nice girl" discourse that often involves notions of controlled sexuality, the tomboy discourse where tomboyism is seen as a phase that girls will or should grow out of because adult female masculinity or transgenderism are not as easily tolerated, and the discourse of girl power in pop culture.[27] I will return to aspects of these and other aged and gendered discourses in greater detail in the analytical chapters. Magic age-shifting is a fascinating narrative device because it can address both material aging and the social and performative aspects of age as well as question normative life stories and trajectories. Where relevant, I will discuss gender and age also in relation to social class and ethnicity; the latter two are also understood as identity categories that are performed within a scene of constraint consisting of norms regulating behavior associated with certain classes or ethnicities.

As regards the concept of discourse, it will here be used mainly in the Foucauldian, social theoretical sense of being a form of social practice. Following Sara Mills's formulation of Foucault's ideas, I see this definition of discourse as relevant "to be able to identify discourses, that is, groups of utterances which seem to be regulated in some way and which seem to have a coherence and a force to them in common ... [such as] a discourse of femininity."[28] As Mills writes, the term "discourse" in the Foucauldian sense refers to a discursive structure that "can be detected because of the systematicity of the ideas, opinions, concepts, ways of thinking and behaving which are formed within a particular context, and because of the effects of those ways of thinking and behaving." What this means in relation to gender is that "we can assume that there is a set of discourses of femininity and masculinity, because women and men behave within a certain range of parameters when defining themselves as gendered subjects."[29] That is, there exist several gendered discourses circulating in society, and these discourses — discourses of femininity and masculinity — involve different ideologies of gender, or belief systems that govern assumptions about gender. Gendered discourses specify ways of being gendered subjects: how one is supposed to look and to behave as a woman and a man, a girl and a boy, and so forth.

In contrast to Foucault's notion of discourses as "practices that systematically form the objects of which they speak,"[30] which indicates that the individual is determined by structures, feminist theory also builds on Foucault's later (1978) definitions of power both as a form of oppression and a form of resistance. Although dominant, privileged gendered discourses can shape individuals' lives, they can also be resisted and transformed by the individuals participating in social situations, institutions and structures that are partly constituted by discourse.[31] While examining texts that rewrite earlier stories, motifs and tropes, I am specifically interested in fiction as a form of critique in the sense that it exposes, challenges or subverts conventional notions of gender. To avoid at least some confusion in relation to the term, I will mainly use the term "discourse" as in Mills's definition above, in reference to different gendered discourses that circulate in society and are reflected in texts.[32] At times, I will refer to rather broad sets of ideas as a discourse — such as "liberal-feminist discourse of empowerment" as realized in feminist theorizings but also in feminist fictions. But, where possible, I will employ the term "discourse" to refer to more specific sets of ideas about gender, such as the "nice girl" discourse or the "radical-feminist discourse of the witch."

Multivoicedness

Whereas early feminist criticism often aimed at recognizing role models and labeling texts as sexist or feminist, a key premise in contemporary feminist discourse analysis is that any text is potentially multivoiced, particularly in terms of gendered discourses. The analysis of multivoicedness is based on Bakhtinian understanding of texts as inherently intertextual, and draws on Bakhtin's original terms "dialogic," "heteroglossia" and "polyphony." All three concepts have connections to intertextuality in a broad sense, and are often used interchangeably. However, it is useful to bear in mind their distinctive meanings; for my purposes, I will differentiate between the terms "intertextuality," "multivoicedness," and "polyphony," which all relate to the different uses of the term "dialogic."

First, "dialogism" or "the dialogic orientation of discourse" refers to the intertextual and interpersonal nature of language and meaning-making in general: words exist in relation to other words, texts exist in relation to other texts, discourses exist in relation to other discourses; in sum, meaning is created only in relation, in dialogue, in a context.[33] To describe this broad phenomenon of dialogism, I will use the term "intertextuality." I will employ intertextuality as a concept to refer both to its narrow sense as a study of traceable references to previous texts in the studied text and to the broader notion of intertextuality as a relation between a text and genres and discourses.[34] I consider the vagueness of the Bakhtinian notion of intertextuality an advantage in the sense that it allows for the investigation of both literary pretexts as well as more vaguely defined linguistic and discursive constructions outside literature — such as gendered discourses circulating in society. However, in my analyses I hope to make it clear in relation to each specific intertextual element whether I am referring to a specific earlier story or text, a generic convention, or a gendered discourse circulating both inside and outside literature.

Second, Bakhtin writes about dialogism specifically in relation to the novel as a genre. Because "the basic distinguishing feature of the stylistics of the novel" is the dialogization of "different languages and speech types" the (modern) novel is, as a genre, dialogic by definition.[35] Dialogism in this sense is related to Bakhtin's use of the term "heteroglossia" which refers to "the social diversity of speech types," that is, to all the different speech types that are part of any single language, including dialects, jargons, genres, sociolects, and "languages of the authorities, of various circles and of passing fashions, languages that serve the specific socio-political purposes of the day, even the hour."[36] The last two references to "languages" in the list resemble Foucault's notions of discourses. All Bakhtin's speech types (or languages) have a socio-political relevance in his theory: "All languages of heteroglossia, whatever the principle underlying them and making each unique, are specific points of view on the world, forms for conceptualizing the world in words, specific world views, each characterized by its own objects, meanings and values."[37] In this sense, "languages" or, in Foucauldian terms, discourses, reflect different worldviews or ideologies. My interest is the ways in which discourses about gender, or gendered discourses that involve certain gender ideologies, are reflected in the studied novels.

The heteroglossia, that is, the different languages or discourses that exist in society, enter the novel through all the different "voices" in the novel, including authorial speech, the speeches of narrators, inserted genres and the speech of characters. These voices exist in a dialogue with each other and are artistically organized or "orchestrated" into a stylistic unity.[38] While this variety of voices in the text is in later interpretations of Bakhtin's theory referred to as "dialogism," "heteroglossia" as well as "polyphony," I will use the English term "multivoicedness" in reference to heteroglossia. Multivoicedness thus indicates that a text involves traces of different discourses, in this study specifically gendered discourses, from outside the text, from society. What the notion of multivoicedness means with respect to gender is that one text, for instance a children's book, may employ several "voices" or discourses representing different assumptions of gender, some of them possibly even oppositional.[39] I will reserve the term "polyphony" to describe the narrative organization of fictional voices in the actual text — the voices of the narrator, characters, cited texts, and so forth — because the term is related to Bakhtin's notion of orchestration of voices in the novel.

Finally, there is a third definition of "dialogic." Bakhtin also uses the term dialogic in relation to the term "monologic"—in this sense, all texts are dialogic, but some texts are more dialogic than others. A dialogic text allows the equal representation of different voices or speech styles (and, accordingly, worldviews or ideologies) and different meanings, whereas a monologic text aims at "unitary language" and emphasizes one voice or speech style (and worldview) over the others and aims towards a fixed meaning.[40] In her Bakhtinian approach to children's texts, McCallum associates monologism "with the hegemony of authorial control and the limitation of narrational techniques, discursive styles and ideological viewpoints represented in novels" and dialogism "with the relinquishing of authorial control, and with narrative techniques which disguise or efface an author's presence so as to construct more active and analytic strategies for reading."[41] A similar distinction between monologism and dialogism is made by Dale M. Bauer, who applies a feminist–Bakhtinian framework—or "feminist dialogics"—in her study of adult fiction.[42] Although I agree that there are certain narrative techniques that leave little room for readers' interpretations and others that encourage complex and critical readings of texts, I will not be using the term monologic or the term dialogic as an antonym of monologic. Obviously, there are ways to highlight certain gendered discourses and undermine others in narrative texts— indeed these ways or techniques are addressed in my analysis—however, I will avoid the term monologic because other discourses in the text are never completely obliterated.

At the same time, it is also true that even a radical rewriting necessarily refers to conventional discourses and notions of gender. No matter how drastic the textual and narrative strategies of rewriting, the texts always remind of the earlier, conventional texts even when revising them. In this sense feminist rewritings are always "double-voiced," a term that Cristina Bacchilega uses in relation to postmodern feminist fairy tales that are "both affirmative and questioning, without necessarily being recuperative or politically subversive."[43] Linda Hutcheon refers to the same phenomenon in her description of postmodernist writing that reworks earlier conventions; it is a kind of writing that both "purveys and challenges [earlier/conventional] ideology."[44] That is, to be able to criticize something, one needs to mention that something. Another challenge is that subverting one convention may not be enough. As Anne Cranny-Francis states, genres are hybrid and thus a writer "must be aware of the dialogic nature of the text and take account of the encoded discourses of all these textual conventions."[45] For instance, if an author rewrites the conventional hero narrative by replacing a male protagonist with a female one, this does not necessarily challenge any other assumption about the hero, such as the notion that using violence for the right purposes is acceptable. A related issue is that representing one radical character, or an exceptional individual, may not be enough. In her analyses of "feminist children's novels," Roberta Seelinger Trites points out that even feminist texts reflect conflicting ideologies; despite the revisionary voices of the girl protagonists, there are other characters (such as the protagonists' mothers) "trapped in stereotypical gender roles."[46]

I do not view these contradictions as flaws in texts — after all, the conventional characters may serve a narrative function by providing the "norm" against which the emancipated characters seem radical. Instead, I propose that the conflicting voices and discourses should be carefully examined. This examination should consider narrative structures: although all texts may be multivoiced, all voices in texts are not equal. Even though the most utopian interpretation of Bakhtin's polyphony in the text might mean that there are several, independent and equal voices in the narrative that may reflect different, even conflicting or oppositional ideologies, in actuality a narrative is not a democratic meeting where everyone is allocated equally long speaking turns and whatever each person says is equally valued. Focalization, for instance, is a key strategy to represent events from a certain point of view — but obviously it also matters how often and for how long certain characters get to speak and how their utterances are evaluated by other characters. It also matters what happens to different gendered discourses in the course of the narrative.[47] Thus, even though I view the studied novels as multivoiced in terms of gendered discourses, I do not expect that the texts will remain completely ambiguous in what gendered discourses are emphasized.

To sum up, drawing on feminist discourse analysis, I view modern children's fantasy fiction novels as multivoiced and suggest that the idea of multivoicedness of texts could be the starting point for the analysis of gendered discourses children's books. In an analysis of gender in children's fiction, the focus should be on taking a critical stance towards taken-for-granted or common-sense assumptions of gender and examining the representation of *multiple* possible gendered identities or gendered discourses in specific texts. In the textual analysis, this would mean focusing on the different voices, that is, on the polyphony in the texts: on analyzing narrator's voice, speech and thought representation and intertextuality, the latter including the study of pretexts, generic conventions, as well as non-fictional discourses of gender. These narrative voices in a specific text include traces of different gendered discourses that echo earlier literary texts as well as reflect the ways of speaking about gender in the society where the text has been produced. While gendered discourses may enter the text through voices speaking out in dialogue or through a representation of a specific character's thoughts on gender, they also enter the text through characterization; the author portrays both narrators and characters in relation to certain understanding, or discourses of gender.

Contextualization

As Mills points out and as I have argued elsewhere with Piia Varis, in feminist criticism contextualization of texts cannot happen simply by assuming a patriarchal society as the main context and then observing forms of oppression of women in relation to that context — this is an oversimplification of the several contexts in which texts exist.[48] The choice of relevant contexts will necessarily affect the meanings found in the texts. In a feminist-stylistic framework, according to Mills, "a critic is ... concerned about charting a range of possible readings which the text negotiates with a reader and which that reader accepts or resists."[49] These possible readings are based on the textual features as well as on the contexts in which the text is interpreted. Because works can be read in relation to various contexts, Jan Blommaert suggests that the contextualization work itself has to be subjected to critical analysis.[50] I will thus briefly explain the ways in which I have contextualized the data of this study. Instead of examining the texts in a vaguely defined socio-historical context which would somehow be self-evident, I will be analyzing the novels in two more specific contexts.

Drawing on Mills, I will assume that the context of a given text includes those discursive practices that pertain to the text in question, and the relevant social practices.[51] To start with the wider context, taking into account the relevant social practices in regard to gender means "simply" to examine the novels in their socio-historical context — obviously this is not as simple as it sounds because any socio-historical context is not a consistent block of ideologies and practices that the analyst can assume and refer to. Since all contexts are constructions, in terms of socio-historical context, I have deliberately decided to examine the novels in the context of different forms of feminism that began to have their impact on children's literature in the United States and Britain in the 1970s and have continued to influence books for young audiences throughout the 1980s, 1990s and 2000s. This is because, as suggested above, in relation to gender I am interested in forms of rewriting of gendered discourses and representations.

Although various gendered discourses in relation to invisibility and ageshifting have been in circulation before second-wave feminism, in its aftermath there emerged a new kind of awareness of gender and about different ways of thinking about gender. When discussing feminist discourses, I will be talking about different forms of feminism, rather than feminism as one coherent ideology. As regards the second level of contextualization, the analysis of the discursive practices around the texts involves investigation of the production and reception of the studied texts. Here I will focus on one major discursive literary practice, genre that both writers and readers draw on when producing and consuming texts. I will analyze the ways in which the examined books draw on earlier representations of invisibility and age-shifting in children's fantasy, and in separate chapters I will be focusing on conventions of different sub-genres, including secondary world fantasy, fairy tale, time-slip narratives, and Gothic horror.

Research Questions and Data

When examining the novels, the following large questions have guided my readings. First of all, I have looked at the ways in which the bodily transformations — invisibility and age-shifting — are represented in the texts by textual and narrative means and how the transformations are connected with representations of girlhood and womanhood. Second, I have analyzed the ways in which the bodily transformations affect power relations in the story world: who has control over the transformations, and over the transformed bodies? Are the transformations about control from outside or about empowerment? Finally, my last two questions focus on invisibility and age-shifting as intertextual devices that are discussed in relation to two main contexts: how do the transformations function in relation to conventional discourses of gender in earlier fantasy, fairy tales and mythological stories? How do the transformations function in relation to non-fictional feminist discourses of invisibility, aging and gender?

These questions will be addressed with the help of close analysis of narrative discourse. Although the representation and shaping of (ideological) knowledge happens at all levels of the narrative, I will in my analysis focus on characterization: on description, actions and speech and thought representation of the transforming females as well as on the ways they are framed in the text both by narrative point of view and intertextual and metafictional elements. What does it, then, mean to analyze the multivoicedness of a fictional narrative, with a specific focus on gendered discourses? The analysis of narrative point of view and representation of speech are essential in examining how the gendered representations and discourses are framed or contextualized inside the narrative — from whose point of view, in whose voice. By narrator's voice and characters' voices I will refer to them as speakers, that is, as sources of speech or thought in the narrative. I will occasionally use the term "voice" in the feminist sense of a girl character finding her voice — or, to be exact, the way to use her voice or speech as a form of agency — but in these cases I hope to make it clear that the key issue is agency.

As regards the narrative point of view, I will be employing the term "focalization" instead of the other common concept, "perspective."[52] As regards transformations and gender, focalization is connected with questions such as from whose point of view are the transformations perceived and interpreted, and, when the protagonists are focalizers, how they perceive others and themselves before, during and after their transformations. The analysis of speech and thought representation is linked to the analysis of focalization — readers will only get access to the thoughts of those characters who focalize (and possibly also the narrator's thoughts) and all the speech in the narrative is represented from someone's point of view. The analysis of speech and thought representation is important when locating the gendered discourses in texts — the narrator, the focalizing character(s) and the other characters may reflect different views on gender.

I will also pay attention to narrative sequencing and closure — this is especially relevant in stories that are thematically about girls' coming of age, as well as in stories that challenge heteronormative patterns of growing up and aging. First, chronological temporal sequence is usually interpreted as not only natural but also causal: what happens first includes the reason for what happens next. As Cranny-Francis suggests, this "natural" or "obvious" connection between chronology and causality enables the encoding of ideological (gendered) discourses by introducing causal relationships between things as natural rather than ideologically determined.[53]

Against this background, disruptions in temporal sequence may offer possibilities for deconstructing other "obviousnesses," for instance, by manipulating the time in fantastic means, as in the case of magic changes in age and time slips. A conventional sense of closure in literature in general involves not only ending the temporal and causal sequence at a convenient point but bringing the narrative into a thematic closure, which creates a sense of the overall significance of the narrative. As Stephens suggests, a fixed closure is typical of children's literature because it often serves didactic or socializing purposes.[54] The expectation of a fixed closure will create a sense of teleology in the text: everything that goes on between the beginning and the end is a part that contributes to the overall meaning of the text that is complete at the end.[55] Often the closure is anticipated already at the beginning of the narrative; the fairy tale formula "Once upon a time" will create expectations of a certain kind of closure, as will the introductory event of finding a dead body in a library at the beginning of a traditional murder mystery.[56] Even when a particular closure is not in any way anticipated at the beginning, a central expectation will be that at the end of the text, a certain explanation for all that has been going on will be offered. Even in cases of an open ending where a fixed or determinate closure is not offered, there will be a sense of "why" the narrative is significant.

In the studied novels, it is important to look at what is the starting point for the transforming girl protagonists and where the girls end up, what kind of femininities appear at the beginning and in the closure and how gendered identities (that are partly result of the transformations) are linked to questions of agency. As regards fantastic transformations, even tropes that are first and foremost about change can have a resolution that signals stability and non-change as ideal states — that is, magic bodily transformations can represent momentary phases that are left behind when young characters reach more stable adult identities.

Since the corpus of analyzed texts consists of what I have called contemporary children's fantasy, I should briefly explain my use of the terms "fantasy," "children" and "contemporary." For the purposes of this study, I will maintain the general idea that fantasy is literature of impossible and supernatural.[57] I will examine fantasy as a hybrid genre or, a "fuzzy set," to follow Attebery's notion: it consists of several different types and subgroups or subgenres.[58] Adopting here the Bakhtinian view of genres as sets of conventions that provide frameworks for both authors and readers and that become institutions through socio-historical developments, defining a genre would involve mapping out the conventions, including textual and stylistic features and typical themes, contents and functions of any particular genre.[59] Describing the conventions of children's fantasy is challenging because as a general category it consists of rather different subtypes ranging from animal stories to epic secondary world fantasy narratives.[60] This is particularly the case if, as I do here, the category of "children" is also understood to include young adult readers. However, in relation to rewriting I will explore specific conventions, and thus I am mainly interested in the subgenres of children's fantasy, rather than finding an ideal general definition for fantasy as a genre. The studied novels employ and rewrite conventions of several different subgenres, related genres and narrative types — including folk tale, myth, ghost story, female Gothic, time-slip fantasy and quest narrative. I will also examine a few works that are categorized as young adult science fiction. I have included these examples because they involve interesting examples of the uses of invisibility and age-shifting. To avoid confusion, whenever I refer to the representational mode that is seen as the oppositional pole to realism, I will use the term *fantastic* instead of fantasy.[61]

While Chapter 1 will review the use of motifs and tropes of invisibility and age-shifting in a broader spectrum of books — including some adult books as well as myths, folktales and earlier children's fiction — in later chapters I have limited my focus to contemporary, that is, post–1970s texts. The last four decades have been a period during which feminist influences have become more common in children's literature and is of special importance to anyone interested in examining rewriting of gendered conventions. Despite the increase of feminist influences on a general level, not all contemporary children's fantasy involving invisibility or age-shifting female characters is radical in terms of gender politics. When searching for children's and young adult books involving invisibility or age-shifting, I encountered plenty of transforming characters that have little to do with rewriting of gendered discourses and representations. Quite often invisibility or age-shifting functions as a plot device that has little or no connection to characters' identities.

The novels selected for closer examination have been chosen on the basis of the criterion that invisibility, age-shifting or both are central motifs in relation to female protagonists in the novels. Special attention will be paid to texts that challenge earlier generic conventions of fantastic narratives. This is because my interest is mainly in the strategies of rewriting gender, rather than in conducting a broad, historical motif study of invisibility and age-shifting. The core data set should therefore not be understood as representative of contemporary children's fantasy in general — what I am interested here is in what has been possible in terms of rewriting of gendered conventions, rather than what are the most typical or common strategies of representing gender in children's fantasy.

The analyzed novels involve different uses of invisibility and age-shifting and the texts vary in the ways in which the transformations are contextualized — these differences provide a point of departure for a comparative analysis of the novels. Some of the texts involve only invisibility or some kind of magic age-shifting, while others include both. In some of the books the protagonists are also able to shape-shift into other forms, such as animals. The causes for the transformations are also various: changes in form may result from a curse or a spell, from drinking a magic potion or getting a medical shot, or, in some cases, from time-slips or even death. Shape-shifting may also be a character's personal ability, whether inherent or acquired through training. The transformations may be desired and voluntary or unwanted and forced upon. In each novel the transformations of the protagonists are thus differently contextualized both in the level of the story and also in terms of (sub)genres and narrative types the texts rely on. Because the novels differ from each other in terms of themes, structure, and use of the motifs or tropes of invisibility and age-shifting, some of them are discussed in greater length than others. Some works that involve both invisibility and age-shifting are examined from different analytical perspectives and concepts in different chapters.

The Structure of This Book

The rest of the chapters will provide critical readings of children's and young adult fantasy involving the motifs or tropes of invisibility and age-shifting. Chapter 1, Magic Cloaks and Potions: Motifs and Tropes of Invisibility and Age-Shifting, provides readers with a broader literary context for the fantastic bodily transformations; both invisibility and magic changes in age have been and remain popular motifs and tropes both in fantastic literature. The chapter opens with a section that explains the uses of metamorphosis and transformations as textual devices and the difference between the usage of transformations — here invisibility and age-shifting — as motifs and tropes. The rest of the chapter will introduce different functions, as well as the conventional and common uses of the motifs and tropes of invisibility and age-shifting in earlier fantastic fictions, including folk literature, fairy tales and earlier literary fantasies for children and adults. Chapter 1 will thus set the background for the following chapters. It will introduce conventional uses of invisibility and age-shifting which are often challenged and rewritten in contemporary works, particularly in relation to gender. The following four analytical chapters will provide more detailed readings of specific contemporary works ranging from secondary world fantasy to fantastic realism, time-slip narratives and Gothic horror.

Chapter 2, Witch Power: Invisibility, Age-Shifting and Empowerment, explores invisibility and magic changes in age as narrative motifs that are associated with female characters' agency and empowerment in texts that rewrite earlier conventional representations of the witch. In the novels examined here, the female protagonists are skillful wizards or witches in training and they can, at least to some extent, control their own transformations. The chapter discusses the transformations of the female characters in the context of earlier fairy tales and fantastic stories and discusses how the motifs are reframed in contemporary fantasy.

Chapter 3, Deconstructing and Reconstructing Female Subjectivity: Magic Transformations and Girls' Coming of Age, examines how invisibility and magic changes in age that are results of a shift in time effect the transforming character's subjectivity and identity in female coming-of-age novels that belong to the genre of fantastic realism. While the previous chapter has focused on novels that can be characterized as secondary world fantasy, this and the following chapter discuss texts in which the magic or supernatural elements occur in a contemporary, urban setting. This chapter considers invisibility and magic changes in age as narrative devices that deconstruct the girl protagonists' subjectivities and thus potentially challenge and question gendered discourses and representations. As in Chapter 2, the issues of agency and subjectivity will be addressed — the focus here is on the role of transformations in identity and subjectivity formation, particularly on the functions of the transformations in the identity narratives of the girl protagonists.

Chapter 4, Discourses of Gender, Power and Desire: Invisibility and

Female Gaze, investigates the invisible girls in a few selected texts in relation to feminist discourses of (in)visibility and gaze. While Chapter 3 has considered invisibility in relation to powerlessness, invisibility is an ambiguous trope that does not only function to communicate ideas of loss of self and powerlessness, even in narratives involving mainly realist, urban settings. The chapter focuses on the relations between invisibility, gaze, power and subjectivity: invisibility as a state where one escapes gaze and a state where the invisible person has power over people whom s/he observes. Both of these possibilities are explored in feminist discourses on (in)visibility and gaze, which will provide the theoretical framework for this chapter. While the different feminist discourses on (in)visibility in relation to females and femininity may seem contradictory, they also illustrate the complexity of gendered discourses and representations in relation to notions of gaze.

Chapter 5, Crossing Borders: Queer Aging, examines characters who depart from conventional heteronormative life trajectories due to their abnormal aging patterns. After briefly introducing queer theorizations about growing up and aging, the first half of the chapter continues to discuss the shape-shifting figure of the shaman and investigates how the shamanic ability to cross boundaries of worlds and different ages is connected with representation of gender and conceptualizations of queer temporalities and identities. The second half of the chapter will analyze the trope of reversed aging in novels where characters are growing younger and have to adapt to going through earlier phases of their lives again. The queerness of the reversed aging patterns challenges heteronormative views because the characters are unable to foresee their futures in relation to conventional views about growing up and growing old.

1

Magic Cloaks and Potions: Motifs and Tropes of Invisibility and Age-Shifting

THE IDEAS OF EVER-CHANGING AND hybrid identities are not exactly new. Yet, contemporary Western theories of literature, poetry and fiction are, as Kai Mikkonen puts it, particularly "metamorphosis-laden": theorists such as Julia Kristeva, Mikhail Bakhtin, and Gilles Deleuze and Felix Guattari employ ideas of metamorphic and hybrid texts and subjects.[1] Second- and third-wave feminist writings also involve a plethora of different theories of both fantastic and real, material metamorphoses and bodily transformations. Feminist theorists, including Donna Haraway and Rosi Braidotti, have been interested in both the material and metaphorical aspects of hybrid bodies, and bodily transformations also appear in writings of women's monstrous bodies, or "the monstrous feminine" to use the film critic Barbara Creed's term.[2]

The theoretical interest is linked to the notion of transformations as ubiquitous in the contemporary world that is characterized by what Vivian Sobchack calls cultures of "quick-change" in the "larger metamorphic technosphere." Discourses of popular culture and marketing are full of descriptions of swift external and internal transformations that seem almost magic.[3] Everything changes at an accelerating pace, which forces people to adapt to the rapid changes, or continuously change themselves — identity politics is less about "being" than about "becoming." Because theorizations and analyses of transformations are particularly popular in contemporary writings, the background literature is both enormous and extremely versatile. I will not provide a comprehensive review, but briefly discuss some central concepts in relation to fantastic transformations in narrative fiction.

The concept of transformation is here used of fantastic bodily transformations that are perceived as actual, rather than figurative, in the story-world by the transformed character herself or himself and by other characters.[4] The changes in physical form studied here are not restricted to one-way developments but can be reversed or occur repeatedly. Following Maria Lassén-Seger, I will use the term shape-shifting of the kind of transformations that are "voluntary, self-induced, multiple and reversible" in contrast to those types of transformations that are forced upon the changing subject.[5]

While in the story-world a transformation is an event, on the textual level transformations can be treated as narrative devices that can be categorized in several ways. As narrative devices, fantastic bodily transformations can function on many levels of the narrative: as motifs, functions (in the Proppian sense, e.g., "villain casting a spell over someone"), or metaphors and tropes that are closely connected to large themes such as identity/selfhood or change in human life.[6] Of these rhetorical or narratological concepts, I find the terms "motif" and "trope" most useful. For my purposes, I will be referring to transformations as motifs when they mainly serve a strategic function in the story or narrative as plot devices, usually understood in the fantasy world merely on the literal level. For instance, in several short narratives about children draping themselves in invisibility cloaks, or consuming invisibility potions, pills or powders, invisibility usually has little to do with issues of identity; in these stories it serves a strategic purpose. In contrast, transformations function as tropes when they can be interpreted metonymically or metaphorically—that is, beyond their strategic, literal function in the text. Invisibility and age-shifting can be employed to describe, for instance, a character's social status or her experience of her own personal identity which may be different from her material body. Whether used as motifs or tropes, transformations can have associations with gender.

In his study of metamorphoses in contemporary adult fiction, Mikkonen examines the figurative metamorphoses as tools that question and deconstruct identities and have a "connection with the openly paradoxical and process-like notion of subjectivity in a lot of contemporary fiction."[7] However, bodily transformations do not necessarily function in any particularly subversive or transgressive ways in children's and young adult fiction. Metamorphosis is not necessarily a radical trope in such fiction, because in the figurative sense it might be the main trope. Identity forming during a period of metamorphosis or radical bodily and psychological change is one of the main concerns of children's and young adult fiction. Among others, the author Natalie Babbitt suggests that children's fiction is about "the great metamorphosis of growing up," while the critic Sue Easun links metamorphosis not to childhood but to adolescence, which is "often considered synonymous with searching for a new sense of self."[8]

Although change is the norm rather than deviation during the process of life and aging, in contemporary Western discourses of aging, drastic bodily and psychological change is associated namely with the passage from childhood to adulthood. An aspect of the discourses of adolescence — the emergence of which is usually located in the Victorian period — is that the end result of the process of metamorphosis is something desirable: adulthood signals agency, empowerment, responsibility and freedom.[9] In this kind of understanding of human development, transformations can be used to fix unique or essential identities instead of questioning them; through a radical, irreversible change young people find their "true," "unique" and more stable adult identities. Indeed, conventionalism might be more expected in children's and young adult literature than any radical questioning of popular discourses of adolescence and adulthood. For instance, in her study of representations of adolescence in contemporary fantastic realism for young adults, Alison Waller concludes that the genre tends to be conventional and reflect liberal humanist impulses: "Adolescence is represented as a minor stage in the process of becoming an adult, whole and empowered within appropriate parameters."[10]

Earlier studies on bodily transformations in children's literature both support and challenge the above notions. Bodily transformations in adult literature have been examined in a number of studies, most of them focusing on Ovidian influences from the Middle Ages to modern classics. However, discussions of the bodily transformations in children's literature are rare, even though the motifs themselves are ubiquitous in fiction for young readers.[11] Maria Lassén-Seger's (2006) study of child metamorphs in late twentieth-century children's literature addresses metamorphoses in connection to child-adult power relations and the image of the child in children's literature. In another recent study of metamorphosis in children's and young adult literature, Shelley Chappell (2007) focuses on selected transformation types (including werewolves and selkies) and their role in the representation of child and young adult identities. In another more specific study, Lois Kuznetz (1994) examines a certain type of metamorphosis: toy characters becoming alive.

These earlier studies have mapped out several different functions of fantastic transformations in children's literature. Kuznetz starts with an assumption that toy characters can act as subversive forces in children's fiction because they embody anxieties about the boundaries of humanity and selfhood. However, the results of her study show that toy stories are "generally conservative in dealing with the givens of a patriarchal culture and subversive largely in the individualistic sense."[12] In her study, Lassén-Seger arrives at a different conclusion: her findings suggest that the motif of metamorphosis became more popular towards the end of twentieth century and that, in contrast to earlier metamorphoses that were often either about punishment or carnevalesque play, recent fiction includes more radical metamorphoses that are used to subvert both generic conventions and conservative values regarding identity.[13] Chappell also concludes that fantastic metamorphoses are flexible metaphors that can address several major issues in relation to adolescence, including embodiment and subjectivity, experiences of otherness, maturation, and changing power relations.[14] In all three studies, the authors show how metamorphosis in children's fiction can function similarly as in myths and adult literature: transformations address questions of identity, are linked to issues of power and (dis)empowerment and can be tragic as well as comic. These notions of different functions of bodily transformations in children's fiction provide a starting point for this study.

While all of the above studies involve discussions about gender and metamorphosis, none of them makes gender its main focus. Furthermore, none of the above studies examines invisibility and age-shifting and, in general, the uses of these two transformation types in children's fiction have not been widely addressed in children's literature criticism. In the following, I will offer a concise review of uses of invisibility and age-shifting in earlier folk literature, classic texts for adults, and children's books.

Invisibility

Invisibility is an immensely popular motif in many types of narratives: Stith Thompson's *Motif-index of Folk-Literature* lists dozens of examples of invisibility and invisible persons, animals, things, fairies and gods that appear in tales all over the world.[15] In myths, legends and folktales invisibility is always in some way connected with uses of power. Influential examples in the Western mythological tradition include the uses of invisibility items in Greco-Roman mythology — such as the Petasus (cap) of Hermes/Mercury and the helmet of Hades — as well as invisibility cloaks in the Icelandic *Eddas* and the German national epic *Nibelungenlied*. Persons who can turn invisible in these stories are either gods or goddesses or people with superhuman powers.

Immortal beings can also help their favorite mortals to turn invisible, whether wrapping them in mist, as Apollo does when concealing his favorite Trojans from their Greek enemies in the battlefield in the *Iliad*, or providing them with magic items or articles of clothing that make them invisible, such as the helmet of Hades given to Perseus by the nymphs to help him to kill Medusa. In a similar vein, the *Tarnkappe* ("magic hood") or the *Nebelkappe* ("mist-cloak") in the *Nibelungenlied* enables Siegfried to help Günther to overcome Queen Brünhild in a fight and deprive her of her supernatural strength. The cloak not only makes Siegfried invisible but also gives him the strength of twelve men.[16] In these examples, invisibility is a plot device, or, strategic — a method to achieve certain aims or to perform a particular task in the narrative.

Folktales and fairy tales also offer examples of strategic invisibility. In the story titled "The Shoes That Were Danced to Pieces" in Grimm's fairy tales,[17] twelve princesses disappear mysteriously each night. An old woman gives a soldier an invisibility cloak to be able to follow the princesses and find out where they go. After spying on the princesses, he reveals to the king that his daughters go to dance with twelve princes each night, and the soldier is rewarded with the hand of the eldest princess. In another Grimms' tale, "The King of the Golden Mountain,"[18] the king, who has been betrayed by his wife, obtains an invisibility cloak, a magic sword and magic boots from giants disputing over these items. The king uses invisibility to get unseen into his palace and to take revenge on his wife, who is being wedded to a new man: he eats unseen all the food from his wife's plate and strikes her in the face, after which he turns visible and tells the magic sword to kill everyone else in the hall. The invisibility coat, along with other magic items, also appears in the English tale "The History of Jack the Giant-Killer,"[19] similarly used for strategic purposes.

This type of invisibility is strategic because it is intentionally used to achieve a specific concrete aim or to accomplish a certain task. Moreover, invisibility is a temporary state: after accomplishing the task at hand, the invisible characters turn visible again. There is no ambiguity about the unseen state, it is always empowering and enables the invisible person to successfully perform whatever task at hand. In strategic invisibility, there are no risks in wearing the invisibility items — the fear of the loss of identity or loss of connection to other people or the corruptive effects of power are not introduced. Although the morals of the invisible persons accomplishing their tasks might be questioned from a perspective outside the story in stories such as "The King of the Golden Mountain," they are not questioned in the stories themselves. Invisibility remains a useful strategy to accomplish certain tasks and thus functions as a motif rather than a trope.

Figurative Uses of Invisibility

Invisibility can, however, have metonymical or metaphorical dimensions and thus become a trope, particularly in stories where persons turn invisible repeatedly or permanently. Michael Haldane's articles offer an extensive discussion of invisibility achieved by a Wishing Hat in an early German prose text, *Fortunatus* (1509/1549), and of the several parallels that the text has with folktales, myths and later fantasy novels.[20] Haldane discusses two significant aspects of invisibility in European traditions: first, the relation between invisibility and (im)morality and, second, the associations between invisibility and death. Both connections exist in Greco-Roman mythology: the two gods who possess the caps of invisibility are Hermes/Mercury who, among other things, is the god of thieves, and Hades, the ruler of the kingdom of the dead.

As regards moral issues raised by invisibility, the story of Gyges in Plato's *The Republic* is a key narrative that has had a major influence on later literary representations of invisibility. In the second book of *The Republic*, Glaucon relates the story of Gyges to demonstrate that people are moral only out of necessity; if no one is able to monitor their behavior, they will act in an unjust and immoral manner. In the story, the shepherd Gyges finds a ring of invisibility and, unseen, seduces the queen, murders the king and takes possession of the throne himself. As Haldane points out, this rather pessimistic view of human beings' capability of moral behavior was challenged by Cicero, who discusses the same tale in *De Officiis* but comes to the conclusion that wise and good people would not use invisibility for immoral purposes; a moral subject is able to behave in a socially acceptable way whether invisible or not.[21]

A similar view is expressed by the character of Socrates in book ten of *The Republic*, where he maintains that a just man who knows that he has an immortal soul and who desires to be like God by the pursuit of virtue will not lose control over himself in any circumstances because acting virtuously is a reward in itself. Invisibility here becomes a metonym for secrecy; people are, of course, capable of doing all kinds of morally unacceptable things unseen without turning literally invisible by using supernatural devices. Whereas Glaucon in *The Republic* views all human beings as inherently corrupt — invisibility would turn anyone into a criminal — Socrates in *The Republic*, as well as Cicero in *De Officiis*, emphasize the integrity of a moral subject whom opportunity does not make a thief. The views share an assumed connection between invisibility and subjectivity: invisibility would reveal a person's "true" nature, whether egoistic or altruistic.

Perhaps the best-known contemporary historian and philosopher to address the issues of (in)visibility, morality and power has been Michel Foucault. Foucault discusses contemporary society as a "disciplinary" or "panoptic" society where norms and regulations are imposed on people by various disciplinary institutions (including school, army, and medical institutions) and maintained through a threat of punishment and a sense of constant surveillance that lead people to monitor their own behavior.[22] That is, when people know that they are constantly observed and thus visible to others, they will aim at behaving in socially acceptable ways. Foucault's phrase "docile bodies" describes the products of disciplinary power, subjects that are disciplined and controlled through punishment and their constant visibility.[23] While regulating behavior, disciplinary systems also aim at normalization, that is, establishing "the division between normal and abnormal" and associating normativity with normality.[24]

Foucault's idea of the panopticon was inspired by the eighteenth-century English philosopher Jeremy Bentham's vision of a new type of a modern prison: a circular building with an inspection center in the middle and the observed subjects' cells in the perimeter. Central to this idea is that those in control inside the inspection house are kept invisible; thus the subjects of surveillance never know whether they are being watched and start to watch themselves because there is always the chance that someone is observing them. Thus, what is visible can be controlled and, moreover, power belongs to those who remain invisible. While in Foucault's theorizations those exercising invisible power are not necessarily corrupt as in the ancient trope of invisibility and morality, visibility is certainly considered a way to control subjects and their morality.

The second major discourse of invisibility involves associations with darkness, death and the underworld. Invisibility, in general, is associated not only with gods and goddesses but also other inhuman creatures such as fairies and nature-spirits. However, as long as these are immortal creatures, invisibility, even if suspicious, is treated as a part of their nature and not as an indication of death. On the other hand, invisibility of deceased humans is a source of another type of anxiety. Ghosts, vampires and other living dead usually invoke horror partly because their invisibility is associated with death. Invisibility here becomes metaphorical since it signifies a new form of existence. Haldane discusses invisibility and death in relation to the helmet of Hades that "encloses its wearer in darkness," and writes that "the wearer may be likened to the dead: he walks the world, seeing but unseen." He then goes on to suggest that "this association of the unseen with death and spirits may have influenced the portrayal of invisibility in legend and literature; one may be at liberty to retire into oneself, or to indulge one's desires, but there is the danger of retreating ever further from mankind, of fading into a wraith, of becoming as the dead."[25]

Whereas in the discourse of invisibility and morals the invisible person's behavior evokes fear and anxiety mainly in other people, in the discourse of invisibility and death the anxiety also concerns the invisible persons themselves. Both discourses highlight the way in which subjectivity is formed in relation to other people. In the morality discourse, invisible persons can enter into subject positions they would or could not take if their behavior was monitored by the gaze of other subjects. In the death, or non-existence discourse, invisible persons are positioned in a liminal space where they have lost or risk losing their (human) subjectivity completely.

Both discourses have frequently been employed in later literature. The discourses are not mutually exclusive. Instead, there is often an indication that loss of one's morality will gradually lead to loss of one's humanity as well. As regards the morality discourse, Haldane suggests that Plato's pessimistic view is more commonly reflected in stories of invisibility. Although pointing out that in *Fortunatus* the author praises morals — when a character uses the Hat to steal, he later settles his account — Haldane suggests that this kind of behavior is untypical, because "with Gyges, Siegfried, and Hermes, invisibility involves murder, deceit and [symbolic or actual] rape" and that in general the stories of invisibility tend to reflect "a moral anxiety as to how the individual would handle the freedom of being unseen.... Wearing Gyges's ring or the Wishing-Hat may also entail corruption, conferring the liberty to fulfill dark, suppressed desires."[26] The grim aspects of invisibility are also reflected in the two best-known English-language fantastic texts involving invisibility: H.G. Wells's *The Invisible Man: A Grotesque Romance* (1897) and J.R.R. Tolkien's *The Lord of the Rings* (1954–1955). Both of these texts combine the morality discourse with the death/non-existence discourse.

In Wells's story the scientist Griffin has invented a formula for invisibility and first declares that invisibility is "strange perhaps, but it's not a crime," but later contemplates his "magnificent vision of all that Invisibility might mean to a man. The mystery, the power, the freedom."[27] Despite, or perhaps because of, his vision, his story ends tragically — Griffin ends up being a thief and a murderer, slides into solitary madness and is later pursued and killed by the authorities.

In Tolkien's epic fantasy, the invisibility ring has different effects on different persons — some are able to resist its powers to a certain extent, some are completely destroyed by it. The ring itself is so dangerous that it must be destroyed because no one is able to completely resist its powers. Although the childlike hobbits are represented as most resistant to the corruptive effects of the ring, the three hobbits who have owned the ring all part from the land of living in the end — Gollum follows the ring into a fiery stream and Frodo and Bilbo join the elves in their journey to the land of eternal youth. Wearing the ring has made them all less human, or at least incapable of continuing to live among other humans.

In all these texts discussed so far, including *Fortunatus*, in which the Hat is destroyed in the end, the assumption is that no one would be able to deal with the power of invisibility, and thus it is better to burn the hats, throw the rings into streams of fire and shoot those who have been clever enough to invent a formula for invisibility but foolish enough not to invent an antidote as well. Eventually, then, it is not humans who can control their invisibility, but invisibility controls its users.

If one accepts these grim views of invisibility as a device that reveals the inherent immorality of any human and associates its users with death and inhumanity, it is perhaps fortunate that invisibility is impossible. It would seem that the world would probably slip into chaos because no social contracts could bind invisible persons. But would everyone be corrupted? Is the moral subjectivity mainly determined by visibility? Are we talking about humanity here or, could we, perhaps, be talking about a negative version of conventional masculinity? It is not a coincidence that all of the invisible persons that Haldane discusses in relation to power, corruption and violence — Hermes, Siegfried, Andolosia in *Fortunatus*, the hero in "The King of the Golden Mountain," Griffin — are adult males. According to Haldane, these gods and heroes "use the freedom of the mist to act like beasts."[28]

It would seem, then, that invisibility brings out the worst aspects of conventional masculinity, including violence. However, these gendered aspects of invisibility only occur in the canonical texts that Haldane has chosen for his discussion. Catharina Raudvere, for instance, writes that in Scandinavian legends, invisible female witches were believed to come to sleep with men during the night and this behavior was considered suspicious.[29] Yet, as regards the canonical texts, there certainly are gendered aspects of (in)visibility in relation to gender, sexuality and desire — I will return to these in Chapter 6, in a discussion of invisibility in connection of feminist discourses of gaze. I do not want to make any general argument about the gendered nature of invisibility as a form of power at this point; rather, in the section on invisibility in Chapter 2, I will consider the invisible witches in relation to both the canonical texts that Haldane uses and Raudvere's discussion of female witches.

Discourses of (In)visibility in Feminist Theory

In feminist theory, (in)visibility has been a central concept not only in relation to theories of gaze but also in discussions of cultural invisibility. As seen above, invisibility as a trope can be used to raise the question of whether invisible persons have unlimited power because no one is able to monitor their behavior. However, invisibility is also typically used to illustrate how invisible persons are completely powerless in a state in which they are outside all social contacts and recognition. Invisibility as a metaphor for powerlessness is commonplace in all kinds of discourses — probably because of its effectiveness in illustrating power relations and because "invisible" can refer to anything that is unnoticed, non-existing, marginal, or "as-if-not-there"; depending on the context, anything can be invisible.

In discourses of cultural invisibility, the metaphor is used as a part of identity politics which aims at the visibility of marginal groups in society. In general, in realist contexts and discourses, cultural invisibility is not a desirable state — for culturally invisible people the issue is not whether they can abuse power because they are invisible, but the fact that since they are ignored, or not recognized, they have little or no power at all. In realist novels as well as in actual socio-historical contexts, invisibility serves as a metaphor for people who are neglected, ignored, or whose voices are not heard — thus we have invisible girls (or sometimes boys or children in general), for instance, in classrooms and third world countries.[30] This kind of cultural invisibility can be associated with whole groups of people — such as ethnic minorities, women, or children — as well as certain individuals. In comparison to realist and real-world texts, there are more possibilities for invisibility as a textual device in fantastic texts, since in a fantastic context it can be interpreted both literally and metaphorically.

In feminist discourses, invisibility is usually defined as an undesirable state in relation to girls and women (whether fictional or real). In fantastic texts, invisible females, such as ghosts or witches, have often served as the frightening female others. As will be shown in Chapter 2, these negative interpretations can be challenged by introducing rewritten versions of the witches as attractive and powerful characters. However, invisibility is also employed in feminist theory to introduce problematics of cultural visibility. According to Lynda Stone, in feminist theory based on liberal or pragmatist feminist discourses, invisibility has been metaphorically used to describe the problematic status of all females in patriarchal orders of history and culture.[31] Consequently, one of the main projects of liberal feminism has been to make women visible, both in real and fictional worlds. While the discourses of invisibility as a troublesome state for females emerged in the 1970s with second-wave feminism, they have by no means disappeared since then, but have taken new forms. For instance, as Sarah Banet-Weiser argues, in third-wave feminist discourses, commercial media visibility and the power connected with it are both embraced and celebrated, while invisibility (absence from the media) is connected with non-existence.[32] In contrast to these common notions about invisibility as a problem for the womankind, other feminist theorists have interpreted invisibility as a potentially positive state associated with safety. I will return to these feminist theories about male/female/queer gaze and (in)visibility in Chapter 4.

Invisibility Narratives for Children: Morality and Fear of Disappearance

As one might expect, children's fantasy fiction offers plenty of examples of the folk-tale type of strategic invisibility as a plot element — different kinds of invisibility "tools" function as magic gimmicks that help their users perform certain tasks. The invisibility cloak in J.K. Rowling's *Harry Potter and the Philosopher's Stone* (1997) and the invisibility ring in J.R.R. Tolkien's *The Hobbit* (1937) function in this way: to turn invisible when one chooses is a convenient trick and enables the carrier of the cloak to sneak around or eavesdrop, for instance. Apart from these famous examples, invisibility devices such as a dematerializer in Margaret Meacham's *Quiet! You're Invisible* (2001) and an act of telling lies in Cora Taylor's *Adventure in Istanbul* (2005) enable the characters to accomplish tasks such as spying, stealing, or tackling a bully conveniently while invisible.

Strategic invisibility is a narrative motif that has a clear function in the plot but is not connected with any larger thematic aspects of the story. While these examples are not particularly interesting in terms of the metaphorical potential of invisibility, several other stories for children raise issues about power and powerlessness and involve traces of the two major discourses of invisibility: both moral behavior and the fear of complete disappearance are addressed.

In several stories for children, the plot mainly revolves around the protagonist's invisibility. In these narratives, as in folktales, invisibility is typically enabled by a magic item or ritual. However, invisibility narratives differ from folktales because they make invisibility the main element of the plot and the emphasis is often on the humorous situations that result from invisibility — the humor partly results from the fact that invisibility is the only, or among the few, supernatural elements that intrude into the otherwise realistic everyday world of the characters. Invisibility is, to start with, usually accidental and associated with absurd events rather than heroic deeds. Moreover, these narratives introduce an experiential level to invisibility by representing characters' reactions to invisibility through focalization.

Many of the elements that occur repeatedly in contemporary invisibility narratives have been inspired by Wells's famous novel. Probably the first children's novel that drew on Wells is Edith Nesbit's *The Enchanted Castle* (1907), where invisibility is enabled by a wishing ring. The greatest differences between Wells's and Nesbit's texts are that the latter changes the mode from tragic to comic and replaces the pseudo-scientific explanation for invisibility with a purely fantastic one. The ring's powers are found out accidentally when one of the protagonists, Mabel, wishes that she was invisible. After an anxious start to her invisibility — she is scared of permanent invisibility which could mean powerlessness, isolation and abnormality — Mabel soon begins "to see all sorts of amusing things coming along,"[33] a turn of phrase characteristic of the mode of the narrative. The children explore activities that invisibility makes possible, including performing "magic" and acting as an invisible detective.

The children also note that invisibility enables one to be a perfect burglar, but this morally unacceptable possibility is abandoned. At the end the wishing ring loses its power, which is the end of fantastic adventures for the protagonists.

The matter-of-fact style in which characters in the books react to invisibility seems absurd in relation to the marvelous events. In *The Enchanted Castle* the absurd humor is highlighted by metafictional comments where the narrator directly addresses the readers and blurs the borders of fiction and reality: "Those of my readers who have gone about much with an invisible companion will not need to be told how awkward the whole business is."[34] By ironically suggesting that her readers might have experienced similar trouble with magic items as the characters in her book, the narrator actually emphasizes the fictionality of invisibility (at least for those readers who do not believe in it in real-life contexts).

The plot in Nesbit's story — the introduction of a magic element in an everyday world, the description of the absurd and humorous events that follow and the destruction or disappearance of the magic element at the end — is typical of more recent invisibility narratives. In stories such as Helen Cresswell's and Judy Brown's *Almost Goodbye, Guzzler* (1990), Eric Houghton's *Vincent the Invisible* (1993), Jeff Brown's *Invisible Stanley* (1995), Mary Hoffman's *A Vanishing Tail* (1996), Marthe Jocelyn's *The Invisible Day* (1997), Dan Greenburg's *Now You See Me ... Now You Don't* (1998), Robert Swindells's *Invisible!* (1999), Sally Gardner's *The Invisible Boy* (2002), and Jim Benton's *The Invisible Fran* (2004), the originality in each narrative is not a result of changing the functions of invisibility, or the mode and closure of the narrative, but a result of replacing invisibility gadgets and rituals with new inventions. These include, for instance, a Hat of Invisibleness made of a lampshade, a saucepan, a glass pig and Sellotape (Houghton), a ritual of eating raisins during a thunderstorm at night (Brown), an invisibility patch provided by an extraterrestrial visitor (Gardner), and a formula that combines cellophane molecules with chameleon DNA and disappearing ink (Benton).

The play with the cause of invisibility suggests to me that it is assumed in the texts that readers are familiar with the more conventional invisibility gadgets, such as cloaks, and thus able to appreciate the humor in the rewriting of the conventional element. Invisibility may be complete or one's clothes may remain visible, or, as in Edgar Eager's (1954) *Half Magic* that explicitly refers to Nesbit's *The Enchanted Castle*, a magic nickel that does spells only by halves turns one of the main characters transparent, rather than completely invisible. In most stories the main characters are children, although in a recent picture book retelling of Wells's tale, Arthur Yorink's and Doug Cushman's (2010) *The Invisible Man*, the main character is an adult. This has only a minimum effect on the plot that closely resembles those invisibility narratives where the main characters are children. The invisible protagonists try the activities introduced by Nesbit, particularly conjuring or magic tricks, spying on people and catching thieves. The texts also maintain a comic mode throughout, mainly building on the absurdity of the characters' invisibility in an everyday world. Puns based on various words related to seeing and vision also abound — there are plenty of possibilities for this in the English language since "seeing" metaphorically refers to understanding.

The characters that turn invisible are portrayed as morally exemplary in the tradition of Cicero — spying on people is allowed if it is for good purposes, such as catching burglars. Invisibility endows the child characters with power, but they neither abuse it nor are corrupted by it. Even though the characters often give in to temptations, such as spying on people in private spaces, doing rude things in front of people or stealing things, soon the characters give up the immoral activities and, in many cases, compensate for the harm that they have done in the end. In Jocelyn's (1997) *The Invisible Day*, for instance, the main character, Billie, avoids paying public transportation fees and steals fruit from a shop while being invisible but later pays for it. In these comic narratives such ethically informed behavior is not linked with gender; the morally exemplary characters can be either boys or girls.

Significantly, invisibility is never completely safe or fun — this conveniently erases the possible problem that, were invisibility safe, the characters might not be able to resist the immoral temptations in the long run. The negative experience of invisibility — the fear of exclusion or complete disappearance — is the reason why most of the children do not want to try invisibility again once they have become visible at the end. While the characters find invisibility funny, it is also treated as a problem, as evidenced by the new, popular motif of a planned or completed visit to a doctor to find a cure for invisibility.[35] It is meaningful that the characters learn the drawbacks of invisibility through their own experience and that invisibility is always associated with the danger of powerlessness and isolation. The negative experiences of invisibility also seem to be non-gendered: both boys and girls experience the fear of permanent invisibility. The irrelevance of gender is unsurprising in terms of the overall characterization — the invisible children here are not rounded characters but actants in short comic stories. Invisibility is not employed as an element of characterization to illustrate the metaphorical condition of any specific person, but used to illustrate the concerns and anxieties associated with invisibility in general.

Unsurprisingly, it is Cicero's view of invisibility and morals that is adopted in the majority of children's invisibility narratives. However, in contrast to the comic invisibility narratives above, another group of texts leans more towards horror than comedy and focuses more clearly on tragic aspects of invisibility. Examples would include Diana Wynne Jones's children's novel *The Ogre Downstairs* (1974), Robert Cormier's young adult novel *Fade* (1988), R.L. Stine's *Let's Get Invisible!* (1993) and Jenny Nimmo's *Charlie Bone and the Blue Boa* (2004).

In *The Ogre Downstairs*, a boy manages to turn himself invisible by the help of a magic chemistry set. He wants to use invisibility to take revenge on his stepfather, and when invisible "doesn't feel like him any more — he's a sort of an angry ghost."[36] Invisibility clearly does not suit him — he tries to kill or, at least, to do serious harm to the stepfather — and everyone is relieved when it is found out that water turns him visible again.

The tragedy of invisibility is also addressed in Cormier's *Fade* that features male characters who, one generation after other, end up using invisibility for violent or immoral purposes, and thus represent a negative version of conventional masculinity. R.L. Stine's *Let's Get Invisible!*, published in the *Goosebumps* horror series for children, features a magic mirror that helps a group of children to turn invisible — albeit that if they do that one time too many, they will be prisoned inside the mirror and replaced by their evil reflections or doppelgangers in the outside world. While invisibility seems fun at the beginning, the characters soon start to fear about complete disappearance, especially after the protagonist, Max, meets his doppelganger, or "dark side," inside the mirror and is asked to give in to it. For Max and his friends, to resist invisibility and thus their evil side is necessary in the end (although, this being a horror story, not everyone manages it).

In contrast, Nimmo's *Charlie Bone and the Blue Boa* is certainly not a horror novel but treats invisibility as a horrifying curse. Ollie Sparks, a minor character, has been turned invisible by a blue boa that hugs its victims not to death but to invisibility. Due to his invisibility, Ollie is cut out of normal life and has to hide in the attic of a school. None of the story is focalized through Ollie but through dialogue it becomes clear the he does not enjoy his invisibility and his state is also pitied by the protagonist, Charlie Bone, who views being invisible as "a pretty miserable existence."[37] In the end, with the help of other children, Ollie is turned visible again.

While in most of the above examples — apart from *Fade*, a significantly more complex narrative in comparison to the other discussed texts — it is suggested that anyone who suddenly turns invisible has the same experiences and faces the same risks and temptations as everyone else, another set of stories associates invisibility with specific persons who have specific histories and personalities; that is, their invisibility is not a happy or unhappy accident but explained by their behavior in the past or their personality, or both. In contrast to narratives where invisibility is achieved by using different magic "tools," here invisibility is a more permanent state, a skill acquired through training, or a gift bestowed upon a certain character. In these cases, invisibility — whether self-chosen or imposed — is more crucially linked to the character's identity and not always a positive feature.

One specific group of texts where invisibility is an inherent or acquired ability of a young female character are stories about witches and other magic users who can become temporarily invisible, usually for strategic purposes. Since invisibility is an ability that the witches can control, it is often an empowering state that enables the characters to, for instance, hide from or spy on their enemies. However, as with magic and witchcraft in general, the ability to turn invisible is not always empowering, even for experienced magic users — both because it raises questions about the invisible subject's moral agency and because invisible female characters are often pursued by others who want to abuse their powers. I will return to this issue in the following chapter that will discuss invisible witches in both secondary world fantasy by Terry Pratchett, Susan Price and Philip Pullman, as well as primary world fantasy set in contemporary urban milieu by Sarah Neufeld, Laura Ruby, and Lynne Ewing.

In another group of texts featuring invisible young women, the focus is on invisibility and powerlessness — the morality discourse is addressed in some texts but pushed to the margins or completely excluded in others. While these stories can be humorous, invisibility is mainly portrayed as an undesirable state that the girl characters need to escape to achieve agentic subjectivity. In examples such as Diana Wynne Jones's *The Time of the Ghost* (1981), Patrice Kindl's *The Woman in the Wall* (1997), Tonya Hurley's *Ghostgirl* (2008) and Marilyn Kaye's *Out of Sight, Out of Mind* (2009), turning invisible is connected with being shy, scared and powerless in the sense that the characters are unable to participate in social networks and communication.[38] In each case at the end of the story the characters become permanently visible again, after becoming braver, gaining recognition by others and developing a more agentic subjectivity.[39]

Although in these texts it first seems that invisibility is an undesired state and a form of powerlessness, it is also a form of power, even if a passive one, because these characters more or less control their invisibility themselves. In the case of these invisible characters the motif of invisibility can become ambiguous: is it actually a form of power or a state of powerlessness, or perhaps a combination of both? Is invisibility necessarily connected with the morality of a subject? I will return to these issues in relation to trauma theory and identity in Chapter 3, where I will discuss the invisible girl protagonists in *The Time of the Ghost*, *Ghostgirl* and *Out of Sight, Out of Mind* in greater detail. These texts share the thematics of cultural invisibility that is also addressed in shorter stories; however, they are in many ways more complex texts, partly because the novels are aimed at an older audience. In Chapter 3 I will specifically discuss the ways in which invisibility can be used as a narrative device to deconstruct girl subjectivities. In Chapter 4 I will address issues of (in)visibility and subjectivity in relation to the concept of gaze and discuss invisible girls and young women as both objects and subjects of gaze in *The Time of the Ghost*, *The Woman in the Wall* and *Ghostgirl*, as well as in Susan Price's *The Ghost Wife* (1999) and Laura Whitcomb's *A Certain Slant of Light* (2005).

Texts in which invisibility is an ability of a boy or a young man exist as well. As mentioned above, in Cormier's *Fade* invisibility is an inherited feature that runs in the male-line of a certain family. While invisibility serves as a source of power for the young male characters — they are able, for instance, to hide from others when they wish and to spy on people — in the end invisibility turns out to be tragic rather than empowering. As Waller argues in her analysis of *Fade*, invisibility is associated with the loss of identity: "The fantastic trope of invisibility ... provides a visual gap in what is already a narrative of spectral subjectivity."[40] Young invisible men who are represented as outsiders also feature in Andrew Clements's *Things Not Seen* (2002) and Neal Shusterman's *The Schwa Was Here* (2004) that depict invisibility in urban, contemporary school settings. In Neil Gaiman's *The Graveyard Book* (2008), the boy protagonist is able to remain unnoticed; in a graveyard he can turn literally invisible, outside it people can see him, but soon forget what they have seen. Will in Philip Pullman's *The Subtle Knife* (1997) also knows how to make himself unnoticeable, if not literally invisible. Each of these texts associate invisibility with the status of the boy/male characters as outsiders in society, but their invisibility has little to do with shyness. Moreover, none of the texts with young, invisible male protagonists associates *visibility* with good looks and beauty, that is, with the status of being a beautiful object for others sexual or erotic gazes. As will be seen, this connection is strong in many of the texts with young invisible female protagonists. In the analytical chapters, I will make occasional comparisons between invisible male and female protagonists but will not provide any systematic discussion of invisibility in regard to masculinity. Next, however, let us turn to motifs and tropes of age-shifting.

Age-Shifting

Stories about magic age-shifting abound in mythologies, folktales and fiction. Like invisibility, magic age-shifting occurs as a motif in folk-literature, although in Thompson's motif index the entries for magic age-shifting are significantly fewer than those for invisibility. Most of the entries concern magic rejuvenation, eternal youth, or people, gods, or fairies who do not age at all, although there are a few examples listed as premature aging, or transformations into an older person. Because aging is a naturally occurring process, to magically change one's age is often not a change at all, but a stop in (natural) aging — hence the stories of the elixir of life and spells to achieve a prolonged or extended life. Whereas invisibility is a flexible transformation that can be used strategically because it enables the transformed person to perform all sorts of tasks unseen, magic changes in age — although sometimes serving a strategic purpose — are more often permanent changes. In the following, I will first review the motif uses of age-shifting in narratives and then move on to uses of age-shifting as a trope that addresses the grand themes of growing up, aging, and changing, as well as (im)mortality in relation to (gendered) human subjectivity.

Given that old age is rarely something people desire, age-shifting often functions as a reward or punishment motif in tales: regained youth is a reward, premature old age is a curse. The regained youth can function as a reward for (good) characters, while on the other hand a false drink or an unsuccessful rejuvenation ritual can be a way to punish vain characters. In a Grimms' fairy tale titled "The White Snake," a princess sets her suitor different tasks; bringing her an apple from the Tree of Life is one of them.[41] Successful in his task, they eat the apple together and live to a great age. In another tale, "The Water of Life," the king's sons bring their sick old father the water of life and he turns strong and healthy again, as in his youth — although it is not clear whether he actually turns young again but merely regains the attributes of youth, strength and health.[42]

Whereas those changes are ambiguous, in a tale titled "The Old Man Made Young Again," a magic change in age definitely takes place — the latter part of the tale involves the punishment motif.[43] In the tale the Lord and St. Peter encounter a poor old beggar, have compassion on him and the Lord turns him young again by putting him first into a blacksmith's forge and then cooling him in a quenching tub. The man comes out looking young and healthy. After this, the tale takes a brutal twist, when the smith decides to try to turn his old mother-in-law young by using the same techniques. He does not succeed, of course, but the vain old woman is horribly burned and mutilated instead, first by the fire and then in the cool water. The smith's wife and his daughter-in-law, both pregnant, hear the old woman's screaming and come to see what is going on: they are terrified by seeing the old woman's face completely mutilated. The following night the smith's wife and his daughter-in-law give birth to two ape-like boys who run into the woods. Whether this is a story including a lesson about human vanity and the danger of humans meddling with godly powers or merely an episode that Maria Tatar describes as one that "blend[s] sadism with slapstick to produce a form of festive violence that targets either the top dog or the underdog as victim" is open to interpretation.[44] In any case, these narratives involve age-shifting as a motif that does address human desires related to (not) aging, but they do not engage in exploring what the changed human subjectivities are like after their magic transformations.

Another common situation where magic age-shifting occurs often as a punishment is a moment of crossing the boundary between the real (or the primary) world and the fairyland, a secondary fantastic world or a parallel universe. In the fairyland occurring in folk literatures time usually, if not always, flies faster than in the land of mortals, and thus those mortals who venture to fairyland and back find that they have returned to their homes several years, decades or centuries later after spending only a day in the magic world. A version of this tale occurs famously in Washington Irving's "Rip Van Winkle" (1819), where the protagonist encounters a group of strange people while wandering in the mountains, spends the night merrymaking with them, wakes up alone the following day and, upon returning to his home village, realizes that he has been away for decades — something that he also feels in his limbs since he has turned into an old man overnight.

In contrast, in children's fantasy, the age-shifting that occurs during boundary-crossing between different worlds does not necessarily have tragic consequences. For instance, in C.S. Lewis's *The Lion, the Witch and the Wardrobe* (1950), the four siblings grow into adults in Narnia but turn back into their young selves upon their return to the primary world; while they miss Narnia, they are not destroyed upon their return (which, of course, has to do with the fact that they have not lost any time in their lives in the primary world). A recent use of this motif can be found in Margo Lanagan's *Tender Morsels* (2008) where an abused young woman escapes into her own magic world with her two children; in the magic world time passes faster than in the primary world, which creates a soothing distance to the traumatic events that the young woman has experienced and thus she is better prepared to return to the primary world later on.

In contrast to magic changes in age (or attempts towards them) as rewards or punishments, there are other transformations that can be considered strategic. In these types of changes one can become either younger or older to accomplish a certain task in the narrative. While ordinary mortals do not repeatedly shift back and forth from youth to old age or vice versa, the ability is a typical one in connection to fairies, gods and goddesses. As with invisibility, human beings that are able to change their age are either helped by supernatural powers, or can themselves do magic. One type of strategic aging occurs when characters, in this case ordinary mortals, need to fill in a typical role in the tale. In two Russian tales, "Tzar Saltan" and "Little Bear's Son" the child protagonists grow "not by days [or years] but by hours" to be able to take the role of the hero.⁴⁵ In these cases, however, it is questionable whether the characters actually age magically by the help of supernatural powers or whether these are merely examples of condensed (or magic fairy tale) time in the narrative.

Another, more famous version of strategic change in age occurs in the Grimms' version of Snow White, "Little Snow White," where the stepmother transforms herself: "She disguised and took the shape of another old woman"— this happens clearly for strategic purposes as she tries to poison Snow White in her disguised form.⁴⁶ Whereas the other magic changes cited above are not really gendered, the image of a female witch who changes her age magically certainly is. This image is associated with the popular figure or the archetype of the triple goddess — a female with supernatural powers who is able to appear in different forms, as a maiden, a mother, or a crone. Often age-shifting that invokes the archetype functions merely as a motif— the narrative itself does not examine the different, aged aspects of femininity or the changing female subjectivity in detail. These versions of the triple goddess frequently occur in English-language children's fantasy that draws on Celtic mythology. For instance, the three witches, Orwen, Orddu and Orgoch, that occur both as crones and young maidens in Lloyd Alexander's *The Chronicles of Prydain* (1964–1973) are based on Welsh goddesses. Their function in the tale is to help the main hero, and little is learned of the witches' subjectivities.

In several tales, what remains of the archetype (other than the portrayals of the old, evil, devouring hag on its own) are characters that are young maidens disguised as or turned into old crones. This typically occurs in tales of monstrous brides which involve the "virtue or true love is rewarded" theme. In Irish stories of the divine Sovereignty of Ireland that Anne Ross cites, the goddess appears to three princes in the form of a hideous old woman, and while two of the brothers reject her sexual advances, the third, the future king, accepts them and the crone turns into a beautiful young maiden.⁴⁷ The same type of monstrous bride occurs in the medieval English "Loathly Lady" stories — Geoffrey Chaucer's "The Wife of Bath's Tale" (in *The Canterbury Tales*, 1958) and a folk ballad, "The Marriage of Sir Gawain" (in Child 1957), involve versions of the story. In all these tales the transformation from a crone into a maiden depends on the true groom's virtue/love, whether the transformed party has voluntarily disguised herself or himself to test the bride or groom, or she is under a curse. Whereas for the goddesses all their forms were equally important, in the "Loathly Lady" stories it is obvious that the form of the old hag is a curse and the form of the lovely young lady is a reward (supposedly both to the lady herself as well as her husband).

However, elsewhere the age-shifting witch or goddess can become a trope to explore female subjectivity in a more complex way. In her Jungian-feminist analysis of women's writing, Annis Pratt suggests that in women's fiction the triple goddess archetype is used to address female experience of life: "The fully matured feminine personality comprehends all three elements and brings any one of them into play at any time."[48] Pratt's optimistic view does not concern all stories involving females that magically (or metaphorically) change their age — in the children's fantasy novels that I will examine, shifting between differently aged identities is not necessarily a sign of maturation, nor is it always connected with voluntary choice.

In Louise Lawrence's *The Earth Witch* (1982) that also draws on Welsh mythology, the age-shifting witch is associated with various goddesses and her changing subjectivity is juxtaposed and compared to a young female character's process of coming of age. Female subjectivity is here portrayed partly as violent and horrifying and, importantly, as something that young girls will naturally and inevitably grow into. In contrast, Diana Wynne Jones's *Howl's Moving Castle* (1986), where a young woman is turned into a 90-year-old granny, involves a somewhat altered version of the "Loathly Lady" story and is a comic take on the character of the age-shifting witch. Rather than putting emphasis on essential womanhood, Jones's text highlights the performativity of gendered subjectivity. I will discuss these two texts in Chapter 2 in relation to female subjectivity, aging and the concept of empowerment. In the following, I will introduce some other children's fantasy texts where age-shifting becomes a trope addressing aged subjectivity and growing up. While fountains of youth and visits to fairyland are among the traditional motifs, age-shifting has remained popular in contemporary children's fiction, particularly in the form of time slips back to one's past or future, (pseudo)scientific techniques that can stop cells from aging, or body swapping experiences. The following texts are not secondary world fantasy, and the move from the mythic or fairy tale setting to contemporary, urban surroundings highlights somewhat different expectations related to aging and subjectivity.

Performing Age in Children's Fiction

In children's fantasy fiction situated in modern, urban settings, age-shifting often occurs as a temporary experiment with subjectivity — this usually involves the lesson of trying to walk in someone else's shoes, be it another person of a different age (as in body swapping) or one's own younger or older self. In narratives situated in a contemporary world, age-shifting often leads to absurd situations, in a similar way as in the invisibility narratives discussed above. As with invisibility, the cause for age-shifting varies, sometimes it is not explained at all. Whatever its cause, age-shifting can be utilized to critically explore embodied subjectivity: how does a subject's material body affect her sense of identity, agency and the ways in which other people regard her in social interaction?

In comparison to invisibility — which potentially allows unseen persons to do almost anything they wish — age-shifting is not such a flexible transformation. The advantages gained from changes in age depend on the social identities and power connected with certain ages. Like gender, age is performative in the sense that it is partly based on the features of the material body, but also on a set of behaviors learned through repetition and by internalizing the discourses of age that circulate in society. Thus it is possible to describe people as younger or older than their biological age (both in terms of appearance and behavior) or to encourage them to "act their age." While in folk tales performativity is not really an issue — the stock characters are connected with certain types of actions and thus their performances are limited anyhow — in children's fantasy texts the (in)ability to act one's (new) age is addressed frequently in relation to magic changes in age. If the age-shifter is not able to "act her age," that is, to perform the new social, aged and gendered identity associated with their transformed material body, the performance can become comic. Abrupt age-shifting highlights the challenges involved in trying to behave like someone else without the time to practice the performance.

A central question in relation to the age-shifting and identity is also the issue of continuity: is it merely the appearance that changes while the inner core stays the same, or does the appearance — the new body and the experience of the new body — affect subjectivity? What happens to the personal identity narrative if a character partly loses her memory — how does she perform age and gender if she does not remember who she is? Fantasy makes it possible to play with identities in a manner that is not tied to psychological realism: the characters that turn into younger or older versions of themselves may turn into completely different persons as well. This is what happens, for instance, in Nesbit's *The Enchanted Castle* when the boy Jimmy makes a wish that he was rich and the wishing ring turns him into an elderly gentleman who no longer recognizes his siblings and is merely concerned about his business affairs. There is no continuity between the young Jimmy and the old man, who is a completely different person and would not himself be recognized by his siblings had they not seen the transformation happen in the front of their eyes. In Penelope Farmer's *The Castle of Bone* (1972), teenage boy Penn accidentally falls into a magic cupboard which turns anything placed inside it into an earlier version of that thing or person — Penn turns first into a toddler and after his second time in the cupboard from the toddler into a newborn baby. As with Jimmy in *The Enchanted Castle*, for Penn the change in his body means an immediate and complete change in subjectivity — or, to be exact, almost a complete loss of subjectivity because he transforms into such a young child that he can no longer talk nor take care of himself.

In narratives where characters are aware of their changing body during and after their transformations, age-shifting is often used for moral purposes: to teach characters a lesson about what it is to walk in another's shoes. Thus the stories reflect a strong sense of the effects of embodiment. In two picture books that involve age-shifting, Anthony Browne's *The Big Baby: A Little Joke* (1993) and Allen Say's *A Stranger in the Mirror* (1995), the age-shifting is caused by the protagonists' desire not to grow up. Browne's text features an adult man who looks and acts young for his age; worried about aging, he one day ends up drinking a bottle of "Elixa de Yoof" and turns into a baby overnight. As a baby, the man has no agency at all and his wife has to take care of him by feeding him and changing his nappies. As the pictures and the text suggest, the man does not enjoy this condition at all. In the end, the man changes back to his normal self, apart form the fact that he sees the first grey hair on his head — this is an indication that the man is on his path to accepting change and aging.

In Say's picture book the age-shifting occurs in the opposite direction: a young boy becomes an old man overnight after he has visited his grandfather in an old people's home and expressed his desire to never grow old. The boy is named "Rip Van Wrinkle" at school and bullied — his tragedy is that he has to enter an unchanged world while he himself has drastically changed. His family and friends are appalled at the way he looks. After a while the boy is about to run away from home but is stopped by a skateboard gliding by; the boy jumps on it, forgets he is old and performs skillful tricks, thus challenging the bystanders' expectations about what an "old man" can do. At the closure, the boy wakes up and finds out he has been dreaming. Readers are left with the idea that while embodiment affects the ways in which other people react to and interact with a subject, inside the body the subject has a unique core identity that is the "real" self that does not need to be molded by other people's expectations. In these two picture books, aged, embodied identity is addressed by demonstrating how other people's relationships to the transformed characters change after their age-shifting.

In other children's narratives, however, the successful or failed performance of a new younger or older identity becomes a major issue, namely because most of the other characters are unaware of the transformations or disguise of the protagonists. In F. Anstey's *Vice Versa* (1881), Mary Rodgers's *Freaky Friday* (1972) and *Summer Switch* (1982), and Marilyn Kaye's novel *Happy Birthday, Dear Amy* (2001), age-shifting is an unanticipated and undesired result of an accident or of another person's spell, and the characters have to adapt to their new bodies as well as they can. In the first three novels, age-shifting results from body-swapping, children changing bodies with their parents, whereas in Kaye's novel the female protagonist changes from a 13-year-old teenager into a 25-year-old woman overnight because her genetically engineered cells take an aging spurt.

Judith Butler emphasizes that gender is performative in the sense that it is produced through discourse and enforced through repetition; it is not a costume or role that a person can easily change at will.[49] The same concerns an aged identity. This is humorously illustrated in Anstey's *Vice Versa* where a father and a son swap bodies. This leads to disaster when the son focuses on all the fun aspects of adulthood, such as partying, while ruining his father's business and earning him a reputation as a lunatic. Meanwhile, the father faces various punishments for his unwanted behavior at a boarding school. The father, in particular, has trouble adapting to his role as a child where he is pushed around by other kids as well as teachers who find his requests to be treated in a more respectful way absurd or impudent. Words such as "mimicry," "burlesque," "caricature" and "farce" are explicitly used in the novel to refer to the characters' failed attempts to perform their (bodily) age — all these terms refer to forms of performance which are based on exaggeration and parodic imitation. In *Vice Versa* the use of parody effectively deconstructs the discourse of "respectable" adult masculinity. The father's failed performance in particular is connected with his difficulty in seeing things from other people's perspective. In the end, he is enlightened by his experience and begins to treat his son in a much more supportive way.

However, in relation to age and gender, in other novels characters are able to change their behavior according to their "costume." When their appearance changes, they are easily able to accommodate their behavior to the expectations that their new bodily identity creates — this happens in Rodgers's *Summer Switch* that plays with a similar scenario as *Vice Versa*. The crucial difference is that in *Summer Switch* both the son and the father manage to play their new roles so well that, when they return to their own bodies in the end, each finds himself in an improved situation. The son in his father's body manages to make his father's business prosper whereas the father in his son's body beats other kids in a summer camp in various games and changes the reputation of his earlier sissy son. Instead of challenging conventional masculinity, each character excels in fields where features traditionally associated with masculinity, such as competitiveness and strength (whether physical or mental), are appreciated.

In Rodgers's *Freaky Friday* that involves a daughter and a mother swapping bodies, as well as in Kaye's *Happy Birthday Amy!*, the age-shifting characters are also quick to adapt to their new bodies. These texts, however, include some aspects that deconstruct certain notions of conventional femininity. I will return to these texts in Chapter 3, where I compare them to narratives with characters who are not conscious about their identity performance but are doing their aged and gendered identities habitually and unconsciously.

The depiction of unconscious performance of identity is possible in texts where characters are unaware that they have gone through bodily changes because of losing their memory at the moment of transformation — this can happen, for instance, in relation to age-shifting that occurs as a result of slips in time. Sometimes this type of age-shifting can become a trope to address the changing subject's experiences of herself at different ages and her sense of identity and agency. Time slips that result in life-transforming age-shifting occur, for instance, in several of Diana Wynne Jones's novels including *The Time of the Ghost* (1981), *Archer's Goon* (1984), *Fire and Hemlock* (1985) and *Hexwood* (1993). In each case, the shifts in time are combined with a memory loss that causes a disruption in the character's identity narrative and functions as a narrative device to address subjectivity construction. In these novels the continuity between the protagonists' present and past selves is lost at the beginning but — unlike in the texts by Nesbit and Farmer mentioned above — is regained later with reconstructed memories of the past. I will return to *Hexwood* in detail in Chapter 3 and argue that the shifts in time and age in the novel are a way to explore the gendered and aged subjectivities of their female protagonists.

Choosing Mortality: Dangers of Eternal Youth

Finally, since age-shifting in the forms of rejuvenation and life extension or arrested aging is frequently connected with immortality, I will briefly address it here. Immortality is a vast theme and here I am only interested in it as much as it is associated with embodied subjectivity and bodily transformations either in the form of age-shifting — usually rejuvenation — or an abnormal halt or suspension in aging. Immortality as a theme has occurred in mythologies, religious writings and fictions throughout human history. In the present, it also occurs in scientific discourses about aging and life extension in medicine and geropsychology. In most cultures, various deities are usually immortal, while humans desire immortality but are mostly denied it; indeed, recognizing one's own mortality is considered a necessary aspect of humanity.

One of the earliest surviving pieces of human writing, *The Epic of Gilgamesh*, involves a story where Gilgamesh — half god, half man — seeks the herb of life in the deepest part of the well of life. He finds the herb but loses it to a snake that eats it and then sheds its skin. Quests for a source of immortality have often ended in failure, other famous examples including Alexander the Great's search for the water of life, or Ponce de León's pursuit of the fountain of youth. It is usually suggested that this failure is for the better for humankind.

While most religions involve an idea of an immortal human soul, physical immortality that involves living eternally in one's flesh and bones is usually treated with more suspicion. As Joseph D. Miller writes in regard to Christianity and the figure of the Wandering Jew, "an archetypal example of the Faustian price of immortality," "physical, secular immortality is a poor substitute for the joys of Christian paradise."[50] Unless granted by some kind of supreme being—other than the devil, as with Faustian figures—immortality is often associated with immorality and the loss of one's humanity. Apart from Faustian figures one only needs to think of, for instance, vampires and other undead creatures.

Immortality may be associated with wisdom, but it can also be associated with immaturity and child-like self-centeredness; the latter because it is so often linked to eternal youth. Several stories about immortality suggest that eternal life is only bearable as long as one stays physically young and healthy. As the story about Eos and Tithonus in Greek mythology shows, immortality can become a curse if one continues to age. The goddess Eon asks Zeus to grant immortality to her mortal love, Tithonus, but forgets to ask for eternal youth as well. Thus Tithonus continues to age and in the end Eos locks her old lover in a room to hide him from the pitying gaze of others and herself.

Old age is associated with decay and powerlessness not only in ancient myths but also in contemporary discourses about growing old. In the present, various technologies of rejuvenation — whether successful or not — are constantly developed and marketed to customers trying to pursue youth. The attitude towards rejuvenation and life extension is ambiguous, however. According to one common belief, adulthood means the ability to accept one's changing, aging and decaying body. Inner growth, rather than aim to preserve one's youthful form, is associated with maturity. Rejuvenation, for instance in the form of cosmetic surgery, is commonly judged as vain and superficial.

One place where this ambiguous attitude towards immortality and life extension is examined in detail is adult science fiction. A great number of works of adult science fiction explore future societies where humans, due to new technologies, might not have to age and die—a vision that challenges the notions of bodily change as necessary altogether.[51] This is unsurprising, given the aim in modern medicine is to preserve human life as long as possible; immortality would only be a logical result of defeating all forms of disease and cellular deterioration.

While adult science fiction may experiment with visions of immortality, in children's fantastic literature an eternal life is a much more challenging theme. Offers of unnaturally long or immortal life are usually refused in stories for children because the (child) protagonists must learn to accept change. This necessity of accepting psychological and bodily change is linked to maturation; the acceptance is a sign of adulthood. This is often highlighted by juxtaposing the abnormal, immortal characters and those characters who choose to grow up and age (and, eventually, die) in a natural way. As Lynne Lundquist writes, one take on immortality is the character of the eternal child. In the stories that Lundquist discusses, J.M. Barrie's *Peter Pan: A Fantasy in Five Acts* (1902/1928) and Rachel Field's *Hitty: Her First Hundred Years* (1929), immortality is "a form of stasis that is clearly undesirable" and the immortal is "someone to be finally disliked or pitied, not admired or emulated."[52] Peter Pan is a boy who has willingly refused to grow up and thus stays eternally young, but he suffers from amnesia and is alone with his condition. Hitty is a doll who is indeed immortal but also lacks agency since she cannot move on her own. These characters, whose existence, Lundquist suggests, is hardly represented as an ideal one, are juxtaposed with the children that they encounter — Wendy, the Lost Boys, Hitty's owners — who go on with their lives, aging and changing. While Peter Pan may be interpreted as a character that challenges normative assumptions about growing up and adulthood, no one else joins him in his challenge.[53]

Accepting change is also the idea pursued in later children's fantasy works such as Penelope Farmer's *The Castle of Bone* (1972), Natalie Babbitt's *Tuck Everlasting* (1975), and Anne Lindbergh's *The People in Pineapple Place* (1982). The main theme in Farmer's text is the acceptance of change and aging; in the mythical world accessed through a magic cupboard everything and everybody changes and yet stays the same. This is, however, the world that the child characters in the novel choose not to live in — they refuse immortality. The child character in Babbitt's novel makes a similar choice — although invited to join the Tuck family who have drunk from the well of life and live eternally never aging, her decision is to age naturally. In Lindbergh's novel the young protagonist also encounters a group of families who live in their own small, traveling world where they do not age at all. At the closure, the families travel on in their unchanging time-space bubble, while the young boy goes on with his normal life. In Lindbergh's text this is not really presented as a conscious choice by the protagonist, although he does view the prospect of "staying in fourth grade for forty-three years, not to speak forever" not exactly appealing.[54] As with the Tuck family in Babbitt, here another tragic aspect of immortality combined with non-aging is that the immortals are forced to move to new places and abandon old homes and friends all the time, to keep from raising suspicion about their abnormal state. The underlying idea in all these novels is that the tragedy is not to change and die but to live forever. In change lies the beauty of life.

In a similar vein, most children's and young adult books about rejuvenation tend to represent the desire to grow younger as an unwanted feature of someone who does not want to accept mortality as a fact of life. Often the characters searching for rejuvenation spells, potions, or treatments are portrayed as downright evil, although sometimes merely misguided. To cite a few examples, in Lois Duncan's teen horror novel *Locked in Time* (1985), a family of mother and her children have managed to keep their youthful appearances for a century by performing voodoo rites that involve sacrificing the life of a husband. This strategy is represented as horrifying and the family is properly destroyed in the end, with the help of its members, as the children are happy to put an end to their extended childhoods.

In Jeanette Winterson's science fiction novel *Tanglewreck* (2006), the powerful scientist Regalia Mason is applying a technique called Time Transfusion to rejuvenate herself: she "borrows" time from young children who, in the process, age while she gets younger. This is not appreciated by the young female protagonist in the novel and eventually she defeats Mason in her play with time. Non-aging adults are also the enemy of young protagonists in Gemma Malley's *The Declaration Trilogy* (2007–2010), where the longevity drugs guaranteed to most people have significantly worsened the problem of overpopulation and thus people who choose longevity cannot have any children by law. Illegal children are treated as problematic surplus who have to serve as slaves or, worse, are used as source materials for rejuvenation technologies for adults. In the end, the young protagonists participating in a resistance movement against the huge corporation producing longevity and rejuvenation drugs manage to overcome the selfish adult leaders. The moral is that renewal should not be about the same people living eternally but about the natural cycle of life where the new replaces the old, new generations replace old generations. This is viewed as natural because the Earth can only accommodate a certain number of people.

In contrast with the general trend illustrated by the above examples, several best-selling books in the paranormal romance genre published in the last few years are actually embracing immortality as well as eternal youth. There is nothing essentially new in these stories; to return to the story of Eos and Tithonus, the idea of lovers desiring to be eternally together is ancient. However, in many contemporary takes on the old trope the tragic ending—one half of the couple growing old while the other stays eternally young—is replaced with a happy fairytale closure. At the moment, the most famous example of this is the enormously successful *Twilight Saga* (2005–2008) by Stephenie Meyer. There the young female protagonist, Bella, chooses the life as an immortal vampire to live happily ever after with her undead boyfriend. Apart from vampire stories, the old trope also occurs in relation to other immortal creatures, including gods and goddesses. Although stylistically rather different from Meyer's novels, Gail Carson Levine's *Ever* (2008) also involves a mortal girl choosing immortality to be with her loved one. *Ever* is a reworking of Middle Eastern myths where the young god Olus falls in love with a mortal girl, Kezi, and the two face a series of trials and tribulations before Kezi can also become divine and immortal.

As in fairy tales, in these books very little is told about the happily ever after when it is finally reached — which may partly have to do with the idea that immortality seems more appealing as an aim rather than as a lived reality. Alyson Noël's *The Immortals* series (2009–2011) ends with the main couple giving up their immortality. For them immortality has included all kinds of peculiar limitations, such as not being able to touch each other, as well as hundreds of years of moments of loss and pain. They give it up for finding happiness in being together for their short lives as mortals. Of course, in regard to the conventional romance closure, it does not actually matter whether the lovers will spend together their whole lives, the eternity, or the next few days; as long as they are together at the end of the narrative and there is the promise of happily ever after, readers that desire conventional endings will be satisfied.

Thus, even though treating immortality as desirable may seem like a transgression in regard to conventions of children's literature, in the above examples it does not really challenge any conventional assumptions about gender and heterosexuality. However, in novels where immortality is treated as a lived reality rather than a mere promise, it has more potential, as a trope, to challenge normative (heterosexual) patterns of growing up and aging. As seen above, when immortal characters are depicted from mortal perspectives, they usually seem suspicious. The situation is different in novels that are focalized through the immortal characters.

Cate Tiernan's *Immortal Beloved* trilogy (2010–2012) features a first-person narrator, Natasha, an immortal, magic human who has trampled the earth for a little over four hundred and sixty years. Immortality is an ambiguous trope in the series. On the one hand, Natasha has experienced all the usual drawbacks of immortality: losses of loved ones, alienation and boredom; her long life has been characterized by tragedy rather than happiness. On the other hand, immortality comes with useful magic skills such as the ability to heal from anything else apart from beheading, as well as the opportunity to maintain one's youthful looks for a long time (the immortals do age but after reaching sixteen, their aging slows down to a pattern where it takes a hundred years to achieve the bodily changes that usually occur during a year). Natasha is "locked in an eternal twilight of adolescence" and to her "normal" is "a freakish concept."[55]

The series raises questions of how to organize one's life if it is not limited by the number of years and whether it is one's personal identity narrative or one's material body that is more crucial to one's subjectivity. Thus the books include potentially subversive elements, although I am expecting a conventional heteronormative romance closure as well as a completed maturation pattern from a reckless adolescent-like character into a responsible, good immortal in the final book of the series since these are already anticipated at the end of book two.[56] For readers of vampire stories there is nothing new in portraying immortal, transgressive characters, and there also exists a bulk of research on the queer character of the vampire that I am not going to review here, since that would draw the focus too far away from the trope of age-shifting.[57]

Instead, in Chapter 5, I will employ concepts from queer theory to discuss texts where age-shifting is combined with either life extension or a situation where a character goes through a series of lives. While the texts discussed there involve associations to immortality, physical immortality is not granted to any of the characters. Like immortality linked to eternal youth, these texts challenge normative patterns of growing up and aging, albeit that they do it by introducing different patterns of change, rather than non-change. The texts discussed include Philip Pullman's *His Dark Materials* trilogy and Susan Price's Ghost World novels where the female witches and shamans age differently from normal people, and Margaret Haddix's *Turnabout* (2000) and Gabrielle Zevin's *Elsewhere* (2005), where characters grow younger. The abnormal patterns of aging challenge normative assumptions about maturation and address issues of embodiment, agency and subjectivity from a specific viewpoint of characters who cannot or choose not to grow into conventional adulthood. Unlike many children's fantasy texts involving magic age-shifting, these novels take a more radical approach towards changing, aging and growing old (or young) as a female subject.

2

Witch Power: Invisibility, Age-Shifting and Empowerment

THIS CHAPTER CONSIDERS invisibility and magic changes in age as narrative motifs that are associated with female characters' agency and empowerment in texts that rewrite earlier representations of the witch. In the novels examined here, the invisible or age-shifting female characters are witches or magic-users who can, at least to some extent, control their own transformations themselves. The chapter explores the transformations in the context of earlier fairy tales and fantastic stories and discusses how the motifs are reframed in contemporary fantasy. The discussion will focus on uses of invisibility in Philip Pullman's *His Dark Materials* trilogy (1995–2000), Susan Price's *The Ghost Drum* (1987) and *Ghost Dance* (1994), Terry Pratchett's *A Hat Full of Sky* (2004), Lynne Ewing's *Goddess of the Night* (2000), Sarah Neufeld's *Visibility* (2004), as well as Laura Ruby's *The Wall and the Wing* (2006) and its sequel *The Chaos King* (2007). Texts examined in relation to magic age-shifting include Louise Lawrence's *The Earth Witch* (1982) and Diana Wynne Jones's *Howl's Moving Castle* (1986). While some of these stories are set in secondary worlds that resemble fairy-tale milieu and others take place in contemporary urban settings, in all novels invisibility or age-shifting are part of the magic or supernatural that characterizes the story-world in general, not merely the transforming female characters.

Unlike several feminist fairy tale rewritings, the novels discussed here are not retellings of any individual tales. Some of them are, rather, "fairy tale novels" (*Märchenroman* in German), that is, fantasy novels that employ narrative elements from fairy tales, including stock characters, motifs, settings, and beginning and ending formulas. A couple of the texts draw on specific tales and myths but combine them with others. However, yet other novels in the data set do not employ any other fairy tale elements apart from the character of the witch or the exceptional woman able to work magic. While witches are stock characters in fairy tales, in these texts they occur as more complex persons that have a more complicated relationship to their magic abilities than simply waving a wand and making things happen. As Maria Nikolajeva writes, the training of a witch or a wizard is a typical theme in fantasy, but not in fairy tales, where magic is usually not elaborated further but is accepted as part of the fairy tale world.[1] In the novels examined below, magic as a form of power is often discussed in detail. Although in all of the texts invisibility and age-shifting are forms of magic power that the transforming characters can control themselves and the transformations often serve a strategic purpose, the transformations and their functions and outcomes are made more complex than in earlier short tales involving strategic invisibility or age-shifting. In several instances, using one's magical powers puts the girls or young women at risk.[2] I will investigate the connections between the transformations, power relations and the young female protagonists' agency by examining the character's actions, representation of the transformations, focalization and the closure in the narratives. Thus, what follows is a close consideration of the girls' transformations and their effects on the girls' agency and power relations in the text. While it might first seem that learning to do magic — and turn invisible or age-shift — is an empowering process, for the young women in the texts discussed below, dealing with their supernatural powers is a complicated experience. Witch power, for some, may turn out to be disempowering, rather than empowering. However, this is also partly due to the different feminist definitions of the concept of "empowerment."

Rewriting the Witch

Although rewriting and re-visioning can take many forms, two patterns of creating new female heroes were typical of feminist texts in the 1970s and 1980s. Both relied on the male hero monomyth that — as perceived by Joseph Campbell in *The Hero with a Thousand Faces* (1949) — was commonplace in myth, folktales and, subsequently, in modern heroic fantasy that emerged as a genre in the aftermath of Tolkien's epic, *The Lord of the Rings* (1954–1955). For some writers challenging the male hero monomyth simply meant replacing the male protagonist with a female one. Others tried to imagine new inherently feminine patterns of coming of age and heroism; often in these patterns linearity was replaced by circularity, a single helper of the hero was replaced by a community of women, conventionally marginalized characters, such as witches, were made central, sympathetic characters, and so forth. As Patricia

Waugh writes, both forms of rewriting were based on a humanist assumption of true, essentialist and unique identity.[3] However, although Waugh labels both forms of rewriting as liberal-feminist, I will refer to the first type of stories (denying the difference) as those reflecting a liberal-feminist discourse and the latter type (celebrating the difference) as stories reflecting a radical-feminist discourse. Here I follow Chris Weedon's differentiation between liberal feminism and radical feminism; although both rely on humanist notions of the subject, they emphasize different aspects of gendered practices.[4]

The stories based on the liberal-feminist discourse of female heroes, that is, those stories which put a female in the conventional male hero's role, emphasize gender equality and the ability of female heroes to be at least "just as good" as males and capable of performing masculine qualities. These stories were soon criticized, since they did not connect with everyday concerns of real women, but simply represented what Lissa Paul has called "heroes in drag," a view supported later by another feminist children's literature critic, Roberta Seelinger Trites, who maintains that "trying to gain power by acting male ... is indeed irritating and retrograde."[5] In this kind of story, according to these critics, women can only be heroes as long as they fill in the norms and expectations set for conventionally masculine heroes.

However, introducing a particularly female or feminine quest or coming-of-age story can also be complicated. Stories based on radical-feminist discourses emphasize the specifically feminine, "natural" or "authentic" qualities of females and often deem those superior to any conventionally masculine or male qualities.[6] The main issue with radical-feminist attempts to introduce a new model for a female hero whose experiences are based on the assumed biological and cultural realities of womanhood is that they often seem to be paralyzed by the idea that there should exist one particularly representative model that captures the female experience as opposed to the male experience. This idea was popular in early 1980s feminist literary criticism, such as Annis Pratt's Jungian study of popular archetypes in women's fiction where she suggested that fiction relying on the female archetypes offers "a pathway to the authentic self, to the roots of our selves beneath consciousness of self, and to our innermost being."[7] In fantasy, perhaps the most popular archetype or stock character to be turned into a rich, authentic representation of female experience has been the witch.

Several fantasy fictions that have incorporated a sympathetic version of the witch reverse the negative stereotypes of old wicked crones and evil enchantresses. These revisions have often been colored by nostalgia — as indeed are the radical or eco-feminist discourses that fantasy fictions frequently draw on.[8] As critics such as Rita Felski and Diane Purkiss point out, the early radical-feminist discourses were, according to Felski, based on "the myth of the fall, the nostalgia for lost innocence" or, in the case of the witch, on what Purkiss calls "the myth of the Burning Times" linked to "the myth of an originary matriarchy, through the themes of mother-daughter learning and of matriarchal religions as sources of witchcraft."[9] The revisions thus offer an imagined vision of a blissful, matriarchal past. Justyna Sempruch also describes the figure of the witch as a political fantasy or as a character in feminist "herstories" or "form[s] of feminist mythology."[10] Apart from the possibilities that representations of witchcraft as a specifically feminine form of power offers for subverting gender stereotypes, the character of the witch is also appealing in the sense that witches often rely on their intelligence rather than physical strength to overcome difficulties and enemies.

In narratives for young audiences, the character of the witch has been popular in feminist revisions of fantastic texts that aim at introducing specifically feminine or female coming-of-age stories. Witches in contemporary children's literature often draw on radical feminist discourses that link witchcraft as a matriarchal religion or belief system with authentic or natural femininity and womanhood. Revised witches in recent children's fantasy replace the two stereotypical figures of the witch, the old crone and the evil beautiful sorceress, with wise healers or other magic-workers who are represented as complex persons with feelings and histories and strongly associated with the stereotype of the green woman leading a simple life close to nature.[11] Sometimes rewritings include the assertion that the fairy tale representations of the witch are "misrepresentations" that radical-feminist writers set out to correct with their more "authentic" depictions of female magic-users.[12] John Stephens refers to the same set of conventions as the wise witch schema — a schema that portrays witches as "conservers of nature and tradition, healers, and agents of renewal."[13] As Stephens suggests, this schema can be used to critique contemporary social attitudes and practices.

How does the character of the witch function as a form of critique of gendered practices? To put it simply, by celebrating features that have conventionally been associated with femininity and been regarded as unimportant, dangerous or inferior in relation to conventional masculine features, and by offering an example of a strong, independent, empowered female hero. In her discussion of "feminist children's novels," Trites relies on Elaine Showalter's notion of the "female novels" and thus on the liberal-feminist notions of choices and the right to be treated equally, whatever one chooses to do: a feminist children's novel is "a novel in which the main character is empowered regardless of gender." This view of equal opportunity is combined with a notion that feminist characters transcend gender roles by "embrac[ing] and celebrat[ing] certain characteristics traditionally linked to femininity ... compassion, interconnectedness, and community."[14]

This notion of celebrating femininity strongly resembles radical-feminist discourses. While it depends very much on each individual critic what exactly is conventional or traditional femininity that should be celebrated, empowerment has been the key word in feminist children's literature criticism regardless of how gender as a category is defined. Empowerment is linked to issues of constructing an agentic subjectivity, individuality and choice. While the concept has been useful in describing character development in fictional texts, it is also problematic since it is frequently very loosely defined. As we are now living in an era where the concept of empowerment has been fully appropriated in late-capitalist marketing discourses so that anything from buying a new lipstick or tasting the latest flavor of a low-fat yogurt to having or not having children or a career can be considered "empowering," the concept needs to be reconsidered if it is to have any useful application in feminist criticism.

How can empowerment then be defined, particularly in connection with the other key concept of agency? Trites writes:

> The most powerful way that feminist children's novels reverse traditional gender roles, however, is by their reliance on the protagonist's agency.... The protagonist is more aware of her own agency, more aware of her ability to assert her own personality and to enact her own decisions, at the end of the novel than she has been at the beginning.... The feminist protagonist need not squelch her individuality in order to fit into society. Instead, her agency, her individuality, her choice, and her nonconformity are affirmed and even celebrated.[15]

The feminist stories — often girls' coming-of-age stories — are here rooted in humanist notions of the individual's personality (something innate) and individual agency that involves free will and choice. Trites adopts Marilyn French's two-fold notion of power — "power over" as opposed to "power to" — and maintains that feminist power (which is the power in "empowerment") is more about being aware of one's agency than it is about controlling other people and thus refers to positive forms of autonomy, self-expression, and self-awareness.[16] This is all very good but this is exactly the same discourse that now characterizes advertising and marketing, particularly in encouragements to "be oneself" and in phrases such as "Just Do It." I will return to postfeminist discourses of visibility, beauty and choice in Chapter 3. While I do not suggest that empowerment and agency are unimportant in relation to girl protagonists, I want to examine the power relations as a complex network in which an individual's location can never be interpreted in a simple manner because gender intersects with other social identities (age, ethnicity, class and so forth). It is not self-evident when a "choice" is a "free choice" (if ever) and what it is exactly that defines one's "authentic" identity or self. Furthermore, cooperation and even power over others also involve agency and cannot be always interpreted merely in a negative sense (i.e., suppressing the individual).

Thus, when examining the fictional texts in the following sections, I will not assume that witchcraft is necessarily empowering, particularly for witches who use it to turn invisible or age-shift. As seen in the previous chapter, invisibility as a trope has often negative connotations — I will here focus particularly on the trope of invisibility and moral subjectivity. As regards age-shifting, recirculating images of the triple goddess do not necessarily lead to representation of empowered characters or characters that challenge stereotypes and norms associated with gender and age. I will examine the representations of invisible and age-shifting witches in the selected novels by addressing the following questions: What does invisibility or age-shifting reveal about the witches' power? What do invisibility and age-shifting show about the power relations between the transforming character and other characters? Are invisibility and age-shifting empowering, disempowering, or, perhaps, both at the same time?

Invisible Women of Power

In the novels discussed here, invisibility is a power controlled by the witch-characters themselves. While at points invisibility is merely strategic, in a more general level it is connected with the trope of invisibility, morality and power. I will first discuss the novels by Pullman, Price and Pratchett where witchcraft occurs in a fairly traditional secondary fantasy world setting and then turn to the books by Ewing, Kaye, Ruby and Neufeld, where girls and young women with the ability to turn invisible occur in modern urban settings.

Spells and Spirit-Traveling: The Powerful, Invisible Witches

In Pullman's *His Dark Materials* trilogy, Price's *The Ghost Drum* and *Ghost Dance* and in Pratchett's *Tiffany Aching* novels, representations of witchcraft clearly draw on radical feminist discourses of the witch. In all these texts, witchcraft (or shamanism in Price) is predominantly a female occupation and transferred matrilineally from one generation of females to another. The female magic-users are wise women who are outsiders to society or have a very specific role in society — in Pullman's and Price's novels the witches live in their own societies mainly without meddling into common people's affairs unless the whole world is in danger, whereas in Pratchett's texts witches live as members of society where they have the responsibility taking care of the common people, for instance, by occupying the role of a village healer.

Despite the similarities in the representation of female witches, there are also significant differences. First, the novels by these three writers are rather different in tone — Pullman writes fairly conventional epic fantasy, while Price's and Pratchett's novels might be termed as postmodern fantasy that employ strategies such as metafiction and irony to draw attention to earlier storytelling conventions, also those that have to do with gender stereotypes. Price's texts also draw attention to the whole process of storytelling as a way of constructing a specific view of the world, characters, and events — at the end of the novels readers are asked to tell their own versions of the stories if they did not like what they have just read or heard.[17]

Second, the witches serve rather different narrative functions. In Pullman's novels the witches are minor characters who help the English protagonists in the story — while parts of the narrative are focalized through witch-characters, they are mainly left to the sidelines and remain as outsiders to the urban society of the protagonists. In contrast, in Price's and Pratchett's novels the witches are among the main characters and focalizers and thus more information about their thoughts and motifs is revealed to readers. However, in regard to the use of invisibility, it is instructive to compare these different novels since, overall, the ways in which invisibility is represented are fairly similar in each case.

Invisibility in these novels is a form of power that is mastered by mental magic, or words and music and, as such, it is only one of the skills that the witches or shamans have. Invisibility is a power that is achieved through several years of training; thus it is the result of hard work rather than simply, or accidentally, achieved by swallowing a magic pill, powder or potion, or wearing an invisibility cloak, ring or helmet. Because the use and abuse of power are among the main themes in the novels, it is worth examining how the invisibility of the witches fits into the discourses of power in each novel. Each text addresses invisibility differently: whereas Pullman's novels and Price's *The Ghost Drum* introduce invisibility as a form of a witch's power that can be strategically used to accomplish certain tasks, in Price's *Ghost Dance* invisibility does not help Shingebiss to achieve her aims. In Pratchett's *A Hat Full of Sky*, invisibility is an ability that Tiffany can control, but it puts her in grave danger.

NORTHERN WITCHES AND INVISIBILITY

In Pullman's and Price's novels the witches live in an alternative world version of Northern Europe. Each writer's texts seem to draw on old Nordic myths where Lappish witches or shamans are, among other things, associated with invisibility. Pullman's *His Dark Materials* novels form a fairly conventional fantasy trilogy, where the battle of good and evil takes a new form in a rewritten story of the biblical Fall: the young protagonists Lyra and Will work against the Magisterium — a fictional institution based on the Roman Catholic Church that experiments with children's souls and tries to maintain its religious and political power by controlling people's lives. Thus Pullman's novels tackle issues of (patriarchal) power and colonialism, specifically in relation to organized religion. In Pullman's novels the Lapland witches are sympathetic minor characters who help the English protagonists Lyra and Will during their quest to fight the Magisterium. To create a sense of Northern "authenticity," the novels involve characters with names that come from the North, be it real names or names from mythological traditions.[18] Despite the various sources for their names, all the witches share a belief system where the goddess who appears to the witches before their death is called Yambe-Akka. *Jábmiidáhkká* is the name of the goddess of the Underworld in Sámi mythology. The novels thus involve a suggestive link between witchcraft and Sámi culture.

Together with a third novel, *Ghost Song* (1992), Price's *The Ghost Drum* and *Ghost Dance* form a loose trilogy. Although the novels are situated in the same fictional world and share some characters, the plot-lines do not form a chronological continuum.[19] Rather, the novels are separate stories situated in the same fictional world, a version of the czardom that we know as Russia and told by the same cat narrator. As in Pullman's novels, the witch-shamans here work against the power, control and colonialist politics of a patriarchal system by either fighting or trying to educate the czars and czaritsas (gods on Earth). The witches and shamans in Price's novels live in the northern parts of the czardom and are associated with northern nomadic people through descriptions of the reindeer-hide clothes, called in the novels as "Lappish," even though the names of the characters come from elsewhere.[20] The Ghost World novels combine motifs and characters from the Russian tradition in general — and some of the narrative devices from Alexandr Pushkin's fairy tales in particular, as well as elements from Norse mythology and anthropological accounts of shamanism. The female protagonists in the novels, Chingis and Shingebiss, are young female witches, shamans' apprentices, adopted by their witch grandmothers, versions of Baba Yaga who live in houses on chicken legs and are here sympathetic mentors, not cannibalistic ogres.

Both Pullman's and Price's novels are reworkings of Nordic mythology, constructing the female shaman, or the witch, not as an malevolent figure but as a woman of power. As regards invisibility, the texts seem to make use of the representations of shape-shifters, shamans and witches in Nordic mythology. In Nordic myths, invisibility and shape-shifting have specific meanings. In her study of female shape-shifters in Scandinavian traditions, Raudvere explains that whether the shape-shifters were males or females, gods or humans, shape-shifting—and invisibility, or spirit-traveling as one form of it—was considered a predominantly evil form of power. Moreover, females who turned invisible (or spirit-traveled) during the night and visited other people's homes were regarded as particularly suspicious. As Raudvere states: "By contrast to many of the male characters with the same [shape-shifting] abilities, the women act almost exclusively out of greed, envy, depravity, corruption and unrequited love. The stories of female shape-shifters are almost always connected with sexuality and witchcraft."[21] The positive image of a female shape-shifter in Pullman's and Price's novels is a rewriting of the version of the witch-woman in Nordic legends — invisibility represents the witches' power that they use out of altruistic rather than selfish motives and thus to construct the moral subjectivity of the witch-women.

There are only a few instances where the witches rely on invisibility as a strategic form of power in the novels — in some of these instances the witches use invisibility successfully, while in other cases invisibility turns out to be disempowering since it does not allow the witch to use her power to change things around her, or turning invisible puts the witch in danger. To start with effective invisibility, Serafina Pekkala and Chingis are witch characters that are able to use invisibility in a strategic way to achieve their aims. While witches occur in all parts of *His Dark Materials* trilogy, invisibility only is used in *The Subtle Knife* (1997) and then only in two main instances. Invisibility as an ability is introduced when Serafina uses it to spy on an imprisoned witch who is kept on a ship populated by members of the Magisterium. Since this brief scene is focalized through Serafina, readers are allowed to see how the witch works with and experiences her invisibility. Invisibility is difficult to achieve, because it is a form of mental magic that controls other people's minds. It is only used when nothing else can be done:

> There was one thing she could do; she was reluctant, because it was desperately risky, and it would leave her exhausted; but it seemed there was no choice. It was a kind of magic she could work to make herself unseen. True invisibility was impossible, of course: this was mental magic, a kind of fiercely-held modesty that could make the spell-worker not invisible but simply unnoticed. Holding it with the right degree of intensity she could pass through a crowded room, or walk beside a solitary traveler, without being seen.[22]

It takes Serafina several minutes to work on her invisibility, and she has to focus on maintaining it while she searches for the imprisoned witch. When Serafina finds the witch, she almost loses control over keeping herself invisible because of the mental agitation that she feels: the prisoned witch is being tortured by Mrs. Coulter, one of the morally susceptible characters in the trilogy, and members of the Magisterium to make her reveal what the witches know about Lyra's destiny. The tortured witch is in horrible pain and about to reveal the secret, which leaves Serafina with few choices of how to act. Serafina could escape from the scene invisibly but she chooses to do the right thing — she turns visible and kills the suffering witch — to release the tortured witch from her pains as well as to stop her revealing the secret about Lyra's destiny that the members of the Magisterium and Mrs. Coulter are after. Afterwards, Serafina manages to escape by fighting her way through rather than using any magic.

For Serafina, invisibility is empowering but difficult to control and exhausting to maintain. As a morality trope, invisibility does not grant the witch the power to do anything that she wishes — here her invisibility does not allow her to save the prisoned witch, even though it does allow her spy on the events successfully. Moreover, as an indication of her moral subjectivity, Serafina is ready to learn the secure, invisible state of a spy to help her fellow witch and to ensure that the malevolent torturers do not achieve their aims.

In *The Ghost Drum*, Chingis is also on a rescuing mission when she uses invisibility. After visiting the Ghost World (the land of the dead) successfully, the witch-shamans in the Ghost World novels have many powers, including the ability to turn invisible. Invisibility can be achieved by writing a spell, singing a song or while traveling as a spirit. Chingis uses invisibility to help the young Safa Czarevich to escape from the czar's palace, where he has been locked up in a tower since his birth. She is not seen in the palace, because she is singing a song that "told all who heard it that she was not there." This is similar to Serafina's spell that alters what the people around her can observe. The reactions to Chingis's invisibility vary from ignoring her to feelings of fear, since people can hear Chingis, even though they cannot see her: "But there was no enemy to be seen, and the doors they heard slam had not, to their eyes, been opened. Only a singing passed through the hall and on into the jewel-colored gloom of the Palace. The soldiers stood to attention, and feared ghosts."[23]

There are three crucial points about Chingis's invisibility. First, as with Serafina, the power of invisibility comes with restrictions: the singing spell only functions when her voice is heard. While this is a restriction, it could also be interpreted as a feminist take on invisibility: a girl or woman who can be heard but not seen is, of course, the opposite of the traditional patriarchal ideal of women as beings who should be seen but not heard. Second, also here invisibility is used to help others and not for selfish purposes — invisibility, again, reveals the character's moral subjectivity and here it is clear that Chingis is using it for the right purposes. Invisibility is based on words that are repeated to create an illusion — as such the invisibility song reflects the notion of power of words and discourses in general, which is addressed earlier in the novel when the shaman grandmother explains the functions of word-magic to Chingis. While some people, such as the czars, use words to deceive others, Chingis's spells are used to help others; there is a clear contrast between using word-magic for "bad" and "good" purposes.

The third important feature of Chingis's invisibility is that her powers arouse fear in others. In the above quote the guards think of her as a ghost — an association based on the connection between invisibility and death — and later a male shaman who is envious of Chingis's powers kills her (although Chingis does return from the dead to set things straight). Killing Chingis is the only way to disempower her — because Chingis's invisibility and other powers are learned abilities, parts of herself, they cannot be stolen from her, as some magic gadget might. The fear of the (invisible) female monster/witch is a convention from earlier tales, which *The Ghost Drum* rewrites. Since the text represents Chingis's opponents, the male shaman and female czaritsa, as people who are obsessed with the idea of power and ready to do away with anyone threatening their position, it shows that the invisible witch-woman is feared because she is powerful and a threat to the social order, rather than because she is evil or frightening. Because Chingis is portrayed as a conventionally good character — caring, kind, brave and in the position of the traditional hero or rescuer — even though she is not a focalizer in the text, readers are invited to sympathize with the witch-character.

In *The Ghost Drum* the significance of invisibility as a useful strategy is put into a new context after the rescuing scene because the tale does not end after the successful rescue (as fairy tales often do). The rescue of Safa has put other people in trouble because the new czaritsa is disturbed by his disappearance. Chingis's further attempts to help the other people fail because she is tricked by Kuzma and killed by soldiers who, in the manner of the seamen in Odysseus's ship, have plugged their ears and make noise by yelling and blowing trumpets in order to not hear Chingis's spells. Her killing shows that there are limits to what a shaman can accomplish and none of her magic powers, invisibility among them, is seen as a guarantee of survival or victory. These limits are addressed even more explicitly in *Ghost Dance* that is, in many ways, a dystopian version of its prequel.

Before turning to Shingebiss in *Ghost Dance*, I will discuss the other instance of invisibility in *The Subtle Knife*; a scene where invisibility turns out to be not empowering at all. This occurs towards the end of the novel when a witch called Lena Feldt is accompanying Lyra and Will on their way and notices that someone is following them. Lena goes back to spy on the trackers and, after finding them, turns invisible to eavesdrop on, again, Mrs. Coulter and her former helper, Carlo, that Mrs. Coulter kills during the scene. Since the scene is focalized through Lena, readers learn that maintaining invisibility takes much of her concentration but also makes her confident enough to focus on the dialogue between Mrs. Coulter and Carlo and ignore everything else that goes on around her:

2. Witch Power

Lena Feldt watched, standing invisibly just two paces from where they sat. Her bowstring was taut, the arrow nocked to it in readiness: she could have pulled and loosed in less than a second, and Mrs. Coulter would have been dead before she finished drawing breath. But the witch was curious. She stood still and silent and wide-eyed.

But while she was watching Mrs. Coulter, she didn't look behind her across the little blue lake.[24]

Shortly after, curiosity kills the witch. Spectres — deadly spirits — come across the lake and catch Lena's daimon. A moment later, Mrs. Coulter suddenly faces Lena and reveals that she has seen her all along — invisibility here has not worked because Mrs. Coulter is immune to the witch's mental magic. Confident in her invisibility, Lena Feldt has only led herself into a trap and ends up being tortured and killed by Mrs. Coulter. Before her death, she reveals the secret of Lyra's destiny and thus Lena's task fails in more than one sense. The blind confidence in one's magic abilities — invisibility in particular — and power that lead one to underestimate enemies and fail is also addressed in Price's *Ghost Dance*.

Other people's immunity to a witch's magic also prevents Shingebiss in *Ghost Dance* to use invisibility to confront the evil rulers, here specifically the czar (or the God on Earth). While Serafina, Chingis, and Lena use invisibility for fairly modest purposes in specific events, to spy on people or to rescue someone from a prison, Shingebiss attempts to use invisibility to change a czar's mind and thus to save the Northlands and the reindeer people that are threatened by the destruction of the land caused by the czar's men. The scale of Shingebiss's task is therefore significantly different. The motivation for Shingebiss's errand is based both on her suitability to fulfill the conventional role of a hero and on ecological concerns. Moreover, while *Ghost Dance* invokes the radical-feminist discourse of witches, the text also presents challenges to the discourse right from the beginning, in the form of a conflict between Shingebiss and her foster grandmother.

When a group of Lappish hunters comes to seek a shaman's help against the czar destroying the land, Shingebiss wants to help her foster grandmother and tells her apprentice that "All things must change.... If that [the czar's people are killing the Northlands] is true, then you must live with the death, or you must die with it, that is all."[25] This seems to be a breach in the wise witch schema — the grandmother is not concerned at all about the conservation of the land; or, as a more experienced shaman, knows that changing the world or people's minds is not a simple task. By first confronting her grandmother and then ignoring the tutor's advice after her death, the good-hearted Shingebiss leaves the shaman community thinking that it is no use being a shaman unless one can help others. She travels to the city to put a spell the czar in the belief that by changing the ruler's mind it is possible to save the people and the land. Her first main strategy in trying use magic on the czar is to rely on invisibility.

Like Chingis, Shingebiss uses invisibility to enter the czar's palace unseen. She sings a song of invisibility that concerns both her visual appearance and any sounds that she makes; unlike Chingis, Shingebiss disguises her voice as well:

> "White hare on white snow, you see me not, see me not, see me not. One flake of snow lost in the drift, see me not, see me not."
> The guards looked at her with open eyes as she walked up to them and among them, and yet somehow they mistook the whites of her eyes and teeth for snow, the black of her hair for the black cobbles where snow had been scraped away, and the flash of brass rings on her coat as the flash of their own pike-blades. They did start and look about as the arrows rustled in her quiver, but she added to her song: "A bird's cheep in the city's din is heard not, heard not."[26]

Shingebiss's magic words do not belong to any special shamanic jargon, but she seems to be composing the spell while she is singing it by adding words that take her surroundings, the city, into consideration. She uses everyday words and images to blend into the everyday surroundings, things that are not only difficult to detect but which people do not usually pay further attention to, "white hare on white snow," "one flake of snow lost in the drift" or "a bird's cheep in the city's din." Thus, her appearance and voice melt into the unremarkable surroundings. The spell is based on persuasion and it functions in a similar way as word-magic in *The Ghost Drum*— through repetition and the use of everyday words. The use of everyday words is different from the conventional notion of spells as consisting of magic or special diction. I will return to this issue in relation to Sophie's magic in *Howl's Moving Castle* below; it is possible to interpret the everydayness of spells as a feminine or female form of magic.

As Serafina, Chingis and Lena, Shingebiss is portrayed as a magic user or illusionist who uses the magic for good purposes. Shingebiss's morality is further emphasized because her way of working magic and illusions is in sharp contrast with the use of fake magic by Master Jenkins, an Englishman in the czar's court who tries to earn riches by deceiving the czar by lies and tricks. Ironically, Master Jenkins relies on the traditional notion of magic as a special language when he pretends to summon a devil, although he knows that his words have no magic quality— his strategy is to speak English that sounds unintelligible and thus magic to his Russian audience. Master Jenkins's use of the fake magic incantations is parodic and he is represented as a greedy character, a complete opposite of the altruistic Shingebiss who has no interest in power or riches. Even though only a small part of the novel is focalized through Shingebiss, as in the case of Chingis, her position as the "good" hero in the story invites readers to align with her rather than the "evil" ones.

For Shingebiss, invisibility is first an empowering ability. She uses it strategically to enter the czar's palace. Because Shingebiss knows that her invisibility spell works, she also believes she can persuade people in other ways. It is later revealed that she has earlier been able to not only persuade people to believe that she is invisible, but when unseen, to persuade people to change their minds according to the whispers of a disembodied voice: "When she had been learning her art, it had been a game to wander invisibly in marketplaces and make those selling change their prices, and those buying change their minds."[27] This is why she thinks she can change the czar's mind as well; however, her earlier (supposedly) innocent play now turns into a tragedy. When Shingebiss tries to appeal to the czar to have mercy on his prisoners, the persuasive whispers by the invisible young woman do not function in the desired way: sometimes the czar releases the prisoners, sometimes he decides to give them even more severe sentences. Shingebiss is shaken by the fact that her power is diminished or almost non-existent; her words have almost no effect, as the czar treats them as the noise made by an irritating insect. Another indication of Shingebiss's loss of her powers is, as with Serafina, that when she gets tired during the trials, she cannot keep her spells in good order and occasionally becomes visible.

Invisibility does not allow Shingebiss to do whatever she wants but her further attempts to try to persuade the czar as visible do not succeed either. Shingebiss's mistake seems to be that she continues to rely on the conventionally feminine form of persuasion which, in her case, is based on telling the truth.[28] Ironically, it seems to be only lies that work on the czar; here, again, Shingebiss is contrasted with the fake magician Master Jenkins. Jenkins promises the czar the elixir of life and gains his favor, whereas Shingebiss tells the czar that eternal life is an impossibility and thus loses his trust. Shingebiss refuses to recognize that power of words can effectively be used by relying on people's desires. The czar only hears what he desires to hear and sees what he desires to see. This is why Shingebiss also fails when she appears to the czar after her unsuccessful attempts to affect him by whispering to him unseen. As I have argued elsewhere, the czar embodies an imperial gaze — his colonialist worldview explains his surroundings in terms of his own desire.[29] The czar creates his own interpretation of what the visible Shingebiss is: a Black Angel sent to God on Earth by God in Heaven, which is supposed to show people that he is favored by God. Ironically, Shingebiss the witch remains invisible to the czar, who only sees what fits into his own logics, guided by his desire for power. At the end Shingebiss manages to overcome the czar and Jenkins, but to achieve that Shingebiss switches to a completely different strategy. After her word magic and persuasions turn out to be ineffective, she invokes the spirit of Loki, a male god, transforms into a giant otter and resorts to violence to deal justice.

Testing the Apprentice Witch

In Pratchett's novels the protagonist, Tiffany Aching, grows up from a 9-year-old girl into a 16-year-old teenager and from an apprentice witch into an independent professional whose duty is to help people in her home village.[30] In Pratchett's Discworld witchcraft is a strictly feminine venue and good witches work as healers or nurses, tasks varying from taking a patient's pain away magically to cutting old women's toenails. Apart from rewriting the evil witch stereotype by introducing a good witch that follows a fairly traditional feminine career path of nursing and healing, fairy tale and fantasy conventions are explicitly addressed at several points in the books, often through (black) humor. Tiffany is constantly pondering her behavior in relation to stereotypical views of witches (and old women) and tries to change people's negative assumptions about witchcraft.

Tiffany's own altruistic behavior changes other people's perceptions of witches in the story world, while her representation that is often done through metafictional commentary alters stereotypical figures of witches in readers' minds: "The storybook pictures of the drooling hag were being wiped away, every time Tiffany helped a young mother with her first baby, or soothed an old man's path to his grave."[31] Elsewhere, stereotypes occur through trivial comments about pointy hats but Tiffany also encounters more serious events where people have killed old women who have been mistakenly suspected of witchcraft. Thus the books address conventional expectations related not only to witches but women in general, albeit that some conventions are challenged (including the assumption that old women are evil) while others are only enforced (such as the assumption that caring and nurturing are specifically feminine skills).

While Tiffany turns occasionally invisible in the other novels, I will here focus on *The Hat Full of Sky* where invisibility as a skill or technique is not yet completely understood by Tiffany and where her use of invisibility puts her in serious danger. In *The Hat Full of Sky* Tiffany is an eleven-year-old apprentice who has just been sent to Miss Level, an experienced witch, to learn about witchcraft. In Pratchett's novels, there are two ways a witch can turn invisible — by leaving her body in spirit, a strategy called "borrowing" since the spirit can enter another person's or animal's body if the witch so wishes, or, as in Pullman's trilogy and *Ghost Dance*, by making oneself unnoticed and blurring into the background. The latter is the preferred strategy if one only wants to become invisible (and not enter someone else's body), but Tiffany does not know it yet. Stepping outside her own body is something that she has learned on her own, unaware of the potentially dangerous consequences. It is constantly emphasized that one needs certain innate abilities to be a witch — especially sharp intelligence and keen observation skills — yet Tiffany's path to witchcraft also shows that guidance from more experienced magic-users is necessary to be able to use one's abilities in a safe and just manner. In *A Hat Full of Sky* invisibility is a skill that metonymically indicates magic use in general.

Tiffany first steps out of her body at the very beginning to see herself from outside in her new outfit that she has put on when about to leave her home for the apprenticeship. In the prequel, *The Wee Free Men*, Tiffany has already done magic without knowing what she is doing and continues to do so here, when she ponders her invisibility trick upon returning to her body:

> Tiffany had done magic, serious magic. Before she had done it she hadn't known that she could; when she had been doing it she hadn't known that she was; and after she had done it she hadn't known how she had. Now she had to learn how.
> "See me not," she said. The vision of her ... or whatever it was, because she was not exactly sure about this trick ... vanished.
> It had been a shock, the first time she'd done this. But she'd always found it easy to see herself, at least in her head. All her memories were like little pictures of herself doing things or watching things, rather than the view from the two holes in the front of her head. There was a part of her that was always watching her.[32]

Tiffany believes that her (in)visibility trick, stepping outside her body to observe herself, works because she has a clear mental image of herself and a part of her is "always watching her." Indeed, later it becomes obvious that this kind of self-monitoring is necessary for any witch to maintain a critical view of herself and avoid abusing her abilities and power, or "going to the bad."[33] However, Tiffany herself does not yet associate her invisibility trick with the more serious considerations connected with one's responsibilities and moral subjectivity as a witch. The phrase that Tiffany uses to step outside her body is "See me," and she has mainly used this skill to check her appearance whenever she does not have a mirror. Although she believes that she should discuss it with a more experienced witch, Tiffany decides not to do that yet since she views this particular skill as a trivial trick. This is her mistake, since continuing to do magic on her own and relying on her own wits rather than more experienced witches' advice puts her in grave danger.

The above instance of momentary invisibility is accompanied with passages describing a strange spirit sensing Tiffany doing magic and starting to hunt her. Later on it is explained that this creature is a "hiver," a kind of parasite that lives on human minds, makes them act upon their secret wishes — also the vain and violent ones — and, in the end, leaves them dead and starts a search for another mind to inhabit. The hiver seeks powerful minds and senses this in Tiffany; every time she does magic, the hiver gets closer and finally enters Tiffany's body after she has once again used her "See me" trick. After taking control of Tiffany's mind, the hiver makes her act upon her secret wishes — she thus attacks her bully, steals money and buys herself fancy witch clothes and attacks adults who try to stop her. While Tiffany has used her "See me" trick also to invisibly eavesdrop on others, it seems that the hiver is sensing the potential vanity involved in the trick if it is used to watch oneself from outside. Tiffany's vanity is connected with her desire to be respected as a talented magic-user, by other witches, apprentices and people in general. To compensate for the lack of respect, the hiver turns Tiffany into a show-off who uses her magic to intimidate others. While Tiffany manages to get rid of the hiver in the end with the help of others and survives the occupation of her mind almost intact — some voices of minds that the hiver has occupied earlier remain in her head — her experiences drastically change her moral subjectivity.

It is ironic that the spell that initiates Tiffany's trials and tribulations by making her an easy target for the hiver is the "See me" spell, since the main lesson that Tiffany needs to learn is to see herself as well as others more clearly and objectively. While Tiffany was earlier represented as a brave and mainly benevolent character, she is, at points, also an irritable know-it-all who underestimates others and is too proud to appreciate the everyday non-magic chores and responsibilities that witches have to do.

Since most of the story is focalized through Tiffany, readers know that the more experienced witches' voices and teachings are frequently in her thoughts, for instance, when she remembers Miss Tick's advice about wishful thinking: "Never wish. Especially don't wish upon a star, which is astronomically stupid. Open your eyes, and then open your eyes again."[34] These particular teachings address the main issues that Tiffany needs to learn if she wants to become a strong witch: instead of wishful thinking, one needs to take responsibility and act oneself to change the world for the better and, to be able to act in a rightful manner, one needs to observe, assess and think critically. This also involves not using spells that one does not truly know. Tiffany's tutor, Miss Level, is shocked when she hears that Tiffany has been playing around with invisibility and soon realizes that what Tiffany has done is actually "borrowing," which is dangerous unless one knows how to protect oneself. Thus Miss Level is incredulous to hear that Tiffany has only invented the spell to replace a mirror. By keeping her spells secret, Tiffany has thus only shown her own inexperience. Invisibility spells — or any magic — should not be used before one has sufficient knowledge over those spells, as well as the ability to discern when to use magic at all. While it is specifically Tiffany's invisibility trick that is under scrutiny here, it is clear that her inexperience concerns her use of her magic powers in general.

As Janet Brennan Croft writes in her article on the witches and morality in Pratchett's Discworld novels, the experienced witches do not aim for niceness or goodness (as described in rigorous, dogmatic rules) but rightness, separating between right and wrong: "Rightness is linked to the fact that witchcraft on Discworld is a neutral power, neither black or white.... A mature witch has to respect the rights of the individual and be willing to take complete responsibility for her own actions."[35] Witches must thus constantly observe the behavior of others and their own to be able to critically assess situations and people. In this, Pratchett's novels reflect a humanist belief in a subject who cares for others and uses her best judgment to assess situations as objectively as possible to be able to do what is right and just.

What is also suggested, however, is that a witch's moral subjectivity is interpersonally constructed — it is not only young apprentices that are monitored by more experienced witches but all the witches are monitoring each other. This is explained by the narrator at the beginning of *A Hat Full of Sky* by comparing witches to cats: "Witches were a bit like cats. They didn't much like one another's company, but they did like to know where all the other witches were, just in case they needed them. And what you might need them for was to tell you, as a friend, that you were beginning to cackle."[36]

Among witches in Discworld, cackling — stereotypical behavior of an old hag — is considered a potential sign of losing one's moral subjectivity and turning into an evil witch. A witch's moral subjectivity is thus dependent on both the individual witch's judgment as well as the community of female peers. At the closure of the novel, Tiffany thinks that she has been put to a test — or to several tests — by the most respected witch, Granny Weatherwax; since Tiffany has shown that she is capable of taking responsibility for her own actions, as well as being able to be a human apart from being a magic-user, she passes the test. It is clear that Tiffany matures during her apprenticeship and gains agency through her profession as a witch. In the fourth novel of the series, *I Shall Wear Midnight*, readers encounter a sixteen-year-old experienced witch who also knows how to use invisibility in a controlled manner: she is able to both step out of her body and fade into the background without much effort and without putting herself at risk. Her training has ensured that as long as she constantly monitors her own methods, motifs and behavior, she is able to do magic — and turn invisible — strategically when necessary.

For the witches in Pullman's, Price's and Pratchett's novels, invisibility is not always empowering but it is always indicative of the moral subjectivity of the witches — whether or not they reach their aims, they are not corrupted by their magic powers. Corruption is unlikely since invisibility is a very limited form of power for these witches; in this these stories resemble the typical invisibility narratives for children where invisibility always comes with limitations. These texts reflect the radical-feminist discourse of witch-women as attractive characters by showing that the witches here are both powerful and good persons — the motivation and justification for their actions are also based on their role as the hero or the hero's helper. However, the texts do not rewrite the fact that the witch-woman, a Woman of Power, remains outside society — the witch-shamans are not only feared by the power-craving, mean characters but also by the common people who do not understand their powers. As Stephens points out, this is, of course, the case with many other (radical) feminist stories of the witch.[37] I will return to this issue in Chapter 5, where the otherness is considered in relation to queer discourses.

Not all witches are goody-goody, however — there are magic-users who join the evil forces or turn themselves evil by using magic for selfish or malevolent purposes. In any of the novels a witch could use her powers in a wrong way, unless she constantly monitors her own behavior and is monitored by the female community around her. The witches are represented as a morally superior characters — their only flaw is inexperience, since witches need to strive for knowledge and truth all the time and never confidently assume that they have reached a level where they can use their powers without a detailed consideration of the situation, other people and their own motives. By suggesting that something good can be achieved through shape-shifting, the texts rewrite the famous stories of the corruptive effects of invisibility, as equated with power: Plato's story of Gyges and Wells's and Tolkien's later extended versions of it.

This, again, brings us back to the radical-feminist discourse of witches, which tends to see the power of the witch as a positive force. In this discourse, moral questions concerning the use of power are introduced only in the sense that the female witches are represented as morally exemplary characters that do not abuse their powers, nor are corrupted by them. However, in all novels the witches are part of female communities and their moral subjectivity is interpersonally constructed and maintained. For these secondary-world fantasy witches, refusal of guidance and rebellion against one's elders will often lead to unpredictable and dangerous results. In contrast, in the urban fantasy discussed in the following, rebellion against adults is often what saves the transforming young characters from being exploited.

Female Invisibility in Urban Fantasy: Power And Abuse

The books about witches or magically talented girls have plenty of similarities with the realist *Künstlerroman* for girls — with the exception that instead of a realistic talent such as writing, art or music these young women have to learn to live with their magical talents. It is then, perhaps, no wonder that girls who can work magic are not restricted to secondary-world fantasy but witches in the primary world have been popular as well. Witches or magically talented girls worrying about their supernatural abilities as well as school life with its common everyday concerns have recently featured not only in Rowling's Harry Potter novels but also in several mass-market book series. Series that feature invisibility as a specific talent of a teenage girl include *Daughters of the Moon* (2000–) by Lynne Ewing and *Gifted* (2009–) by Marilyn Kaye. Both series feature a group of teenagers who each have a special magical talent that is somehow related to their identity and has to be properly mastered. Apart from book series, invisible girls have recently featured in such urban fantasy novels as *The Wall and the Wing* (2006) and its sequel *The Chaos King* (2007) by Laura Ruby and *Visibility* (2004) by Sarah Neufeld. In comparison with the groups of teenagers in Ewing's and Kaye's series, as well as the witches in Pullman, Price and Pratchett, the young women in Ruby and Neufeld are different in that they are unique in their abilities and have no one to guide or instruct them. Yet, whether guided or learning on their own, in all the novels discussed below, coming to terms with one's magical abilities means coming to terms with one's identity and responsibilities as well.

I am not going to repeat the argument about invisibility and moral subjectivity here, apart from saying that the invisible girls here have also high moral standards and mainly use invisibility to help others rather than themselves. Instead, I will here address the question of whether invisibility is empowering for girls and young women who become targets of abuse when other people try to force them to use their ability to turn invisible for evil, immoral or illegal purposes.

The invisible goddess and female collaboration

Both Ewing's and Kaye's series involve a structure where each book focuses on a different member of the group of teenagers with magical or supernatural abilities. While the overall story runs through all the books, each part of the series can also be read as a stand-alone book. The set-up of characters with different extraordinary abilities is familiar, for instance, from superhero team comics such as the *X-Men*, but also typical of the genre of school story where characters often represent different talents, although their extraordinariness is reflected in such realist forums as writing, sports or music. In these types of stories, one of the key themes is often learning how to collaborate, since the different characters are not as strong on their own as when they work in the team, where the abilities of its members complement each other. In Ewing's and Kaye's series invisibility is treated as a supernatural power among other extraordinary talents. While in each series the supernaturally talented teenagers run the risk of becoming targets of exploitation, I will here focus on Ewing's series where invisibility is clearly a form of power but linked to discourses of sexual exploitation. Since in Kaye's novels embodied invisibility — while partly strategic — is strongly associated with metaphorical invisibility and a conventional, passive, powerless female status, I will return to them in the following chapter.

Ewing's *Daughters of the Moon* series resembles the novels about secondary world witches in its representation of a group of mortal goddesses with supernatural abilities — the series certainly reflects some aspects of the radical-feminist discourses of the witch. *Daughters of the Moon* draws on Greek mythology mixed with Latin names and presents the moon goddess Selene as the protector of a group of females (her daughters) with supernatural abilities who battle against the evil forces called the Atrox. Despite the main Greek connection, the language of the spells and prayers that the goddesses use is Latin. Clearly any authenticity in regard to Greek mythology is not the main issue here; references to mythology are merely used to build up a background narrative for the female goddesses who have protected humankind against the evil powers for millennia. The present group of mortal goddesses in the novels consists of teenage girls living in contemporary Los Angeles. I will here focus on the first book of the series, *Goddess of the Night* (2000), that introduces Vanessa Cleveland, a girl who has the ability to become invisible by expanding her molecules.

At the beginning, Vanessa is not aware of her divine heritage and has kept her special skill secret from everyone else except her best friend, Catty, who has another ability; she can travel in time. The secrecy is partly explained by the fact that Vanessa is ashamed of her ability that she cannot yet control at will. Moreover, she is a beautiful, clever girl who is among the most popular students in her school and feels that her invisibility makes her too different, positioned "in the freak category," and thus she does not want to reveal it: "Maybe kids at school liked her now, but what if they knew the truth?"[38] Interestingly, Vanessa's invisibility is also associated with sexuality, since she has more trouble controlling her molecules every time she has an intimate moment with the boy that she is attracted to: "Her breath caught, and then her mouth opened slightly as she felt his tongue. Her molecules danced in pleasure and bounded outward. She tried to pull them back, but the kiss was too powerful."[39]

Vanessa turns only half invisible and gets a control over her "molecules" when she pulls away. Invisibility highlights the corporeal aspects of subjectivity — Vanessa is not always in control of her own body and thus not able to perform what she understands as "normal" teenage femininity, which includes intimate moments with boyfriends. Later on, when she learns to control her invisibility, it serves as a form of pleasure, which makes her ability rather different from the other girls' abilities to travel in time, read thoughts or see into the future. Controlling her invisibility also means control over her own sexuality and desire. This can, of course, be read as a very conventional take on female sexuality, but the closure of the novel also suggests that control and better knowledge of her invisibility allows Vanessa to take pleasure in it. However, invisibility has strategic uses as well, mainly for spying, and as a form of divine power, it makes its user a target for evil exploiters.

Vanessa is chased by unseen enemies already at the beginning of the book and later on learns from her mentor, Maggie, that the Atrox is specifically after the daughters of the moon since they are destined to be the ones who at some point defeat the evil completely. The destiny of the girls lies in their genes, since their abilities are innate, and, furthermore, used intuitively rather than by applying a specific, rehearsed technique, even though a greater control of one's ability can be attained in time. Maggie explains to her mentees that while her responsibility is to guide the girls, the girls' responsibility is to fight the evil because that is what they have been born to do. With special abilities comes the responsibility to use them for good purposes, according to the adult mentor who is there to ensure that the girls are not seduced to the wrong side. Invisibility as a supernatural ability is here, again, associated with moral subjectivity, but the question is not what the invisible person can do out of her own will if she chooses the side of the evil but what she can be forced to do by others.

Especially for Vanessa, whose invisibility is linked to her own desire, the exploitation is potentially also sexual—here the text plays on conventional notions about heterosexuality. First, in moments of seduction that could lead to exploitation it is Vanessa's visibility/appearance, rather than invisibility, that is emphasized in her male enemies' sexual gaze. This happens when Vanessa meets her main adversary, the handsome Stanton, a follower of the Atrox, for the first time: "His gaze lingered over her body as if she had invited him to look and take all the time in the world."[40] Vanessa is not amused and attacks Stanton verbally to tackle his unwanted attention. A similar scene occurs also later when Vanessa is dancing with Stanton and approached by another follower of the Atrox who boldly gazes her: "His eyes held frank sexual suggestion and kept returning to her see-through camisole."[41] This is followed by unwelcome touches and mocking laughter by the young men, which make Vanessa feel vulnerable.

Second, Vanessa also contemplates whether she could fall in love with her seducer/exploiter when Stanton has just kissed her, and she compares her own feelings to those of Persephone, who was abducted by Hades. For the time being she is able to resist even though she wants to rescue Stanton from the evil forces. What we see in operation here are discourses of heterosexuality that position the beautiful woman as the sexual object of active male pursuers, as well as the conventional "Beauty and the Beast" syndrome: a woman believes that her kindness and love will be powerful enough to turn the monster into a gentle man. Indeed, it seems that on her own Vanessa would become an easy target for exploitation, despite her good motives; it is only with the help of her girl friends that she is saved from the followers of Atrox, who try to seduce her to their side.

The necessity of intersubjective female agency is explicitly emphasized in the novel. Apart from following the advice of their adult mentor, the girls need to stay together and collaborate to avoid becoming vessels of evil. The Atrox tries to target the girls separately, because while on their own, they are more vulnerable. The female collaboration only lasts while the girls are teenagers, however. When the daughters of the moon reach seventeen, they have to make a choice between losing one's powers and memory of what she has been or disappearing and becoming a guardian spirit. This is represented as a difficult choice, since, for Vanessa her invisibility has become a pleasurable and empowering ability. In the final passage in the novel, focalized through Vanessa, she has control over her ability, which feels liberating: "The wind picked her up and carried her away. She could stay invisible forever. She didn't completely understand her power, but she was beginning to understand who she was. *Goddess*, she thought, and her molecules formed a smile before she rode the breeze with arc-shaped leaps, like a dolphin, up and down toward home."[42]

Goddess of the Night thus ends with a clear sense of empowerment, described through Vanessa's own experience of invisibility as a gift that provides her with a sense of freedom, felt on a bodily level. However, while Vanessa grows more comfortable with her special ability as the series progresses, in the final book she chooses normal life over life as a guardian spirit. Invisibility and her divine heritage have provided Vanessa with agency — which is strongly associated with her femininity and sexuality — but after her choice Vanessa has no recollection of it and thus her adult subjectivity will not be built on her discoveries of her extraordinary abilities as a teenager. The indication that to become "normal" adults, teenage girls need to give up their special powers echoes the early girls' stories where, according to Pratt, girls need to "grow down" rather than grow up since adult femininity means giving up their girlhood freedom and accepting conventional female roles as wives and mothers.[43] On the other hand, forgetting her past as a beautiful goddess who is born to a role where she is constantly the target of male (sexual) predators might be read as liberating in regard to conventional discourses of femininity.

EXPLOITED, LONELY GIRLS

Laura Ruby's *The Wall and the Wing* (2006) with its sequel *The Chaos King* (2007) and Sarah Neufeld's *Visibility* (2004) feature protagonists who learn about their ability to turn invisible on their own, have no support to acquire more knowledge about their talent and are exploited by adult characters. Ruby's books are clearly aimed for a younger audience than Neufeld's young adult novel, and this reflects not only in the age of the protagonists but also in the ways in which issues related to invisibility, power and subjectivity are dealt with at the closure of the narratives. The protagonists in these novels are not described as witches, since in each novel invisibility is a genetic ability.

In Ruby's novels, Gurl, the protagonist, is the first "Wall" (someone able to blend into their surroundings and thus become invisible) in a hundred years and her talent is explained to be a genetic anomaly. Exactly the same explanation is mentioned in Neufeld's text in relation to the invisibility of Natalie, the protagonist, and her mother, although people are also speculating about the possibility of acquiring the ability to turn invisible through brain surgery. However, in these novels, the extraordinary abilities of the protagonists put them in a similar position to the witch as a female with supernatural talents. This similarity is referred to in *The Wall and the Wing* when a character called The Professor explains to Gurl that "many of the witches hanged or burned in the fourteenth, fifteenth, sixteenth and seventeenth centuries were Walls"; this is because people do not trust what they cannot see and "don't like the idea that someone could be watching them, overhearing all their dirty secrets and observing all their dirty tricks."[44] Also in *Visibility*, Natalie — who is the internal first-person narrator of the story — describes her paranoid sense of being watched by her invisible mother: "When I was younger, I was absolutely panicked that my mother came into my room while I was sleeping.... She lurked in the hallways, watching me."[45]

Thus, both Ruby's and Neufeld's texts address the situation where people are afraid of becoming the targets of invisible people's monitoring gaze. As seen above with Price's novels, this fear can be associated with old legends about invisible, malevolent female shape-shifters, but the fear of the unseen is also, of course, what power in the Foucauldian notion of the panopticon is based on. I will return to the issue of gaze and power in Chapter 4 and focus here on how the invisible girls' abilities to serve as perfect spies or thieves makes them appealing targets for exploitation.

In both novels, the girl protagonists' literal invisibility is linked to their metaphorical invisibility as unnoticed, unremarkable persons. In *The Wall and the Wing*, Gurl is a shy thirteen-year-old living in an orphanage called Hope House for the Homeless and Hopeless. Her literal invisibility is an extension of her social condition, one step further from being "not the type of girl that people noticed — she was too thin, too pale, too quiet."[46] Natalie, the seventeen-year-old protagonist and narrator in *Visibility*, describes herself as a daughter who is overshadowed and controlled by her strong-willed, famous mother, who is gorgeous when visible and powerful when invisible. In Natalie's view, she herself becomes unnoticed in her mother's presence: "Any guy who comes here, no matter how old or young, is interested in some aspect of my mother. Not me. They generally don't even *see* me."[47] However, after they learn that they can turn literally invisible, both Gurl and Natalie find invisibility an empowering ability that they can control themselves. Yet, namely because invisibility is a controllable, useful ability, the characters in Ruby's and Neufeld's novels are involuntarily drawn into positions where their invisibility is exploited by adults.

Ruby's *The Wall and the Wing* is situated in an alternative version of modern New York, where magic events and supernatural creatures are regularly encountered and where most people have the ability to fly. In this world, the orphan Gurl is an outcast even among other orphan children at the Hope House because she is a "leadfoot," that is, she cannot fly. Because of this, she is bullied by other children and often humiliated by the adults working at the Hope House during the compulsory flying lessons. In this world, invisibility is a rare ability and very few people are aware that it even exists. At the beginning of the book readers learn from The Professor's notes that Walls only occur once in a century and that they are usually females. Why Walls are mostly females is not explained. What is explained is that, due to their abilities, they have been both persecuted as witches as well as exploited. The gangster Sweetcheeks Grabowski is after Gurl, the current Wall, because he views an invisible girl a perfect tool to reach power and control: "Why, an invisible girl could turn everything around. An invisible girl could help change a better-than-average thief with marital problems into the greatest gangster of all time. Imagine what you could steal if you were invisible. You could steal the most powerful weapon in the world!"[48]

This passage clearly echoes the visions that Wells's invisible man has about his unlimited power and possibilities. The most powerful weapon here is a magic pen that makes things written by it come true, thus a pen that can potentially guarantee its owner control of everything and everyone. Here it is not necessary for Grabowski to turn invisible himself, as long as he finds someone invisible that he can exploit — the novel presents a whole history of adult, criminal men exploiting young, powerless girls. For Walls invisibility has always been an ambiguous form of power — as it is indeed for Gurl.

Gurl finds out about her ability accidentally while trying to hide from a busboy behind a pizzeria and realizes that she has turned literally invisible, a sort of chameleon who changes color to match her background. While invisible, she saves a cat from the busboy, who is beating it, and thus uses her ability to do good. Gurl soon understands that she can turn invisible especially when she feels empathy for someone in danger; later, when she learns how to control her ability, she finds out that her invisibility is not only limited to situations where she tries to help someone else. Not unlike the witches described above, she uses a mantra of her own to blend into her surroundings: "I am the wall and the ground and the air."[49]

She does not have anyone to guide her — even the strange professor knows very little about it — and thus she has to learn about her talent intuitively and through her own experience. Gurl often enjoys her invisibility because it enables her to wander around the city undetected, and later she is able to turn others invisible by touching them; thus her increasing knowledge about her special ability makes her gradually more powerful. Moreover, while invisibility does not directly allow Gurl to deal with her bullies at the Hope House because she tries to keep it a secret, it provides her with confidence that allows her to challenge her bullies when she is visible. Invisibility is a talent that affects both Gurl's self-worth and agency in general.

However, the fact that Gurl turns invisible out of empathy is also part of why she is an easy target for exploitation. When the greedy, vain matron of the Hope House, Mrs. Terwiliger, finds out about Gurl's invisibility, she locks away the cat that Gurl has saved and blackmails Gurl into stealing things for her:

"But it just happens!" Gurl said. "I can't control it!"
"Oh, you'll learn," said Mrs. Terwiliger.
"I don't want to learn. I don't *want* to become a thief."
"What does it matter what you want?" Mrs. Terwiliger said sharply, then caught herself. "You're an orphan, Gurl. I'm offering you an opportunity. You act as if I'm asking you to commit a crime!"
"You *are* asking me to commit a crime," said Gurl.
"Just a little one. It barely even counts. It's not like robbing a bank."[50]

This piece of dialogue where Gurl openly confronts the matron is indicative of several larger tropes related to invisibility as a form of power that operate on the level of the whole narrative. First, Gurl is, as the witches described above, unwilling to use her ability for immoral purposes. The dialogue juxtaposes an adult person who, due to her position as the head of a charity house, should be ethically sound but is something completely different, and Gurl, a powerless orphan child who is dependent on the matron but still opposes her while trying to maintain her moral principles.

Second, Mrs. Terwiliger is correct in her notion that Gurl will learn how to use her ability and thus grasp agency if she only wants to do so. Ironically, it is the stealing trips during which Gurl also experiences the wonderful city unseen and gains more self-confidence after every successful theft, even though this makes her also ashamed and suspecting whether she is an inherently bad person. Because she is forced to use her ability to achieve concrete things, she learns that invisibility increases her agency. Together with an orphan boy, Bug, Gurl manages to make a plan to save the cat Noodle and escape from the orphanage. Soon Gurl finds that she has escaped one exploiter only to land in the hands of another: the gangster Sweetcheeks Grabowski. However, with the help of Bug and The Professor, Sweetcheeks is stopped before he manages to make Gurl steal the magic pen. The fairy-tale ending of the novel also involves Gurl finding her parents, who happen to be the richest people in the universe. While it is unclear at the end of this novel what Gurl will do about her invisibility after finding a safe place at her parents', the sequel to *The Wall and the Wing*, *The Chaos King*, continues to address issues related to invisibility, power and agency.

In *The Chaos King*, Gurl, now called by her real name, Georgie, is living with her rich parents and attending a private school for girls where she is, again bullied, this time by the second-richest-girl in the universe and her followers. Although her parents have asked her not to use invisibility, Georgie occasionally turns invisible to escape awkward situations and notices that her teenage growth spurt has also affected her invisibility: parts of her body do not disappear unless she concentrates very hard. In a lengthy passage focalized through Georgie, she complains about the unfairness of all the changes that she has to go through:

> It wasn't fair that things changed so quickly. First she was invisible to the world, and then she really was invisible, and then she wasn't supposed to be invisible, and now her power didn't work right all the time, and she had to worry about her feet showing or her nose showing or whatever.... Shouldn't a person be allowed to get used to things before they change? It wasn't right![51]

This passage can be read as an allegory of early teenage life in general, during which one has to adapt to rapid bodily, mental and social changes — social changes are involved because the changes in one's body also alter the ways in which other people perceive and respond to the changing or changed individual. Georgie is here represented as a young girl who feels that she is not yet prepared to go through all kinds of changes and yearns for some kind of stability instead. Despite her challenges, Georgie is able to use invisibility strategically to overcome the new villains that threaten her and her family but, in the end, does not want to go on playing the role of the hero all the time. During her young, mainly orphan life, Georgie has been forced to take responsibility for not only herself but also for other children and her parents — at the end of the novel it is indicated that she should now learn to accept that she is still a child who should be taken care of by her parents. Thus, at the closure, the thirteen-year-old Georgie does not grow into greater independence but dependence. Her friend Bug is also brought into closer parental control when Georgie's parents ask him to move in their building instead of continuing to live alone elsewhere.

This is a fairly typical closure in children's fantasy books where the fantastic adventures offer the children a carnivalesque "time-out" from their usual lives, including the surveillance of (adult) authorities, and, in the end, the children return to the safety of their old homes or find a safe haven in their new homes.[52] In a conventional sense, this is, of course, a happy end, although, in terms of child-adult power relations, it is hardly subversive. Georgie is empowered in the end in the sense that she is recognized and accepted as an individual whose choices are respected (the text clearly states that it is her choice to stay with her parents). Yet, it seems that she is not going to use her special ability, invisibility, to achieve greater independence and agency — instead, her father once more highlights the issue that because Georgie is special, she is always vulnerable to other people's exploitation: "You are special. And because of that, people are going to notice you and not always for the right reasons."[53]

While Gurl/Georgie is forced to commit illegal actions while invisible, Natalie in *Visibility* is blackmailed by the police and forced to help them to spy on criminals. Like the orphan Gurl, Natalie is let down by her caretaker, who here is her own mother. The novel is situated in modern Chicago, and in the American society portrayed in the text, it is assumed to be an individual citizen's civic duty to use her extraordinary talents and abilities for the common good. Since Jadyn Irving, Natalie's mother and the only known person to be able to turn invisible at will, has refused to work for the police or the government, she is considered a dangerous, unpredictable citizen and a potential traitor who collaborates with criminals. It is later revealed that the speculations about Jadyn's criminal activities are not completely unfounded, since Jadyn has been working for the drug lord Javier Nadal, but also collected evidence against him at the same time. While Jadyn is a strong figure who has earned a fortune as a invisible spy working in the private sector, following no one else's orders apart from her own and only stopped at the end when she is busted by Natalie and the police, Natalie is unable to use her invisibility for her own purposes.

Natalie is a girl with no friends, apart from the bodyguard Peter, who is keeping an eye over her for Jadyn. This makes her vulnerable, since there is no one who would support her in her attempts to challenge her mother's control. Natalie finds out about her ability to become invisible accidentally during her own birthday party organized by her mother where Natalie is a reluctant hostess. When she escapes the distressing social situation into her own room and wishes to be unnoticed, she experiences a terrible headache, the painful, physical effect of turning invisible:

> The trembly feeling isn't going away. I put a hand behind my head, trying to ignore the stickiness, and rub at the place carefully; it twinges alarmingly, and I force myself to stop. It's dangerous. Every doctor I've talked to thinks the places are only weak spots in my skull now that anything special is gone, and I've been told that if I do the wrong thing I could put myself into a coma. I'm supposed to take aspirin, and use a hot pack, and either fall asleep or try to ignore it until it goes away.[54]

Natalie is not yet aware that she is actually turning invisible, since she assumes that the symptoms are only the result of her losing her genetic ability to turn invisible as a child. Ironically, doctors have advised Natalie to avoid her special headaches and have thus unwittingly kept her from finding out that her ability is still functional. The doctors assume that Natalie has been in an accident that has caused her to lose her talent, but Natalie herself remembers that it is her mother who has done some damage to her as a child to prevent Natalie from developing her ability. This is in line with Natalie's characterization of Jadyn as a mother who exploits her daughter by making her run errands for Jadyn and organizing her life according to Jadyn's orders. It is not only Natalie's mother who has wanted to exploit her, however. Later on, Natalie's personal bodyguard, Peter, reveals that several years ago Natalie's parents both claimed custody over Natalie after their divorce. The court ruled that, because Jadyn is not a reliable citizen, Natalie's father will get custody if Natalie develops her ability to become invisible. While it is unclear whether Jadyn has harmed Natalie out of desire to keep her child near her or out of desire to control Natalie and avoid any competition that her daughter's invisibility might cause, it is clear that Natalie's father has been mainly interested in his daughter's special ability. For Natalie, then, the possibility of exploitation seems to be necessarily connected to her special ability.

First Natalie finds invisibility exhilarating and empowering; she manages to embarrass her bullies and thinks that she will now be free from the control of her mother. In contrast to all the other invisibility narratives discussed here (or any other that I have encountered), Natalie's invisibility is characterized by the scientifically logical consequence of being blind while invisible. However, her blindness does fairly little to stop her from moving around and spying on people, since her other senses, most notably her hearing, are heightened while she is invisible. While invisibility could offer Natalie an escape from her mother and everyone else, she is a person whose subjectivity has been built on following other people's orders in the past; thus she herself admits that she is unable to fathom a plan to leave her current depressing life behind. Although Jadyn cannot exploit her daughter's invisibility because Natalie keeps it a secret, it is exactly because Natalie is terrified of her mother finding out about her that Natalie ends up being blackmailed by the police, who demand that she spy on criminals. Even though being blackmailed, Natalie still finds the situation partly an empowering one, since she now has one aspect in her life that is out of the control of her mother.

During the police operations, Natalie gets into near-fatal situations and it seems that the police have little consideration for her safety, as long as she manages to perform the tasks that she is supposed to do. In the final operation, Natalie is caught by the drug lord Nadal and blackmailed by him in turn. Nadal tries to convince Natalie that since she will get exploited anyway, she might as well join his criminal forces, which can at least ensure her safety:

> "It's life, Natalie." Nadal doesn't blink. "It's in your genes, along with the rest. You were born into it. You are special, and you will be used. There will always be someone behind you, watching you, waiting for you to make a mistake, and you'll always slip. Best to control it as much as possible I'd think. While you still have the option."[55]

What is suggested here is that Natalie's genetic, embodied invisibility will be her destiny, or, in other words, form her subjectivity as someone who is born to be exploited. This fatalistic discourse is challenged when Jadyn kills Nadal to protect Natalie, who can then no longer be blackmailed by the police. After this, for the first time, Natalie is able to act upon her own wishes and motivations. While Peter suggests two possibilities in relation to Natalie's invisibility — either stop doing it and stay safe or turn it into a career at an institution such as the CIA — the final passages suggest that Natalie is now able to make up her own mind and figure out how to use or not to use invisibility for the purposes that she herself views worthwhile.

What helps Natalie in the end, though, is the encouragement from her new friend, Monica, who does not want to exploit her — although, pessimistically speaking, she is not aware of Natalie's ability either — but only asks Natalie to hang around with her and forget about what other people think. At the closure, Natalie is thus urged to stop building her subjectivity on the wishes and expectations of other people. While teenage protagonists in young adult fiction often need to grow out of their irresponsibility and selfishness to reach maturity and adulthood, Natalie has to learn to be less considerate and responsible in the end.

It is easy to see why this pattern is more appealing if the protagonist is someone who has been exploited for most of her life. However, unlike the early teenager Georgie in Ruby's novels, the almost grown-up Natalie is released from parental control — that in her case has been rather oppressive — and represented as capable of taking care of herself. Yet, to build an agentic subjectivity, it is visibility rather than invisibility that Natalie needs; visibility in the sense of recognition that Monica offers at the end. Invisibility, as a state where one is completely isolated from other people, is not the solution if one is to become a socially viable human being. Instead, recognition by others — here in the positive sense of acknowledging other people as worthy human beings in their own right — is necessary in constructing both a positive self-image and an agentic subjectivity. This pattern will be even more obvious in the novels discussed in the following chapter.

To conclude, when invisibility is transported from a fairy tale universe to urban fantasy and modern settings, it becomes even more obviously an ability that is not automatically empowering, strategic or exciting. Invisibility is represented as a form of power that does have strategic uses but these are usually rather limited — while this is often due to the fact that the young protagonists' agency is limited because of their age and the social position that comes along with it, in Ewing's novel invisibility is associated with female sexuality and thus not something that can be interpreted as a simple form of power. While it might be tempting to interpret all the above the narratives about exploitation of female character's ability to become invisible as allegories of the real-world forms of exploitation of women — gendered violence, including rape, human trade and slavery — the exploitation of abilities and talents does not concern only women and girls, not even in children's literature about invisibility. For instance, the possibility of becoming an interesting research object and forced labor for the government is also addressed in Andrew Clements's *Things Not Seen* (2002), where a fifteen-year-old boy turns suddenly invisible. What all of these novels reflect, however, is a discourse where power and empowerment are not understood in any simple manner.

Maidens, Mothers and Crones

This section considers the age-shifting female characters in two fantasy novels from the 1980s, Louise Lawrence's *The Earth Witch* (1982) and Diana Wynne Jones's *Howl's Moving Castle* (1986). Each novel involves characters that shift between youth and old age, yet in each the transforming female characters are portrayed rather differently. In *The Earth Witch* the age-shifting witch-goddess is not the protagonist of the story; instead, the young Katherine's coming of age is represented in juxtaposition to the Earth Witch's transformations. *Howl's Moving Castle* is also a female coming-of-age story, but here the young protagonist goes through age-shifting herself. While the age-shifting in Lawrence's novel might be characterized as a typical radical-feminist take on female subjectivity, the magic changes in age in Jones's text more effectively challenge conventional assumptions about the subjectivity and agency of young girls as well as old women.

The Beautiful and Terrifying Females: Age-Shifting and the Earth Witch

Lawrence's *The Earth Witch* is a novel that builds upon the common metaphor of the earth as a woman. The metaphor has been popular among feminist writers since the 1970s to address women's (assumably) closer relationship to the earth and nature and represent female subjectivity that, unlike the (assumably) more stable and rational male subjectivity, is constantly in change, following cyclical patterns. *The Earth Witch* clearly reflects the radical-feminist discourses of female subjectivity that associate women with nature, as well as witchcraft.

The Earth Witch is situated in a Welsh countryside in the 1970s or early 1980s. The old myths come alive in an otherwise realist setting when the Earth Witch takes the form of a woman, Bronwen Davis, who moves into an abandoned cottage in the woods. The character of the Earth Witch, or the witch-goddess, draws on the image of the triple goddess and its three aspects of maiden, mother and crone. However, the Earth Witch is, according to the witch-character in the novel, actually a combination of several female deities from Welsh mythology: "You haven't heard of her? Rhiannon of the underworld? Blodeuwedd of the owls? Angharad of the lake? Cerridwen the shape changer? She has many names but it is all one woman."[56]

As Donna R. White suggests in her discussion of Welsh influences in children's literature, Lawrence has drawn more inspiration from Robert Graves's *The White Goddess* than *The Mabinogi*, and combines motifs from Welsh mythology to aspects borrowed from Arthurian legends.[57] My specific interest here is not in how "authentic" Lawrence's use of Welsh, or any other, myth is, but in how the image of the triple goddess is employed to represent female subjectivity and associated with the coming-of-age process of the young female protagonist, Katherine/Kate, who herself is not a witch. As C.W. Sullivan argues, one appeal of drawing on Welsh Celtic mythology is that it involves strong women figures that can be transformed into strong female heroes in modern fantasy.[58] Certainly, in *The Earth Witch*, the mythic Celtic women are portrayed as a source of strength for the female characters in the contemporary setting of the novel. None of the narrative is focalized through the witch, although a significant amount of information about the witch is revealed through dialogue because she certainly makes no secret of who she actually is. The two main focalizers in the novel are Owen, the boy whom the witch seduces, and Katherine; their views of and relationship towards the witch are conventionally gendered.

Bronwen Davis appears in the abandoned cottage in late winter in February — she is first despised and feared by the three young protagonists, Owen,

Jonathan and Kate, but Owen soon starts to feel pity for the old woman and agrees to help her with chores. Right from the beginning, Bronwen is associated with the other woman who has lived in the cottage earlier, Megan Davis, an old, unclean woman considered to be a witch. Kate in particular is afraid of Bronwen and intuitively senses that something is wrong. During one scene when she is walking alone in the fields, she feels that she is attacked by the earth and things growing on it, controlled by "some huge formless existence, ancient and undying" that has, despite its formlessness, a feminine gender: "cold and ruthlessly she came ... harsh and cruel was her cry."[59] As the narrative unfolds, it becomes clear that even though the earth witch also has more benevolent forms, in the end she is a ruthless figure who demands human lives for the gifts of the earth that *men* reap — it is namely male lives that must be sacrificed to the witch-goddess. While women are associated with the earth, men are exploiters of the earth (and women); thus the references to the ancient rituals of sacrifice where young men were given to the Earth Witch to ensure that the earth will be fertile also in the following year.

While Katherine is suspicious and afraid of the witch, later, also out of jealousy, Owen soon falls under Bronwen's magic, womanly spells and soon changes from a kind helper of an old woman into the woman's surrogate son, then into her lover and finally into the victim of the devouring crone. These changes occur in sync with the age-shifting of Bronwen/the earth witch: during her relationship with Owen, the witch grows younger when the spring turns to the summer and then rapidly ages and withers away in the autumn. Bronwen's age-shifting clearly builds on the image of the triple goddess and its three aspects of maiden, mother and crone — these aspects not only say something about women as such but also about their relationship to men. The representation of femininity is conventional and occurs in a thoroughly heteronormative framework. The portrayal of Bronwen suggests that during their lives, women change from sweet, beautiful maidens into loving and caring mothers and finally into irritable, angry hags — they are man-eaters (here quite literally) who turn from sexual beings into care-givers and finally into devouring hags, the older, the uglier; the uglier, the more evil.

Bronwen herself changes from a malevolent hag into a motherly woman who tends to her garden and consoles Owen, who has been abandoned by his own mother as a child: "She smelled of soil and flowers, and all the lost years of his childhood were being crammed into one embrace."[60] This is followed by a gradual transformation into a beautiful young woman who takes up a job at the local school as a teacher and plays the role of the Queen of May during the spring carnival, or, rather, seems to embody the spring as the goddess Blodeuwedd. In the autumn, the changes in age occur in a reversed order: Bronwen gets older, uglier and meaner and first kicks Owen out of her cottage and then lures him back there to be fed to her pet sow, aptly named as Cerridwen.

While Owen's foster parents, his friends and villagers view Owen's and Bronwen's relationship as indecent — after all, Owen is sixteen and the witch is, in the spring, middle-aged — Owen himself sees Bronwen as ageless right from the beginning and is later completely dependent on her. At the beginning, Owen explains his own behavior to himself as altruistic — he only wants to aid a weak, lonely woman — but soon he needs no other motive than his love to do whatever the witch-goddess asks of him. Towards the end, Owen seems to lose all his agentic subjectivity due to his relationship with the witch-goddess; when Bronwen leaves him, he gets seriously depressed and later fatally ill after Cerridwen the sow has tasted his leg. Owen only survives the sow's attack because Katherine comes to save him and, in a violent frenzy, kills the pig.

While Owen owes his life to the human-girl Katherine, it seems that this may not essentially affect his almost non-existent sense of self and worth, since he strongly associates Kate with Bronwen — not only because they look alike to him but because Kate is, like Bronwen, very determined. In the closing passage of the book, Owen, seeing Katherine, knows that he will see "the same pattern repeating itself": to him, Katherine, like the witch Bronwen, is also "beautiful and terrifying" and "[l]ike the flowers, like the earth, she could be cruel or gentle."[61] Katherine — like all women, supposedly — is like the earth, something that cannot be controlled by men, although they will always try to exploit it.

Moreover, Katherine herself identifies with the true, wild femininity or femaleness that the witch represents. This first occurs when Katherine sees the earth-witch at the carnival in her young form and both hates her and identifies with her power to enchant and destroy men. A moment later, she strongly recognizes the witch's violent aspects in herself:

> Below the surface of herself Kate could feel something so hideous she could not bear to think of it ... an instinct of blood sacrifices and fertility rites, ancient rituals of birth and death, a woman wanting to come free ... sensuous, savage, uninhibited, earthy and sexual as nature, beautiful as Bronwen, cruel and gentle as the land. What Kate saw, loved and feared and hated in Bronwen were the secret parts of herself. It was a kind of recognition. Bronwen was not just white and pure ... she was also deadly and poison.[62]

Kate intuitively knows that she — as a budding woman — is similar to the witch, especially if she releases the "woman wanting to come free." This does happen, in fact, at the closure when Katherine saves Owen. She explains to herself that she does it out of love, rather than out of hate or want to consume Owen, and in this she is different from the witch. However, during the killing scene Katherine turns into a violent, almost inhuman female avenger, and the whole scene is represented as a coming-of-age moment. Significantly, in her brother's view, there is something different about her: "the shape of a girl standing tall and still ... only she was not a girl. She was a woman. Her stance, her bearing, the curves of her body, the reason she had come was that of a woman."[63] During violently hacking at the sow, Kate realizes that people not only die for what they love but also kill for it. Clearly, this reflects one of the authentic female purposes, to bring death — the other authentic purpose is to create, or give birth. As Kate puts it earlier in the text, men have mostly lost their "basic instinct" because they are "too bound up with each other, cars and technology and earning money"; women, on the other hand, "give birth and rear children and tend sickbeds" and are "still part of the natural cycle. Women and land share the same purpose ... creation and death."[64] This not only reflects radical-feminist discourses but produces key parts of the discourse and explains the argument about the essential, natural differences between men and women, emphasizing the strong, intuitive, natural power of women.

In *The Earth Witch*, the young male protagonist ends up almost completely devoured by the hag, while the young female protagonist finds her own feminine subjectivity through her relationship to, and encounters with, the witch. It seems that, as a mature woman, Katherine might draw into different aspects of her femininity when needed — like the strong women in Pratt's (1982) vision of full womanhood. While the "natural" power that women have in the novel, drawing on the image of the triple goddess, is definitely effective in the sense that Bronwen and Katherine both achieve their aims, whether in love or hate, it is worth considering what their agency consists of. Clearly neither of these women only uses "power to" do something but they are also using their "power over" others as women over men. From a liberal-feminist view, this is not empowerment, since the power relations between genders are hardly equal, even though the conventionally passive and subordinate gender is here dominative. From a radical-feminist view, this may well be a form of empowerment where a young woman gets in touch with her authentic femininity and womanhood. From a poststructuralist or a queer feminist point of view, the concept of empowerment seems simply irrelevant. If one draws on the Foucauldian notion of power as a relation rather than something that a person has, power only occurs in intersubjective frameworks and thus anyone's "empowerment" cannot be considered without taking into account everyone else involved. This is, of course, where issues get more complicated. Thus, asking whether or not Katherine is empowered, one might want to consider how in this particular representation of female coming-of-age is associated with control not only over oneself but also over men and how traditional femininity is inherently linked to femaleness. While celebrating authentic, strong femininity, the novel does little to interrogate gendered power relations — apart from turning the tables — and gendered stereotypes.

Whereas *The Earth Witch* suggests that women can recognize themselves in old myths and draw strength from the nature-bound, authentic femininity, Diana Wynne Jones's *Howl's Moving Castle* does quite the opposite: the novel challenges the conventional fairy tale discourse of predestined life (cycles) by showing that old stories are based on beliefs rather than facts, also in relation to gendered subjectivity.

Rewriting the Crone: The Metamorphosis of a Loathly Lady

Diana Wynne Jones is a fantasist who has frequently employed magic age-shifting in novels that thematize identity construction. As Deborah Kaplan writes, Jones's oeuvre involves "a continuing theme of disguised age and age disruption ... protagonists who age in more than one direction, protagonists who don't know their own age, protagonists in disguise as characters older or younger than themselves."[65] Jones's *Howl's Moving Castle* is one of her novels in which a character goes through an abrupt change in age, here from a young woman into an old hag. As Pratchett's Tiffany Aching books, Jones's novel employs a parodic mode and draws on fairy tale tradition and conventions on a general level, although it also involves links to specific tales, most notably "Bluebeard" and the "Loathly Lady" stories.

Already the opening of the novel invokes a framework of fairy tale conventions and employs a metafictional, parodic discourse: "In the land of Ingary, where such things as seven-league boots and cloaks of invisibility really exist, it is quite a misfortune to be born the eldest of the three. Everyone knows you are the one who will fail first, and worst, if the three of you set out to seek your fortunes."[66] Ingary is a secondary world where magic is a part of everyday life and people's fates seem to be predestined according to fairy-tale rules; this is, at least, what the protagonist, Sophie, the eldest of three daughters, believes at the beginning.

In the following, I will examine the ways in which the novel challenges gendered fairy tale conventions through parody and metafiction and consider the ways in which Sophie's transformation and her performance of new gendered and aged roles function as a parody when analyzed in relation to notions of embodiment and performativity. As suggested earlier, the strategic parodic or mimetic repetition of conventionally gendered behaviors can be a subversive form of agency. In *Howl's Moving Castle*, the textual strategies call readers' attention both to internalized regulatory gendered discourses and experience of embodiment as well as to a parodic performance of conventionally feminine behaviors.

In the case of the twenty-year-old Sophie, the novel demonstrates explicitly how (gendered) discourses regulate subjects' lives — in the novel's fairy-tale world of Ingary these discourses appear in the form of fairy-tale conventions. Before her transformation, Sophie is obsessed with the fairy-tale convention according to which the eldest of three is inevitably doomed to fail. Sophie's internalization of the convention turns her into a character that reflects some of the negative aspects of conventional, passive femininity. Although the narrator describes Sophie as pretty, hard-working and compassionate — all conventionally positive feminine qualities — before her transformation Sophie thinks negatively of herself. The lack of self-confidence and control over her own life as well as the utter unselfishness to the point of self-sacrifice are evident in Sophie's acceptance of her supposedly predestined fate as the eldest child to continue her father's business as a shop assistant and never go out to seek her fortune. The metafictional passages where Sophie as a character recognizes the fairy-tale conventions seem humorous to the reader, but for Sophie the awareness of the conventions prevents her from making any free choices and thus limits her agency. In addition to her non-existing sense of agency, Sophie does not feel comfortable in her young woman's body that to her seems that of "an old woman or a semi-invalid" after months of sitting and sewing.[67] Her feelings about her body are also associated with sexuality — Sophie is afraid to go out and incapable of facing an attractive young man interested in her.

The girl–Sophie that readers encounter at the beginning is an exaggerated representation of the conventional "nice girl," including her sexual uncertainty and inexperience. The nice girl discourse is still very much in circulation in Western societies, not only as an ideal model set up for some girls but as a discourse that is realized as an experienced identity in the lives of many girls and women. In relation to the liberal-feminist discourse operating on the level of the whole novel, the conventional, "nice" and passive feminine identity that the young Sophie portrays is an undesirable one that she should grow out of. The expectation of a change is built into the narrative itself.

First, the nice and shy Sophie is almost a caricature — her niceness and shyness are exaggerated to a humorous effect — and one might anticipate more complexity from a fantasy (if not a traditional fairy-tale) protagonist. Second, Sophie is not the caricature she first seems; her character is made more complex because she is the main focalizer in the novel. In the focalized passages it is revealed that she is both aware of and unhappy about her situation and her wish to change combined with her inability to act upon her wish creates the expectation of a change.

Ironically, it is Sophie's transformation into a ninety-year-old crone that forces her to leave the dull shop and go against her pre-destined fate. Sophie's transformation occurs as the Witch of the Waste appears in the hat shop and puts a spell on Sophie because she thinks Sophie is plotting against her. In this context, as in the "Loathly Lady" stories, it is a punishment to be transformed into an old woman. Sophie's whole transformation is physical, and real to her:

> Sophie put her hands to her face, wondering what the man had stared at. She felt soft, leathery wrinkles. She looked at her hands. They were wrinkled too, and skinny, with large veins in the back and knuckles like knobs. She pulled her gray skirt against her legs and looked down at skinny, decrepit ankles and feet which had made her shoes all knobbly. They were the legs of someone about ninety and they seemed to be real.
> Sophie got herself to the mirror, and found she had to hobble. The face in the mirror was quite calm, because it was what she expected to see. It was the face of a gaunt old woman, withered and brownish, surrounded by wispy white hair. Her own eyes, yellow and watery, stared out at her, looking rather tragic.
> "Don't worry old thing," Sophie said to the face. "You look quite healthy. Besides, this is much more like you really are."[68]

The extended description of the bodily effects of the transformation is a reworking of the folktale motif, as is the point of view: here the transformation is focalized through Sophie and not through an external narrator. As an embodied experience, old age is represented as a painful punishment; Sophie is not merely in a disguise, but her young body truly changes into an old woman's body with all the drawbacks coming with the age. As regards Sophie's material form, then, the transformation is a disempowering one and, as in fairy tales where people are put under a curse, right from the start a central element of the plot is Sophie's task to find out a way to undo the spell she is under.

However, while her body becomes physically weaker, her new ways of behavior empower her in other ways. Sophie is calm about her situation, probably because of the sense of continuity with her former and present self: she has already felt "old" before the transformation. Moreover, although Sophie does not realize it herself, she is enforcing the transformation spell herself, although this only becomes apparent towards the end of the story when all the necessary clues are put together. Retrospectively, it seems that Sophie's transformation is partly psychosomatic — she feels old and suddenly also appears old; she enforces the witch's curse herself by confirming that her new appearance reflects the way she really feels.

If the girl Sophie's body and behavior are quite literally shaped by fairy-tale conventions — which reflect a regulatory discourse of gender — after her transformation it is her new bodily form that enables her to enter into new, empowering subject positions: that of an old woman and a witch. In the real world, as Cruikshank suggests, old women have to deal with "a culturally determined idea that 'old' limits certain behaviors or style choices."[69] This is what the irony in *Howl's Moving Castle* is based on: the old Sophie is less restricted in her behaviors than the young one. Sophie's new bodily form has a direct effect on her way of thinking and behaving; with her new body she seems to acquire a new perspective and experience that people usually only gain with age, that is, during a longer period of time. Sophie's transformation highlights how subjectivity is embodied — the way in which the body a person inhabits shapes her own views — both physically (her pains make her angry) and because she is treated differently by others that perceive her as an old woman.

After her bodily transformation Sophie's feelings of shame, fear and inability have, quite magically, gone — both in relation to her agency as well as her body. Sophie is able to enter the wizard Howl's castle in her new form without fear — this is a reworking of the earlier versions of the Bluebeard tale. In Charles Perrault's "Bluebeard" as well as in variants such as "The Robber Bridegroom" and "The Fitcher's Bird" in Grimms' tales and the English tale "Mr. Fox,"[70] the young women that enter the homes of their new or future husbands are not disguised and therefore are potential victims, although the heroines ultimately do escape from the violent men either because of their own cunning or with the help of relatives or kind strangers. Although Howl is not a killer, he is literally heartless (he has given his heart to a fire demon Calcifer as a part of a contract) and therefore forced to accost young ladies and make them fall in love with him although he is incapable of returning their feelings. In her disguise, Sophie thinks she is safe from Howl — her old body is not prone to being sexually abused.

The major change, however, is Sophie's newly found freedom of speech and action. After realizing that other people perceive her not only as an old woman, but as a witch, she willingly enters into two subject positions conventionally associated with old women: a cleaning lady and a witch. Sophie herself declares her new positions and her announcements function as performative utterances — what she states becomes a socially accepted condition. By making the announcements, Sophie insists an authoritative position, partly granted by her old age. Her old woman's authority is reflected in the way she addresses the people to whom she makes the announcements, as in the scene where she explains to Howl why she has entered his castle:

> "Why I came, young man?" she said. It was obvious after what she had seen of the castle. "I came because I'm your new cleaning lady, of course."
>
> "Are you indeed?" Howl said, cracking the eggs one-handed and tossing the shells among the logs where Calcifer seemed to be eating them with a lot of snarling and gobbling. "Who says you are?"

"*I* do," said Sophie, and she added piously, "I can clean the dirt from this place even if I can't clean you from your wickedness, young man."⁷¹

In the castle, Sophie continues to use speech to control others, often by using the imperative.⁷²

Sophie's new roles are conventional female roles and they occur in a "natural" way to Sophie. The decision to be a cleaning lady, for example, is obvious because as a woman she has immediately spotted the untidiness of the place. It is ironic that the powerful new Sophie is based on a conventional portrayal of an old crone; the young Sophie who was confined to a domestic setting and sewing turns into another type of domestic witch. It is significant that she does not have to adopt any conventional male role to acquire power. Although Sophie is in disguise, she is certainly not a "hero in drag," but a conventionally feminine young woman that enters into conventional female roles — which do not involve passivity.

This is also reflected in her acceptance of the role of the witch. When a young girl asks Sophie about her occupation, Sophie embraces the identity of a witch connected with her appearance as an old hag and her home (a wizard's castle) by stating that she is the best witch in Ingary, even though she at this point believes she knows nothing about magic. While other magic-users have recognized Sophie's magic qualities, Sophie becomes aware of her gift only after a powerful witch tells her directly that she likes Sophie's strong magic. After she realizes that the fairy-tale rule of an eldest being an automatic failure does not prevent her doing magic, she begins to speak her spells out more confidently, which reflects her development and a greater awareness of her agency.

What might also have kept Sophie unaware of her magic is that she has not learned any. The way she works spells is by addressing things and people in a conversational way; spells also occur as she talks to herself. This is similar to the way that the witches do magic in Price's and Pratchett's novels discussed above. In a fantasy world, a witch needs not only to be careful of what she wishes for but also of what she says, because in the fantasy world words meant metaphorically can come true literally. This is a challenge to the conventional view of magic as based on a special language that is only available to specific speakers with a specific training, that is, the view of magic as an institutionalized practice.⁷³ Sophie — as the witches in Price and Pratchett — does not need to learn institutionalized language to perform spells, and her individual style of doing magic is subversive in the sense that although it functions similarly as conventional magic — performatively — it challenges the traditional power structures and hierarchy connected with institutionalized magic.

Yet, other characters do not always perceive Sophie's new subjectivity in a positive light, and this is at least partly due to her conventional performance of the role of a grumpy old granny. A nagging, grumpy and nosy old woman is, of course, a rather conventional figure, even a caricature. Nevertheless, Sophie has chosen herself to play this role, which she feels to be an empowering one: "As a girl, Sophie would have shrivelled with embarrassment at the way she was behaving. As an old woman, she did not mind what she did or said. She found that a great relief."[74]

It is crucial that the events are focalized through Sophie; readers get to see Sophie's experiences both as a girl and as an old woman and thus have a more complex picture of Sophie's behavior than of the other characters. Here lies the paradox in her transformation: by being both young and old at the same time, her character questions power structures connected with age along with stereotypes of both young and old women.

The change in agency — or even the decision to try to change one's behavior — is here only made possible by a very radical bodily transformation. From a material feminist perspective, Sophie's transformation shows that a subject's agency is effectively restricted by corporeality. While this puts her newly gained agency into question — is it agency at all if her actions only result from her new bodily condition that makes certain actions not only possible but necessary?— her transformation also offers possibilities of subverting conventional gendered discourses. As suggested above, Sophie's performance of an old woman's behavior can be interpreted as what Butler calls "a strategy of parodic repetition" and Braidotti describes as "mimetic repetition of [the] imaginary and material institution of femininity." Sophie's appropriation of the conventional roles of an old woman and a witch exposes and challenges the gendered norms by exaggerating them. Even if the parodic performance is not Sophie's intention as a character, her performance of the conventional role of the old woman is parodic from the perspective of readers. This is only possible because she is masquerading, and, moreover, because readers are aware that she is actually not what she appears and pretends to be. In general, a ninety-year-old granny hopping around in seven-league boots is a parodic character, but not necessarily in a subversive sense. In Sophie's case the subversiveness of her behavior results from her conscious choice to perform the role of a grumpy old lady and her relief in finding the new forms of behavior satisfactory.[75]

At the end Sophie is freed from the spell and turns back into a young woman, but she has grown up into adulthood by finding her subjective agency as a witch. Even though she might lose the authority she had as an old woman, her magic remains. Obviously, it is possible to read the transformation undone otherwise: it could mark a shift back to the conventional discourse of femininity reflected in the traditional romance closure and Sophie's decision to marry Howl. However, in opposition to the "Loathly Lady" stories where it is something that the husband does that lifts the curse off the lady, here the curse is lifted mainly due to the Loathly Sophie's own efforts. Although the story follows fairy tale conventions in that the monster/crone turns back into a young, lovely maiden, it is the maiden herself who is the agent of this transformation.

As a rewritten version of the "Bluebeard" story, the novel is a feminist revision, because it rewrites the female traits the Perrault and nineteenth century versions of the story were warning of: female curiosity and disobedience.[76] In the rewritten tale the female protagonist, Sophie's curiosity and agency are shown as necessary features in saving oneself and others, as in some of the earlier folktale versions of "Bluebeard" and in other feminist revisions of the tale.[77]

One might argue that the romance ending not only celebrates marriage as the real fortune of a female hero but also supports heteronormativity, and thus does not make the novel truly subversive in the context of gender. However, because it is possible for texts to include contradictory discourses, I would argue that these conventional aspects do not prevent the text from being revisionist in some other sense. Sexuality in general is not explicitly addressed in Jones's children's fantasy novels. They have more in common with Jane Austen's romances from the nineteenth century than many of the contemporary realist young adult novels that offer much more radical accounts of girls' sexuality. Whichever interpretation one prefers, it is certain that Sophie's "strategy of parodic repetition" is no longer possible after she has returned into her real form — indeed, whatever she now does is interpreted as her "true" identity, because this is what she has gained at the end of the narrative, both in terms of her body and her magic agency.

Complex Powers Among Strong Characters

All the novels examined here depict the tropes of invisibility and age-shifting in complex ways and, in all cases, somewhat differently from the conventional uses of the motifs in earlier tales. Invisibility is empowering for most witches and magically talented girls, yet it can also put the characters at risk or make them appealing targets for exploitation. Moreover, even though invisibility is a skill that the witches can control, it does not always enable its users to achieve their aims.

In *The Earth Witch*, the three different ages of a woman are seen as natural phases and as something that every woman needs to recognize in herself to become fully aware of her womanhood and power. In contrast, in *Howl's Moving Castle* the transformation from youth to old age starts as a curse, but turns out to be useful and empowering in the long run. The connection between the transformations and power is not represented as a simple one.

All the tales involve strong, brave, initiative-taking female heroes. Many of the texts rely on the radical-feminist discourses of the witch and depict female communities where knowledge of magic is transferred from one female generation to another. The witches are portrayed as morally exemplary characters that do not abuse their powers, including invisibility. Other novels, such as *Howl's Moving Castle*, portray a strong female hero to whom conventional feminine features are not a hindrance after she abandons her earlier passivity as a nice girl. While most of these novels reflect a humanist meta-ethics that involves a belief in characters' rounded personality, agency, humanness, abilities, and individual freedom,[78] the dystopian *Ghost Dance* does not comfortably fit in the humanist discourse because it is characterized by a sense of hopelessness and a lack of individual agency. This does not, however, make the novel a failure in feminist terms — when the novel is examined in a queer framework and the focus is shifted from individual agency to the ways in which the shamans as a group challenge normative discourses of gender and age in the fictional society, different interpretations become possible, as will be argued in Chapter 5.

Sempruch has suggested that the radical-feminist myth of the witch "was logically unavoidable at one stage in the feminist past," although it later lost its usefulness.[79] This may be true about the adult fiction that Sempruch discusses but it is certainly not true about children's literature. Judging by the novels that have been published in the last decade, strong witches have only become more popular. While several texts continue to circulate gender stereotypes, the witches that draw on radical-feminist imagery of female or feminine power continue to be radical, because the more conventional images of the witch as a malevolent hag or an evil sorceress have remained in circulation both in children's stories and popular fictions. All the texts discussed above challenge in one way or another the conventional images of the witch and do this partly by employing the tropes of invisibility and age-shifting.

3

Deconstructing and Reconstructing Female Subjectivity: Magic Transformations and Girls' Coming of Age

THIS CHAPTER EXAMINES how invisibility and age-shifting affect the transforming character's subjectivity and identity in female coming-of-age novels that belong to the genre of fantastic realism. The characters here are ordinary girls to whom the transformations happen either inexplicably or as the result of actions by others and who do not necessarily learn how to control their own invisibility or age-shifting. This chapter considers invisibility and age-shifting as narrative devices that deconstruct the girl protagonists' subjectivities and thus potentially challenge and question gendered discourses and representations. I am interpreting the term *deconstruction* here in a broad sense: it refers to any textual and narrative strategies that are used to represent a character who experiences a sense of losing her identity or sense of self. This may involve detailed linguistic play or be, for instance, explicitly described in straightforward speech or thought representation.

As in the previous chapter, the issues of agency and subjectivity will be addressed — the focus here is on the role of transformations in identity and subjectivity formation, particularly on the functions of the transformations in the identity narratives of the girl protagonists. In the novels discussed here, invisibility and age-shifting are caused by various reasons, including time slips, body swapping, unexpected bodily reactions, or death. Even though the bodily transformations as narrative tropes are initially employed to deconstruct or question the identities of the protagonists, the new identities and subjectivities that are (re)constructed towards the closure of the novels are based on coherent, intersubjectively constructed identity narratives.

The first part of this chapter addresses briefly how deconstruction and reconstruction of subjectivity can be interpreted from the perspective of post-structuralist feminist theory. The subsequent sections focus on the narrative tropes of invisibility and age-shifting, from different perspectives. First, invisibility is mainly discussed as a metaphor for powerlessness and exclusion in stories that are thematically about invisibility: invisibility is not merely a minor motif but it is a central or even the main trope in the narrative. Invisibility is connected with the loss of subjectivity and can thus be fruitfully interpreted from the perspective of trauma theory. The texts discussed are Diana Wynne Jones's *The Time of the Ghost* (1981), Tonya Hurley's *Ghostgirl* (2008), and Marilyn Kaye's *Out of Sight, Out of Mind* (2009) and *Now You See Me* (2010).

The second part of the chapter examines how age-shifting as a narrative trope can be used to experiment with aged subjectivity. As seen with Jones's *Howl's Moving Castle*, magic age-shifting can address issues related to embodiment and social expectations related to age. Unlike Sophie's transformation, however, in the texts discussed here the protagonists are themselves not responsible for their transformations. Moreover, the transformations do not occur in a fairy tale setting and have little to do with fairy tale conventions — thus the challenge to any norms related to age and gender happens in relation to contemporary discourses of gender, rather than fairy tale conventions. I will examine how the age-shifting enables the juxtaposing of gendered identities at different ages. The texts discussed include Mary Rodgers's *Freaky Friday* (1972), Marilyn Kaye's *Happy Birthday, Dear Amy* (2001), and Diana Wynne Jones's *Hexwood* (1993).

Feminist Theory and Postmodern Identity

Deconstruction of identity categories and identity narratives can be linked with poststructuralist theory, where essentialist notions of identity categories — such as gender — are challenged and replaced by an understanding of subjectivity as a flexible, changing, multifaceted construction. While this might sound useful for challenging norms and conventions related to gender, feminist theorists have not always embraced notions of unstable, postmodern identities. Several critics have pointed out that the postmodern projects aiming at the deconstruction of subjectivity and at revealing the relativity of truth and experience emerged at the time of cultural revolutions in the 1960s and 1970s as marginalized groups in society were beginning to get their voices heard and were redefining their subjectivity. The poststructuralist view of subjectivity as decentered, unstable, and non-unified seems less desirable from the perspective of the margins. As Braidotti and Waugh suggest, it is not possible to deconstruct a subjectivity that one has not been granted control over, or to challenge representations of identities that have been earlier non-existent or invisible.[1]

However, other feminist thinkers have emphasized the deconstructive potential of feminist criticism as such. Comparing postmodern and feminist thought, Jane Flax, for instance, suggests that both of these are "deconstructive in that they seek to distance us from and make us skeptical about beliefs concerning truth, knowledge, power, the self, and language that are often taken for granted within and serve as legitimation for contemporary Western culture."[2] This view is shared by several feminist poststructuralist critics, such as Weedon, who suggests that poststructuralist feminists have mobilized the postmodern critique of knowledge and subjectivity and have brought "a transformative gender dimension to postmodern theory and [developed] new ways of understanding sexual difference."[3]

Moreover, many poststructuralist feminist theorists maintain the notion of decentered subjectivity, albeit that the feminist theorists do not focus on complete deconstruction or annihilation of subjectivity but emphasize the role of intersubjectivity, narrativity and embodiment in the formation of non-unitary, changing, dependent but yet empowered subjects. Figurations of non-unitary identities, such as cyborgs, metamorphing monsters, or performers switching between visibility and invisibility are viewed as both postmodern and potentially feminist by several theorists.[4] These postmodern figurations are seen as possible ways to challenge and question conventional gendered subjectivities.

Female (or feminist) postmodernist representations would question essentialist identities but not completely obliterate subjective agency and a sense of self. In her discussion of the "female postmodern," Waugh suggests that feminist writers employ postmodernist strategies but, in relation to the representation of subjectivity, show "less concern with 'splitting' and disintegration than with merging and connection; are less interested in the quest of isolated individuals than in positing an individual whose maturity will involve the recognition of her construction through the collective."[5] In Waugh's theory the female postmodernist fictional characters seem to represent poststructuralist subjectivities. For Waugh, "the 'postmodernist' moment of feminist writing" reflects "a core belief in a self which, although contradictory, non-unitary, and historically produced through 'discursive' and ideological formations, nevertheless has a material existence and history in actual human relationships, beginning crucially with those between infant and caretakers at the start of life."[6]

In Waugh's female postmodern, then, postmodernist narrative strategies are employed both to represent and question gendered subjectivities.[7]

In relation to representations of subjectivity, it has been suggested that this type of postmodernism exists in children's books. In her study of the feminine subject in children's literature, Christine Wilkie-Stibbs argues that a decentered but not dissolved subject of psychoanalysis — a sort of poststructuralist subject — is evident in certain types of children's literature. Wilkie-Stibbs defines this type of subject as characteristic of what she terms as "the feminine postmodern." Relying on Waugh's notions of female postmodern aesthetic, *l'écriture féminine* of French feminism, and psychoanalytic theory, Wilkie-Stibbs writes that texts that "exhibit postmodern narrative techniques and the kinds of decentered subjectivities, which accord with Lacanian psychoanalytic descriptions of the subject" but "resist the classic postmodern dissolution and objectification of psycho-textual identity distinguishes them as texts of *the feminine postmodern*." Postmodernist children's texts that represent decentered subjects also rely on "quasi-humanist" notions of subjectivity in that they represent the child subjects as rather stable, capable of agency and dependent on human relationships.[8]

Wilkie-Stibbs's notions of subjectivity in the feminine postmodern come fairly close to the feminist theory of subjectivity that I rely on, and the characters in the text discussed below can be fruitfully interpreted by examining them in regard to both postmodern and quasi-humanist notions of subjectivity. However, I find Wilkie-Stibbs's concept of the feminine postmodern problematic in its binary notion of gender — that is, the separation between *the* feminine and *the* masculine in feminist psychoanalytic theory and the resulting assumption that writing can be described as reflecting the feminine or the masculine. I am not interested in defining feminine-masculine writing or feminine-masculine postmodernism. Instead, I will explore the ways in which characters in the selected texts are represented as persons whose subjectivities are first deconstructed due to their bodily transformations but, in the end, reconstructed at moments of coming of age when the characters' subjectivities are more clearly based on what Wilkie-Stibbs calls quasi-humanism.

Powerlessness and Invisibility

Invisibility has been examined as an ability that is not necessarily empowering but is certainly treated as a controllable superpower in the texts about female magic users. Here invisibility is associated with powerlessness and functions as a trope that deconstructs a young feminine subjectivity. In all the texts examined below, the invisible characters aim to achieve visibility, that is, a strong sense of self that is combined with recognition by others. In *The Time of the Ghost, Ghostgirl, Out of Sight, Out of Mind* and *Now You See Me*, invisibility is used metaphorically to address issues linked to a conventional powerless and passive feminine status and is connected with the deconstruction of identity in texts that resemble trauma narratives. The trauma narrative is here understood as a narrative of a personal, experienced physiological and psychological trauma, that is, in the novels, caused by physical or emotional abuse and neglect, or a violent accident.[9] Apart from *Out of Sight, Out of Mind*, these novels also play with the conventions of the ghost story, although only in *Ghostgirl* is the protagonist actually dead. I will discuss these novels in relation to the conventions of the ghost story and compare *Out of Sight, Out of Mind* with *Ghostgirl*, since each book combines invisibility with another trope of bodily transformation: body swapping.

The narrative structure in conventional ghost stories is the same as in other mystery narratives, such as detective novels. In brief, the plot involves a mystery of a ghost and attempts to solve it, usually what has happened to the ghost before its death. The attempts are typically successful: after the mystery is solved and the culprits are punished (the ghosts have often died because of some kind of mischief), the ghost disappears.

Following Judith Armstrong, I make the differentiation between "ghost stories proper" and "spook stories." Both involve ghosts, but whereas spook stories mainly aim at frightening the readers, ghost stories use the supernatural characters to "find expression via narration for various kinds of psychological experience" and therefore are more complex both on narrative and psychological levels.[10] Ghost stories in this definition, then, are not merely mystery stories but also narratives about identity and self. *The Time of the Ghost* and *Ghostgirl*, as well as Patrice Kindl's *The Woman in the Wall* (1997), Susan Price's *The Ghost Wife* (1999) and Laura Whitcombe's *A Certain Slant of Light* (2005) that will be discussed in Chapter 4, belong to the category of ghost stories, even though each of the texts reworks the traditional ghost story structure by placing the ghosts among the main focalizers.

Armstrong suggests that ghosts function as rhetorical devices that can be interpreted as the protagonists' "psychological possibilities personified."[11] The ghosts are important in relation to the protagonists, the haunted people, because the ghosts can portray certain unrealized psychological dimensions of the protagonists, or, in contrast, highlight features that are in opposition to what the protagonists are like. In the stories that Armstrong discusses, such as Penelope Lively's *The Ghost of Thomas Kempe* (1973), the ghosts are typically reduced to "personified essences rather than rounded characters" and are therefore different from the protagonists who are able to change and develop.[12] The novels discussed here depart from these conventions; in each novel the ghost-character is among the main focalizers, which shifts the perspective from observing the ghosts from outside as others. The ghost-characters here are more complex than "personified essences," mainly because of their unconventional position in the narratives as focalizers.[13] The ghosts thus function as rhetorical devices in the sense that they illustrate certain psychological aspects of the protagonists in the novels. In *The Woman in the Wall*, *The Time of the Ghost*, *Ghostgirl* and *A Certain Slant of Light*, the ghosts are the protagonists and therefore illuminate aspects of themselves, whereas in *The Ghost Wife*, the ghost — who is also a focalizer in several passages — parallels another focalizing female character.

In relation to identity construction in ghost stories, Armstrong also notes that the ghosts, as hidden or unrealized aspects of protagonist's self, enable the representation of "a conceptual model of the personality as an interaction between various parts of the self, recognized and unrecognized, now and not-now, realized and unrealized, active and passive. There is no fixed and static 'real' self hidden at some notional core normally disguised by appearances, but a fluid and even bizarre association of a limitless number of selves."[14] Armstrong's view seems to involve a poststructuralist notion of subjectivity as a play between a number of selves and others. A similar view is reflected in Lidia Curti's interpretation of ghosts as literary devices that combine a set of opposites: the evident and the hidden, the familiar and the unknown, the identity between mystery and truth, the enigma and its solution. While the play with opposites is an aspect of identity construction, Curti suggests that the set of opposites is what renders the ghost uncanny, from an outsider's viewpoint.[15] The opposites become even more disturbing when realized from the ghost's own perspective.

I want to move beyond the binary oppositions and consider Armstrong's more flexible notion of the process of identification as "a fluid and even bizarre association of limitless number of selves" in relation to the invisible girls' search for identity in the novels discussed below. As an experienced state this boundlessness — whether based on losing one's body completely or losing control over it to someone else — is not necessarily positive if the subject has no sense of continuity. As suggested in the introduction, the necessary continuity on which subjectivity is based is, on one hand, found in the experienced, material body and, on the other hand, in the personal identity narrative located in (embodied) memories and often enforced by narrating it to others. There are various ways in which this continuity is both broken and reconstructed in the discussed novels.

My focus is not specifically on the ghost as a rhetorical device, but, instead, on the ghost's invisibility as a narrative device. Not all ghost stories involve invisibility — quite the contrary, the ghosts have to be visible or, at least, audible for people to notice them. While both the ghost story and trauma narrative

3. Deconstructing and Reconstructing Female Subjectivity 105

share the structure of a mystery that must be solved (and this mystery is related to someone's identity), invisibility has somewhat different functions in each genre. In the mystery narrative, invisibility at the beginning omits the identity of the protagonist and becomes the secret to be solved.

Invisibility, Neglect and Trauma

In *The Time of the Ghost*, the female ghost has lost both her body and her memories, which, at the beginning, leaves her in a fluid state, but her experience of it is not a positive one — therefore the novel becomes a rather peculiar quest for identity. According to the conventions of ghost stories, the "truth" must be brought to light, and in the case of Sally, the protagonist in *The Time of the Ghost*, this "truth" involves not only finding out the past events but her own identity.

As a trauma narrative, it is significant that invisibility as an ellipsis in the narrative does not obliterate everything. The process of reconstructing an identity narrative is about putting together what the ghost already knows about herself and merely has to remember again, albeit that the remembering happens from a new perspective gained after a major traumatic incident. This is a more complex process than the simple case of solving a mystery, and whereas the ending of the novel is closed in terms of the mystery narrative, in relation to trauma, the ending is partly open. The thematics of identity in *The Time of the Ghost* have been discussed by several critics, all of whom maintain, in general, that the narrative is mainly about the protagonist's successful quest for self.[16] While this is true — there is a liberal-feminist discourse operating on the level of the novel as a whole — I want to focus on the actual process of how this happens in more detail in the narrative, because several aspects of the process of identity construction are, in Sally's case, gendered. The unconventional strategy of representing the events from the ghost's perspective allows her the active role of the detective who tries to solve the mystery.

In *The Time of the Ghost*, one of the main strategies to find out the ghost's identity is the process of (mis)identification based on attempts to differentiate one's self from the other(s): in the process, Sally tries to identify with her own past self and her three sisters. It is precisely Sally's invisibility which makes the whole play with (mis)identifications possible — because she cannot see herself, she continues to misperceive her identity. Furthermore, it is her invisibility that allows her to take the role of the detective, as she has access to the past to invisibly witness scenes that she otherwise could not observe.

Sally (a short form for Selina), one of four sisters, is a ghost who has lost her memory but gradually recognizes familiar places and people at the boys' boarding school that her parents run. Halfway through the narrative the ghost and readers learn that she is actually lying in a hospital seven years in the future after being in a severe car accident caused by her boyfriend, Julian Addiman, and has been visiting her past as a ghost.[17] After this discovery, Sally willingly travels back to the past trying to fill in the gaps in her memory and to find out the reason for her accident. The events leading to the accident consist, on one level, of a realistic account of Sally's disastrous relationship with Julian and, on another level, of a fantastic story of a female goddess, Monigan, whom the girls have worshipped in the past. Both "versions" of the past are revealed partly through Sally's own memories, partly through the events that she witnesses unseen and, finally, through her sisters' recollections of the past that Sally listens to during the short intervals in the present time at the hospital. By contrasting Sally's memories to the "real" past, the twenty-year-old Sally's nostalgic views of her own past are shown to be very different from the past scenes that she witnesses as a ghost — thus the time slip allows the narrative to question the validity of memories.[18]

The ghost's invisibility functions as a narrative ellipsis — an ellipsis that omits the focalizer's identity — but it is also a horrifying state for the protagonist: the ghost is terrified when she realizes that she has turned into nothing. The horror of invisibility is the result of losing one's body and being cut off from all communication; Sally is not only invisible but her voice cannot be heard either, although readers can see her italicized speech and thoughts. Later in the novel Sally can voluntarily visit her past and, thus, turn invisible, but at the beginning she cannot control her invisibility at all. She feels almost non-existent; invisibility is an undesired state of almost complete powerlessness. As in conventional ghost stories, ghosts and horror are connected, but here the horror or the uncanniness is experienced by the ghost and caused by her powerless, unexplained bodily state. Sally's panic emphasizes the necessity and urgency of solving the mystery of her invisibility — she is an embodied form of the ellipsis, but later in the novel it also becomes clear that her literal invisibility is connected to her metaphorical invisibility in her life before the accident. The reader depends completely on Sally's perceptions and thoughts and thus has to share the ghost's limited point of view. The limited point of view also puts the reader in a powerless position alongside the ghost, to share the fear and anguish caused by her invisibility as much as her unawareness of what is happening.

As in conventional mystery stories, clues are offered to the ghost-detective and readers to deduce her identity. The first chapter includes a scene in which Sally's mother addresses the ghost entering the room as Sally, and she believes that the identification is correct because the person does the identifying is important and familiar to her — emphasized through the repetition of "Mother":

"Mother had seen her. Mother knew her. Mother knew who she was. She was Sally. Of course she was Sally."[19] At first, another person's identification seems to be more important to Sally than her own sense of who she is. Sally's identity is reconfirmed in the following scene in which her younger sister senses the ghost's presence and addresses her as Sally. After the firm belief in her own identity, it comes as a surprise to Sally as well as to readers that when she later goes to see her bodily self, she cannot identify with that girl:

> *Where am I going? I mean, what are you doing?* she said. She was now thoroughly perplexed. Not the least of her troubles was that she could not bring herself to think of this girl firmly creeping through Audrey's house as herself. She knew the girl was Sally. There had been no mistake there. Yet she had no sense of identity with her. She had no idea what this Sally thought and felt. She seemed just someone else she was forced to hover and watch, as she had watched Sally's sisters.[20]

Here the ghost is perplexed, first referring to the bodily Sally with "I" and then immediately switching it to "you," separating between herself and the girl. The girl is, indeed, an other, because the ghost does not know what the girl is thinking or feeling and can merely observe her from outside. This discontinuity between the two makes the ghost suspect that she might not be Sally. In the scene that follows, the ghost watches the girl Sally and Julian dedicate themselves to the service of the goddess Monigan, which is the fantastic explanation for why she is almost dead seven years later (the goddess craves a life). Even though the ghost cannot remember the scene—which to her seems to indicate that she might not be Sally, although in relation to trauma the feeling of otherness has another explanation, as will be suggested below—she still half thinks she is Sally and the narrator echoes this by referring to both the ghost and the girl as Sally, although at points separating between the "bodily Sally" and the ghost.

In relation to trauma, invisibility in *The Time of the Ghost* functions on two different levels. First, invisibility is employed metaphorically to describe the state of a person who has been through a traumatic event and has lost her selfhood—in *The Time of the Ghost* the metaphor becomes literalized in Sally's embodied invisibility. However, the loss of selfhood is connected with the loss of memory and therefore, on the second level, invisibility is connected with an actual lack of continuity, or ellipsis, in the traumatized person's identity narrative. As Bal points out, in psychological terms the ellipsis would be referred to as repression.[21] In *The Time of the Ghost*, the loss or repression of memories is a narrative ellipsis but, interestingly, explained partly by Sally's embodied invisibility—her non-existent head is not capable of containing all her memories. In this sense, her invisibility is a fantastic representation of the effects of trauma.

What is more, her disembodied, invisible state also makes it possible to represent literally the discontinuity between her present and past selves. This discontinuity, however, is not the result of ellipsis, but, in psychological terms, dissociation which, as Bal writes, "doubles the strand of the narrative series of events by splitting off a sideline" which, in narratological terms, is called paralipsis.[22] The sideline, or paralipsis, that shows the younger Sally in the forest is not, first, incorporated into Sally's personal identity narrative because she cannot remember the event ever happening to her. Technically, the information omitted by the ellipsis is the same as that omitted in the mystery narrative — that is, Sally's identity and the course of events in the past — but, in terms of trauma, the motivation for reconstructing the past and Sally's identity is a psychological one.

As Susan J. Brison writes on real-life trauma, "The ability to envision a future, along with the ability to remember a past, enable a person to self-identify as the same person over time. When these abilities are lost the ability to have or to be a self is lost as well."[23] Thus, unless Sally can reconstruct her identity after the trauma — "to envision a future" as well as "remember a past"— she will not be able to regain a sense of self and agency after her accident. It is significant that everything is not omitted by the ellipsis: there is a vast amount of information about the character revealed through her gradually surfacing memories. It is necessary that Sally's invisibility is gradually replaced by her own memories of herself with which she can identify — that is, memories that are no longer omitted from her identity narrative by repression or dissociation brought about by trauma.

The Time of the Ghost involves a description of the traumatic incident that Sally has experienced. In psychological terms, a traumatic event is "one in which a person feels utterly helpless in the face of a force that is perceived to be life-threatening. The immediate psychological responses to such trauma include terror, loss of control, and intense fear of annihilation."[24] Sally's accident — including the events leading to it — certainly fulfils the criteria for a traumatic event. The events leading to her accident, including physical and emotional abuse and neglect by her boyfriend and parents, may seem less serious than the accident but, as Kim Etherington writes, when this type of trauma "accumulates over a prolonged period of time ... [it] will probably have long-term and profound impact on the child's sense of self and identity."[25] Sally indeed experiences all of these psychological responses to trauma. At the beginning of the novel Sally's thoughts are a fictional representation and her invisible bodily state a metaphorical representation of the real-life psychological effects of trauma:

> *I've turned into nothing!* she thought. Panic swelled again. *There's been an accident. STOP IT!* she told herself. *Stop and think.* She made herself to do that. It took a while because thinking seemed so difficult and panic kept swelling through her

thoughts and threatening to whirl her away again, but she eventually thought something like: *I'm all right. I'm here. I'm me. If I wasn't, I wouldn't even be frightened. I wouldn't know. But something has happened to me. I can't see myself at all, not even a smear of shadow on the road. There's been an accident! STOP THAT! I keep thinking about an accident so there must have been one, but it does no good to say so, because every time I do, things just get vaguer. So I must stop thinking that and start thinking what's the matter with me. I may be just invisible.*[26]

The intense fear of annihilation here has a very concrete cause. Sally's disembodied state is an extension of her experienced loss of self (even a somatic response to trauma); she does not merely feel like she does not exist but has literally turned invisible. The narrator explicitly describes Sally's main feeling as panic, whereas the loss of control is represented both metaphorically and through the direct representation of her thoughts, which shows that she has lost control of her thoughts about the accident — they are repeated, or keep coming back to her involuntarily. The capitalized commands to herself seem to reflect her panic and attempts to gain control by "shouting" to herself. Moreover, it is precisely the thought that is connected to the traumatic event ("There's been an accident!") that partly triggers off her panic because every time she thinks about it, "things just get vaguer." Her panic is not only related to her invisible state, but it has occurred already before when the ghost notices that she has lost her memory. Importantly, even though she first refuses to realize it, it is her amnesia that causes her invisibility: she will remain invisible as long as she is unable (or unwilling) to remember her own narrative.

The loss of memory means that the ghost can only exist in the present time — at first she has no access to the past through her memories, although the fantastic time slips make it possible for the ghost to actually go back to the past. However, the fantastic time slips also enable the ghost to visit the past in her present, experienced time and thus (re)witness the past, not merely remember it. Sally's present time — or the time of the ghost — is the time in which most of the novel takes place: the visits to the past are experienced by the ghost in the present, which is right after her accident. The representation of the ghost's direct thoughts emphasize the immediateness of the ghost's existence and experiences because the direct thoughts are represented in the present tense.

This makes sense in terms of trauma. "The shrinking of time to the immediate present," Brison, writes, "is experienced not only during the traumatizing events, but also in their aftermath, at least until the traumatic episode is integrated into the survivor's life narrative."[27] This "shrinking of time to the immediate present" is reflected in *The Time of the Ghost* in the use of the very limited point of view — almost everything is focalized through the amnesic ghost. The lack of memories that would help the ghost to interpret the events that she witnesses results in a very limited perspective on events. The immediateness of Sally's presence has replaced the continuity that is needed to maintain a sense of identity, continuity constructed through memories. Furthermore, because almost everything is focalized through the ghost, to be able to make sense of the story, readers also need to be released from the immediateness of events and experiences, that is, the discontinuities must be replaced with a coherent narrative.

The ghost is represented as a traumatized girl, and although this representation is, at points, ironic — it is namely her literal invisibility that often results in situational irony and allows distance to the experienced trauma — it is also realistic in terms of Sally's reactions to her traumatic incident. Sally's accident is first represented in a short embedded narrative, describing a memory that involuntarily comes back to Sally and is, in a sense, somatic or embodied; it is embedded in her mind and she cannot but think about it, as is typical of traumatic memories. Moreover, the memory has a dissociating effect:

> The car gave a sharp wobble, and its left-hand door came open. It continued to go at a furious speed. The door was blown almost shut with the speed and then forced open again to let a lady tumble out. She tumbled just like a doll, helplessly, to the rushing road and, like a doll, went on tumbling for yards and yards, because her foot was hooked in a long black loop of seat belt. When at last her foot came loose, the car door slammed shut, and the car sped away, leaving the doll-like, crumpled lady lying at the side of the road.
>
> Although she had no sense that this had happened to *her*, it was not a pleasant thing to see. The strong one driving that car had intended to throw the lady out.[28]

The whole incident is described from a third-person perspective, although here it is clear that the memory is really the ghost's own — she is not spirit-traveling, but knows she is lying in the hospital bed when the memory comes, dreamlike, back to her. It makes perfect sense that the ghost cannot identify with the victim, who is represented in very feminine terms as a helpless doll; dissociation, or the feeling that "she had no sense that this had happened to *her*," is a typical reaction to a traumatic memory. Soon after, however, the ghost remembers that the driver was Julian and that it was she who was thrown out of the car (although at this point she is unsure of who she is). The disturbing doll imagery is connected with Sally's experience of her relationship with Julian — she has been his plaything, which is revealed later through her returning memories: "She had devoted herself wholly to pleasing the demanding Julian Addiman."[29]

Sally's traumatic event reflects the conventional (and also actually common) form of gendered violence in which the female is the victim and the male is the perpetrator. While her doll-like condition is connected to her metaphorical invisibility that operates in the novel on a larger scale, the gendered nature of her trauma adds a feminist level to the necessity of reconstructing her subjectivity after the accident. Not only must she reconstruct a sense of self, but she must reconstruct a subjectivity that is not regulated by violence and formed only in relation to her boyfriend and her father. In this respect, she has also been invisible to herself—not only after the trauma, but earlier in her life because she has ignored her own aspirations and entered into the conventional female position in which she only exists in relation to males.

It is suggested that the discontinuity between Sally's different selves may not result only from the actual trauma but from her unwillingness to identify with her younger self, a person she does not particularly like: "She wondered if this was why she had forgotten she was Sally: she did not like herself."[30] In terms of her doll-like role, this is not surprising, and from a feminist perspective it is necessary to replace the negative sense of identity with a more positive one. Sally must learn to challenge the patriarchal control, represented by her father and her boyfriend, as well as her angel-in-the-house mother who supports the father unquestioningly. In this sense, the novel reflects the liberal-feminist discourse of invisibility: it is an undesirable and horrifying state for women — strongly connected with conventional femininity as a powerless and passive status — and the only way out is to become empowered by gaining visibility, voice and agency. This necessity is solved in the novel in two ways: first, by Sally's decision to become an artist and therefore gain independence and agency and, second, by showing that subjectivity can (and must) be negotiated in more positive relationships with others.

While unaware of her own identity, the ghost tries to identify with all the other young females in the narrative, each and every Melford sister in turn. The series of misidentifications, or the ghost's attempts to identify with her sisters, make sense, on one hand, in relation to the discontinuity between the ghost and everyone else — Sally has not been able to identify with any of the four girls in the past, not even herself, and therefore she tries to use logical reasoning to decide which one of the sisters she is. On the other hand, it is in relation to the similarity or unity among the girls that the series of attempted identifications seems relevant — she knows right from the beginning that she is one of the sisters. In relation to gendered subjectivity, both discontinuity and similarity challenge the essentialist idea of a unique and unified identity-subjectivity. Instead of an inner core, subjectivity is partly based on an identity narrative (therefore personal identity can be deconstructed if there is a discontinuity in the narrative created by memory) and partly on the intersubjective negotiations between similarity and difference (subjectivity is not only based on uniqueness, or difference, but also on similarity with others).

Despite their rather remarkable differences, in several passages the matter of differentiating between the sisters seems insignificant. When the ghost is wandering in the schoolyard, she remembers that the boys "being boys, they were of course quite unable to tell you and your sisters apart, and called all four of you Slimy Semolina impartially."[31] From the boys' perspective, then (as Sally remembers it), all girls are the same. However, it is not only the schoolboys who think that the sisters are similar. When the ghost is later summoned in the past and appears to Cart, Imogen, Fenella and a group of boys, no one knows who the ghost is; it could be any of the four sisters. Moreover, it is not only the sisters' appearance that makes them alike. Cart herself explains to Sally at the hospital that all of them were keen on the same guy but never jealous of each other because "we were so — such a unity, that when one of us got him it almost didn't matter which of us it was"; a view against which Sally protests because it makes them "sound like vultures — or female spiders."[32] This is not the whole truth, however, because Imogen and Fenella are consistently represented as hostile to Julian, both in the past and the present.

Furthermore, the girls seem to be a sort of unity to their father, whom they call Himself. The animal imagery that Sally uses of the sisters ("vultures ... female spiders") is also employed by their father, who, during his angry moments, wants to act violently. For instance, trying to avoid the use of the word "bitch" in a scene that involves another adult witness, Himself ends up referring to his daughters as "a coven of witches" followed by a repeated use of "you little bi — beastly girls ... bestial display" and "you ignorant little bi — beast."[33] The imagery — while also suggesting the uncontrollable, animal-like nature of the girls who are misbehaving — groups the girls together as similar creatures with no separate identities that would matter. This is an effective example of othering discourse used by a representative of patriarchal order; it is not coincidental that the father is called Himself (with the capital "H").

It is made clear that the father cannot differentiate between his daughters at all. The father "never forgot a single boy he had ever taught, could never remember which of his daughters was which," and therefore, when addressing them "always had to go through at least three of their names before he chanced on the right one."[34] This is indeed reflected in the dialogues between the father and the daughters. The whole situation is represented as ironic, but the problem of (mis)identification is real. The daughters' identities do not matter to Himself at all — nor does their well-being; the girls are almost completely neglected by both of their parents to the point of malnutrition because they are solely interested in educating the boys in the school. In this respect all the sisters are metaphorically invisible — they are not recognized as individuals, or important.

The similarity discourse seems conventional in the sense that girls' individual identities do not matter, but this discourse is undermined in the text — it is strongly associated with the less sympathetic characters, particularly the father. The similarity that leads to misidentifications is, then, represented as a misconception of the girls' identities. From Sally's perspective, each sister is distinctive; it does matter who each of them is as an individual. The distinctiveness, a sense of identity that is separate from others, is therefore crucially important to Sally at the close — both in terms of the narrative ending (as a solution to the mystery/ellipsis) and the psychological closure (she must know who she is as an individual). Invisibility is replaced with distinctiveness, which is most clearly marked in Sally's career choice that is based on her artistic talent and desire to create powerful pictures. As regards agency, Sally's artistic talent provides a positive link between her past and present identities.

Whereas Sally's career choice is non-gendered (although the career of an artist is a popular choice in girls' coming-of-age narratives), it is not only her career that determines her subjectivity. In relation to the fantastic course of past events, the ending is satisfactory, the goddess Monigan is defeated, at least in the sense that Sally survives. Thus, the mystery is solved, the evil is defeated and Sally has a promising future ahead of her. There is nothing specifically gendered in this survival or coming-of-age pattern, which reflects a liberal-feminist discourse of agency and empowerment: gender does not matter, girls and boys are equal and can grasp agency and make right and responsible choices if they only want to. However, in terms of the more realistic course of past events — which involve the summarized mini-narratives of Sally's teenage years and her accident — it is disturbing that gaining agency involves taking the responsibility for her own earlier choices.

Sally's own thoughts involve an interpretation where it seems that she has "chosen" her position as a victim. Her responsibility is stated in explicit terms, when she thinks about her relationship with Julian and thinks that "she had known it was her fault for letting Julian Addiman take her over like this. And she had decided to break with him. She knew she had to, if she was ever to do anything of her own accord."[35] It is indicated that Sally has not been without agency before, but that she has made choices for which she has to take responsibility. Sally believes that she is partly to blame for her accident, whether as a result of entering into a relationship with Julian in the first place, or as a result of provoking the violent behavior by confronting him just before the accident. This reflects a disturbing discourse of victims' responsibility of acts of violence — the discourse that involves the idea of a victim's provocative behavior that triggers the perpetrator's violent action. The violent behavior is not accepted in the novel, but the perpetrator's responsibility is backgrounded by the notions of the victim's responsibility in provoking the violent behavior.

Although Sally's recognition of her own responsibility also adds complexity to her character from a feminist perspective, it is better that her artistry, a positive form of agency, is emphasized at the end, even if it means that the trauma is not satisfactorily dealt with. Sally has reconstructed a functional self, or subjectivity as an artist, but as a victim she still blames herself. In the final scene in the novel it is revealed that Justin has been killed in a car crash after being chased by the police. There is a sense that he has been justly punished, although there is explicitly only a mention of the worship of the goddess Monigan and not of what he has done to Sally. The death of Julian is a convenient solution in relation to Sally's trauma; she will never have to face her perpetrator again and thus does not have to fear that meeting him some time in the future might trigger the trauma again.

While the definition of individual agency thus becomes problematic, the novel also reflects a take on subjectivity that is not based on individualism, but intersubjectivity and dependence on others. Sally is dependent on others to recognize her, fill in her narrative and, finally, help her to defeat the goddess. As Trites suggests, interdependency between characters can work as a positive (feminist) force in a novel.[36] In Sally's case, interdependency can be seen as a positive factor rather than as a proof of her lack of independence, skills or potential. Moreover, interdependency is a necessary factor in a third-wave feminist understanding of how subjectivity is constructed. This does not only concern the subject's actions and relation to others, but also the subject's internal identity narrative. As a traumatized victim and an amnesiac, Sally is an extreme example that reflects the necessity of interaction with others — this necessity is emphasized by feminist theorists.

Brison suggests that trauma survivors gain control over the traces left of the trauma by "narrating memories to others (who are strong enough and empathic enough to be able to listen)" — they need the others to listen to and accept their narratives.[37] This is what Sally does in the hospital as she relates her experiences as a ghost to Cart. However, because she has lost her memory, she cannot offer a complete narrative. To use Cavarero's term that has been introduced earlier, the necessary other, another person completing one's story, must always be present, since we are unable to remember and tell our own stories fully from birth to death — a situation that is at its extreme in the case of the amnesiac who is completely dependent on others filling in her story and, thus, identity. Sally's necessary others are her sisters, who share their own views of the past with Sally to help her complete her own story.

Interpersonal relationships and interdependency thus play a remarkable part in Sally's search for her identity. While her artistry has a central place in her new subjectivity, she must also relate to others to find out who she is. The novel is not postmodern in the sense that it would deny the possibility of a valid knowledge of the past and identities based on that past — quite the opposite, because Sally goes back to the past as a ghost to witness it exactly as it happened — but it shows that the past as well as subjectivities are interpersonally constructed in the present.

Invisibility and Body Swapping: Intersubjective Construction of Feminine Identity

While invisibility is a common trope to address a character's identity, it is more rarely connected with another popular transformation trope in children's literature, body swapping. When invisibility is experienced by a character while she is in someone else's body, it is framed rather differently. In Hurley's *Ghostgirl* and Kaye's *Out of Sight, Out of Mind*, the girls who have swapped bodies with the invisible girls assist the real owners of the bodies to get control over their invisibility as well as to construct new, stronger visible identities. As in *The Time of the Ghost*, intersubjectivity is crucially important for the invisible girls to gain self-respect, a strong sense of self and an agentic subjectivity — a subjectivity that has been deconstructed at the beginning of the narrative due to the protagonist's invisibility. In contrast to the complex narrative of *The Time of the Ghost*, the novels by Hurley and Kaye are fairly straightforward high school stories that do not directly link invisibility with psychological experiences of trauma but mainly focus on the invisible characters' lack of self-respect and popularity.

Hurley's *Ghostgirl* involves a teenage character, Charlotte, who goes through an ultimate form of shape-shifting: she dies by choking on a candy but continues to exist as a ghost. While alive, Charlotte has been the geeky outcast girl in her high school, struggling for popularity by trying to look good and befriend the popular students in the school. Earlier ignored and bullied by others, Charlotte has spent her summer styling herself and crafting a popularity plan to re-model her subjectivity: "Instead of being forever etched in her classmates' high school memories as the girl who just took up space, the seat filler, the one who sucked up precious air that could be put to better use, she was going to start off this year on the other foot, a foot with the hottest, most uncomfortable shoes that money could buy."[38] While she is aware that her transformation project is superficial, her metaphorical invisibility suggests to her that "all that 'inner beauty' sermonizing was a load of crap anyway. 'Inner beauty' does not get you invited to the greatest parties with the coolest people."[39] For Charlotte, popularity is all about visibility — visibility in the sense of good looks and cool appearance that guarantee recognition and admiration from others.

In her afterlife, Charlotte finds herself in a class of dead teenagers who have to come to terms with whatever has caused their death, let go of their earlier lives and move on. Charlotte does quite the opposite: she continues to pursue her quest for popularity and refuses to accept her literal non-existence that is, rather, a continuation of her metaphorical non-existence as an outcast before. While the death is depicted humorously for Charlotte, her own death is also traumatic: "Dying was horrible enough, but to die in such a pathetic and stupid way ... choking on a bear-shaped semisoft gelatinous candy was an indignity almost too much for Charlotte to bear. It would validate everything they'd always thought about her and confirm her worst fears about herself."[40] The shame that Charlotte has felt as the unpopular, bullied outcast is also linked to her "pathetic" way of dying. Charlotte, however, wants to redo her identity and strives for visibility; after finding out that she is able to possess bodies, she aims to do this through body swapping. After attempting to possess the body of the most popular girl in the school, Petula, without any success, Charlotte makes a pact with Petula's younger sister, the Goth girl Scarlet, who is the only living person that can see Charlotte.

A Goth girl who sees ghosts or talks to the dead is a stereotype that is employed in the novel to a humorous effect. Scarlet's function is not only to build up a contrast between popular cheerleaders and a rebellious rocker but also to suggest that to be able to construct a visible subjectivity, the invisible Charlotte should not imitate the all-alike bimbos but the individual rebel. The whole book series is characterized by references to Goth subcultures, including the color schemes in the cover art as well as references to and quotations from songs by Goth, punk and alternative '80s bands and authors associated with either Gothic or the theme of existential anguish in general.[41]

The representation of Goth subculture is rather stereotypical, but since Scarlet is portrayed as a sympathetic character, Goths seem much more appealing than the also stereotypically portrayed cheerleaders who are obsessed with their looks, mean and stupid. While her big sister, Petula, the most popular girl in the school, is depicted as an air-headed cheerleader, Scarlet is a rock-chic who dresses in punk–Goth clothes and plays the guitar. In comparison to the invisible, non-individual Charlotte, Scarlet is portrayed as a very visible, unique teenager. The contrast between Charlotte and Scarlet is also represented through their different reactions to invisibility.

Unlike Charlotte, for whom literal invisibility is only a slight change from her metaphorical invisibility, Scarlet, who has no trouble with her visibility and agency, enjoys invisibility while effortlessly floating around and playing pranks at school, avenging both mean teachers as well as snobby students. For Scarlet the appeal of invisibility lies in its rebelliousness, as Charlotte suggests to Scarlet when she tries to persuade her to swap bodies again: "Come on, admit it, it was cool ... no boundaries, no limitations, no authority."[42] Moreover, Scarlet knows that her invisibility is temporary and she can return to her own body. It is ironic that Charlotte continues to strive for the stereotypical popular girl's subjectivity even when in Scarlet's punk girl body; the mismatch between Charlotte's spirit and Scarlet's bodily appearance results in comic scenes such as the Goth girl participating in cheerleader tryouts. Charlotte does not want to perform a unique identity — be it her own or the peculiar, schizophrenic Goth girl with two spirits alternating inside — but only wants to be like all the other popular girls and thus recognized as a member of a group rather than an individual. From Charlotte's point of view as a character, the body swapping happens because she wants to date the most popular boy in the school, Damen, and Scarlet wants to help her, but in the level of the whole text the body swapping helps Charlotte to realize that a unique identity, "being herself," might be a better goal than trying to fit in the crowd.

In the end, Charlotte reaches visibility, first in Scarlet's body at the prom, where she gets to dance with the handsome Damen, an experience which turns the ghost–Charlotte visible not only to Scarlet but to everyone else. "Charlotte ascended above the crowd, shining like a thousand Glosticks at a sold-out concert. Her dress transformed her into her smoky-gray chiffon dream dress, the one from her screen saver, as she rose up. She looked beautiful."[43] Expectedly, the visible Charlotte appears in a conventionally feminine outfit. Already earlier when possessing Scarlet's body, the way the body looks and moves has changed from Scarlet's normal performance, described in a parodic tone that imitates the ways in which 19th century romance heroines might be portrayed: "Her posture became more upright, her gait became less prodding, and her demeanor — heaven forbid — even became more feminine."[44] While Scarlet avoids performing conventional femininity at all costs, Charlotte aims for it.

Charlotte's new visible identity is greeted by the applauding prom audience, and while Charlotte herself thinks that she has become visible because she is ready to be seen as who she really is, it seems that this is best reflected in her beautiful appearance. Or, because Charlotte has also a stronger subjective agency at the end — she takes responsibility for actions and is able to change her own script for her life — it seems that her agency is, in the eyes of her audience, reflected in her appearance.

Either way, visibility is associated with beauty that becomes a metonym for self-confidence and strong sense of self; an empowered girl is also visibly beautiful. Since Charlotte is mainly characterized only through her invisibility as the bullied, ignored girl, her visible beauty at the end becomes a rather significant feature. Apart from her beauty, readers know that she is stubborn and good at physics and not much else. A geeky ghostgirl thus transforms into a stunning prom queen at the end and moves on in her afterlife — not very far, though, since in the sequels she is still completing tasks that are linked to her living friends and earlier life and that further help her to realize her "true" identity. Ironically, it is Scarlet who ends up dating Damen by just being herself—and mocking all the "easily influenced poseurs" that quickly pick up her Goth looks and musical interests after they have "studied and memorized her MySpace profile," merely because Damen has taken interest in Scarlet and all girls are after him.[45] What is suggested, of course, is that an authentic (subcultural) identity is not only based on visibility, or imitating appearances, but on doing and experiencing the identity on a more profound, emotional level, which, in Scarlet's case, means really liking her outfit, adoring the bands she listens to and playing her favorite songs on a guitar.

Ghostgirl is a comic approach to serious themes, including identity, loneliness, and the need to belong: the novel is a parody of all the tween and teen romance stories where the Ugly Duckling transforms into a beautiful girl and goes to the prom with the handsome prince of the high school at the end. As a character, Charlotte—similar to Sally in *The Time of the Ghost*—is an example of what Wilkie-Stibbs has called "the feminine postmodern" in children's literature—as a dead, invisible girl, she is a character with a deconstructed "postmodern" self, but her existential crisis is resolved at the end of the book when, with the help of other people and by gaining a deeper understanding of herself, she accepts her fate. Rather than a role model, Charlotte is a character that allows the text to expose various stereotypical expectations associated with teenage girls. While in *Ghostgirl* it is the invisible girl who possesses a visible girl's body, in Kaye's *Out of Sight, Out of Mind* a popular girl finds herself in the body of a both metaphorically and literally invisible geek.

Kaye's series features a group of "gifted" students that consists of both boys and girls. Kaye's books do not play with the idea of certain supernatural abilities as specifically feminine, although, as will be seen, invisibility attains meanings associated with conventional femininity. As with the witch characters discussed in the previous chapter, a central theme here is to learn how to use one's special talent or ability, or the "question of getting better at being yourself" and finding "the extent of your gifts—your true potential," as Madame, the instructor of the gifted class, tells her students in a discourse familiar from counseling and self-help guides.[46] All the teenagers in the gifted class have different talents—including mind reading, telekinesis, clairvoyance, invisibility and body possession; the last two are the main transformation tropes in the books discussed here, *Out of Sight, Out of Mind* (2009, *Gifted 1*) and *Now You See Me* (2010, *Gifted 5*). The characters are stereotypical and exaggerated to a humorous effect, yet the texts manage to address issues related to subjectivity by exploring embodiment and sense of self through the supernatural bodily transformations.

The character with the ability to become invisible, Tracey, only becomes the main focalizer in the fifth book of the series, but invisibility occurs in the first book, *Out of Sight, Out of Mind*, in connection with body swapping. While the novel opens up with a brief prologue where Tracey is the first-person narrator talking about her experience of invisibility, the main focalizer in the novel is Amanda, whose special gift is her ability to possess other people's bodies. Amanda is depicted as the opposite of the shy Tracey, as she is "the coolest girl at Meadowbrook Middle School, the Queen of Mean."[47]

The popular, stylish Amanda is particularly mean in her habitual criticism of the way other girls dress and behave. Amanda's meanness is calculated in the sense that she tries to avoid feeling empathy for other people because that is what triggers her body possession ability: she moves into the body of the person she feels for, while her own body that she leaves behind is a zombie-like half-person who is able to habitually go through Amanda's daily routines. This is what happens when she feels sorry for Tracey, one of her usual bullying targets whom Amanda views as a complete failure, and finds herself in Tracey's body the next morning.

Tracey is, again, an example of a girl character whose embodied, literal invisibility is clearly associated with her metaphorical invisibility as a shy, unnoticed girl. In the opening passage of *Out of Sight, Out of Mind* Tracey narrates her experience of being a girl who makes "very little noise at all" and who is "not a ghost" but "living, breathing, flesh-and blood thirteen-year-old girl"; yet she is often invisible even to herself: "Sometimes I look in a mirror and I don't see anyone looking back."[48] Amanda — for whom appearances are everything — is appalled to find herself in a body that in her view is ugly and ungroomed. Her project is to make Tracey's body look more acceptable, a project that culminates in a complete makeover:

> There was something very significant that she could do for this poor girl — she could make Tracey look better! Now, this day, while she had control of Tracey's body, she could get the girl a decent haircut, some cool clothes, lipgloss and maybe some blusher to brighten her drab complexion. She'd be helping herself too — if Tracey wasn't so pathetic, Amanda wouldn't have to worry about feeling sorry for her and finding herself in this situation again.[49]

Soon Amanda realizes, however, that while the appearance of Tracey's body can be fixed, its continuous disappearance is a more severe challenge. Amanda tries to find clues about Tracey's identity by searching her room and even reading her diary, but finds "nothing that gave her the tiniest hint to what Tracey Devon was all about. There were no books, no CDs, no magazines.... Tracey definitely sounded like an ordinary person in her diary, Amanda thought. This was all so normal, it was boring."[50] Tracey seems to have no identity at all and she is also ignored and neglected by most people at school as well as at home.

At the beginning it is difficult to tell whether the borrowed body is literally invisible or merely unnoticed by others — in each case, results are similar, Amanda in Tracey's body is not paid attention to, which means that at home her mother, who is more worried about Tracey's seven younger sisters, forgets to provide food for her and on her way to school the bus driver fails to notice her and she has to walk all the way back home. However, Amanda in Tracey's body does not accept this treatment, and begins to challenge people who ignore her: "For as long as she had to be this sad girl, she wasn't going to suffer like Tracey did. It was time for Tracey to take some responsibility for herself."[51] While making Tracey more noticeable includes the change in her appearance, it also includes speaking in a louder voice, as well as asking Tracey's parents for money for babysitting the little sisters; changes that others notice and increase Tracey's agency.

For Amanda herself the subjectivity of an invisible girl is an exploration into a shy, unpopular girl's life and, as can be expected, she becomes more empathetic in the end. Despite this, Amanda believes that Tracey's invisibility is due to the fact that she cannot take responsibility for herself. Thus a visible, strong identity is the result of one's own choices and one's personality and social status are things that can be willingly changed.

While dealing with experiences of invisibility, *Out of Sight, Out of Mind* mainly focuses on Amanda's experiences in a borrowed body. The narrative does not reveal how Tracey finds her newly styled body that is now "dressing a lot better" in the view of Amanda's picky friends as well as Amanda herself, who thinks that she is "actually rather proud of her work."[52]

Tracey's transformed subjectivity becomes the focus of the fifth book of the series, *Now You See Me*, where Tracey is still not in complete control over her literal invisibility but is no longer metaphorically completely invisible. Tracey continues to turn invisible involuntarily and even without noticing it herself— this is explained by the fact that, even when visible, she is used to being unnoticed: "Years of feeling unimportant and not worthy of attention had caused her to go invisible on a regular basis."[53] Clearly the experiences as an invisible person have affected her subjectivity in a rather permanent way, and this is still reflected in Tracey's "spell" to become invisible. While invisibility is her gift and enables her to be a good spy, the way she reaches invisibility is by thinking about all her sad memories of feeling alienated. Thus, to be able to use her literal invisibility as a strategic power, Tracey has to imagine her metaphorical invisibility that is only associated with negative feelings.

However, in the passages focalized through Tracey, she views herself as a person who has changed from an "emotionally" invisible girl into someone who could "assert herself and demand the attention she deserved as a human being."[54] Tracey enjoys her new self who is more confident, is noticed by her parents, has friends and, moreover, looks better. Most of this, she thinks, is Amanda's doing; whereas her friends still view Amanda as a "selfish snob," Tracey feels that Amanda is capable of empathy: "When she had my body, she did a lot for me. She got my parents to pay attention to me. She bought me decent clothes, she got me a haircut...."[55]

Readers who are familiar with the earlier book know that Amanda has indeed felt sorry for Tracey — the more interesting thing here is Tracey's acknowledgement that another person in her body has helped her to change her subjectivity, something that she has not been able to do on her own. While body-swapping is a fantastic trope, the realistic equivalent of this kind of subjectivity construction is, of course, the popular make-over stories and programs where an expert or a group of experts groom hopeless women into stylish, confident ladies. It is assumed is that a nice appearance will grant the subject also self-confidence and transform her whole life. In *Out of Sight, Out of Mind*, a girl's visibility — in the sense of bodily appearance — is completely controlled by a female community: girls who monitor each other's bodies and criticize or praise each other according to whether the evaluated bodies meet the latest trends and fashions. In this the novel reflects the discourse of "consumer femininity" that, according to Mary Talbot, "enters into women's daily lives in the material and visual resources that they draw upon to feminize themselves."[56] Women can only maintain a beautiful, feminine appearance by becoming consumers of various goods, including clothes, cosmetics and beauty treatments — the use of these resources forms a practice where women share their knowledge about maintaining a feminine appearance, but also monitor and evaluate each other in regard to how successful their performance of femininity is.

Consumer femininity is associated with neoliberalist and postfeminist discourses by feminist critics such as Anne M. Cronin, Rosalind Gill and Angela McRobbie. While neoliberalist and postfeminist discourses of freedom of choice, agency and empowerment view individuals "as entrepreneurial actors who are rational, calculating, and self-regulating,"[57] these feminist critics maintain that the agency and freedom of choice that "empowered" women have actually come with severe restrictions. Neoliberalist discourses of advertising suggest that it is possible to "just do yourself" and thus perform one's "unique" identity.[58] However, as McRobbie writes, in a lifestyle culture, choice is "a modality of constraint. The individual is compelled to be the kind of subject who can make the right choices."[59] Choices are fairly limited if one wants to be recognized as a fashionable subject — in this sense intersubjectivity means that women control each other's visible identity and appearance.

Thus *Out of Mind, Out of Sight* shows that the intersubjective construction of female subjectivity is not necessarily about any radical approach to gendered norms. Perhaps one should not expect radical critique of gender in a mass-market series where all the characters are, more or less, stereotypes, including a popular girl and a boy, a nerd, and a Goth. Amanda's project to make Tracey more self-assertive clearly echoes liberal-feminist discourses of empowerment, yet the other part of the project, making Tracey look good, reflects the conventional notion of femininity that is mainly realized through one's beautiful appearance. While turning Tracey into a more self-assertive subject, at the same time Amanda makes Tracey less unique by dressing her up just like everyone in the latest girls' magazines. I will return to the issues of visibility, beauty and intersubjective constructions of feminine identity in the following chapter in relation to invisibility and gendered gaze. Before that, I will discuss age-shifting as a trope that can be employed to deconstruct subjectivity, but, as with invisibility, also to celebrate consumer femininity.

Experimenting with Age

This section discusses three novels where age-shifting occurs for various reasons: in Rodgers's *Freaky Friday* age-shifting is connected to body swapping; in Kaye's *Happy Birthday, Dear Amy*, the protagonist's genetically manipulated cells suddenly turn her older; in Jones's *Hexwood* age-shifting occurs in a computer-manipulated game where peculiar time slips take place. The protagonists in these three novels do not identify themselves with "naturally" transforming magic beings such as the Earth Witch or find themselves transformed into something that they feel they are "really like," as the young Sophie who feels old in *Howl's Moving Castle*. Instead, they suddenly and unwillingly find themselves in significantly younger or older bodies — either their own or those of someone else — and have to adapt to the changes the best that they can, except in those cases where the characters have also lost their memory upon the moment of transformation. Moreover, while in *The Earth Witch* and *Howl's Moving Castle* the age-shifting characters occur in settings drawing on mythological or fairy tale conventions, the characters discussed below are situated in settings where their transformations are represented in relation to contemporary norms regarding age and gender. *Hexwood*, as well as *The Time of the Ghost*, can be defined as a girls' coming-of-age story that involve fantastic time slips as part of the process — I have discussed the similarities between the two novels elsewhere and will here focus on *Hexwood* only.[60] *Freaky Friday* and *Happy Birthday, Dear Amy*, on the other hand, are not typical girls' coming-of-age narratives since the protagonists visit adulthood only temporarily and return to their teenage bodies. Yet, in each book the short experience of adulthood triggers issues commonly associated with coming of age: sexuality and responsibility.

Age-Shifting into Maturity: Performing Adulthood

Mary Rodgers's extremely popular *Freaky Friday* (1972)[61] is a story about a mother and a daughter swapping bodies that involves the daughter as the first-person narrator. As revealed at the end of the narrative, the body-swapping is maneuvered by the mother (by some mysterious means) because she wants to teach her daughter a lesson about the responsibilities that adult women have to face. At the beginning Annabel describes herself as a strong-minded girl whom her mother tries to control by telling her what to eat, wear and do. Later descriptions — by Annabel herself as well as her teachers — portray Annabel as a tomboy who does not clean her room, pays little attention to her looks, and, at school, is "outspoken (sometimes to the point of belligerence) on such topics as our environment and the Women's Liberation Movement" and "a natural athlete" whose "boundless energy has led her to investigate karate and wrestling."[62]

While her girlfriends like her, others are more critical. Her mother criticizes Annabel for not keeping her room clean, as well as for biting her nails and not trimming her hair. The boy from next door, Boris, views Annabel as a freak who hit him with a shovel in the playground a few years back. Annabel's teachers view her outspokenness as not completely positive and think she is irresponsible because she is not doing very well at school, despite the fact that she has "a fine mind, with an IQ of a hundred and fifty-five, whose verbal aptitude scores are higher than a freshman in college."[63] The criticism thus concerns both Annabel's looks as well as her "wild" behavior; behavior that, were she a boy, would perhaps get far less attention from others.

The body-swapping enables Annabel to get a view of her young self from a different perspective and lets her mother work on changes in her daughter's young body. In the end, the story that includes criticism of both teenage and adult subjectivities in its use of the trope of body-swapping and situational irony turns into a fairly conventional girls' coming-of-age story, transforming the tomboy into a groomed, domesticated young lady.

The situational irony results from the fact that while Annabel and readers know that she is still, in spirit, her thirteen-year-old self, all the other characters believe that she is the thirty-five-year old Ellen Andrews. Thus other characters view Annabel's behavior as peculiar for an adult. This set-up allows the text to make fun of both stereotypical, impulsive teenage behavior, as well as of strict norms guiding the behavior of adult housewives. On the other hand, at the same time the text suggests that while there are ridiculous aspects in both types of behavior, it is still desirable from a young woman to abandon the first and embrace the latter as she comes of age.

While Annabel finds it first liberating to be in her mother's body, which enables her to avoid going to school, she also thinks that it is her responsibility to try to perform her mother's role as well as possible. She checks her mother's agenda, and tries to take care of all her domestic duties, including ironing her father's shirts, which she is quite happy to try to do: "Imagine letting that poor cute man run almost out of shirts! I decided the first thing to do, before I even turned on the boob tube or picked out my dress for tonight, was those shirts."[64] Despite her good intentions, Annabel lacks the practice and the patience needed to play the role of a pretty housewife successfully. The only thing she does succeed in is choosing a pretty outfit, although even this is criticized by other adults since a normal housewife does not dress up in a velvet outfit to go out to the liquor store and to do the washing. While Annabel is mostly frustrated by the responsibilities that she now has as her mother, the delight that she takes in the good looks of her mother's adult female body is repeated in the end when Annabel's own young body has been made beautiful as well.

During her day, Annabel challenges almost all the adults she talks to, she fires the cleaning lady, confronts the police, and argues with her teachers, who criticize Annabel at a parents' meeting. This leads to comic situations where Annabel's performance as her mother is viewed as peculiar, or even insane; what might be viewed as suitable behavior for a teenage girl is not suitable for an adult, married mother. As the school psychologist puts it, her "behavior is inappropriate and your attitudes bizarre."[65]

While it seems that Annabel is failing in her performance of adult femininity, it is suggested, however, that the femininity of her mother is something that she should not even try to imitate too closely. Mrs. Andrews, the domesticated housewife, is often too polite, kind and controlled; she has not been able to fire the cleaning lady herself even though she has been wanting to do so and is later glad that Annabel has done that. Thus Annabel's impulsivity and strong-mindedness are not only ridiculed but also appreciated; her peculiar behavior challenges the norms set for good housewives. Apart from this, however, the day turns more disastrous as it proceeds and Annabel has to admit that she is not able to take care of all the adult female domestic responsibilities at all: she manages to break down the washing machine, almost forgets the meeting with her daughter's teachers, loses the child that she should care for, and ruins her father's/husband's dinner party. All of this leads to deconstruction of Annabel's careless attitudes and her earlier young identity that she has held in esteem, despite the fact that others have not appreciated her reckless behavior.

Before things get completely out of hand, Annabel's mother reappears, switches them into their own bodies and takes control. While being away in Annabel's body, her mother has worked on another kind of transformation: she has gone to the dentist to get Annabel's braces removed, as well as got her a new haircut and new set of clothes. This has resulted in a complete makeover of Annabel: she is no longer the shabby tomboy but the beautiful girl that Boris has seen with her little brother earlier that day, a transformation that makes Annabel cry out of joy. This comes as no surprise since already at the beginning Annabel has enjoyed the best part of being her mother, which is looking good: she has been excited to experiment with makeup, because she knows how to do it: "I've watched her do it a hundred and thousand times when she was going out on a festive occasion."[66]

Annabel's new looks are not only appreciated by her mother and herself but all the important males in her life: her father seems very proud and her little brother and Boris, the boy Annabel is attracted to, both view her now as pretty. Moreover, Annabel's new beautiful form is presented as necessary for the successful, conventional romance closure of the text:

> But first, I have to ask you a question: Have you been waiting for this? Have you been waiting for the moment when the chest-nut haired, hazel-eyed, three inches taller, champion Nok Hockey player, maker of meatloaves Boris finds out that the metal-mouthed killer ghoul of Central Park *is* no longer? That in her place is Annabel the Beautiful? You *have* been waiting. Yeah, but not as long as I have. I've been waiting for three years.[67]

This metafictional passage refers to the fairy tale and romance conventions that readers might have had in their minds and both highlights and fulfills these expectations at the same time. While in the real world it takes longer for the ghoulish teenage girl to turn into the beautiful princess, for Annabel this happens during a day. The most important transformation for Annabel, then, is not her quick visit into adulthood but the changes that her mother has done to Annabel's young body to make it prettier.

A liberal-feminist interpretation might be that the closure involves a young, feisty girl who has not lost her feistiness and agency even though she has become prettier and learned to be more responsible. This is what Annabel seems to suggest in her description of her new self: "Because now that I am more beautiful, I am also a helpful, domestic (still Women's Lib, though) person."[68] However, a more pessimistic interpretation could be that Annabel is following her mother's path into conventional femininity — it is not explained what exactly the "Women's Lib" aspect of her subjectivity is if she is conventionally beautiful and domestic. It is also unclear why her beauty should also guarantee her meek behavior — it seems as if she no longer wishes to be a tomboy after she has secured the long-desired male attention by her pretty looks.

While all of this is narrated in a humorous tone, the romance closure emphasizes the importance of good looks for a young woman; while it is indicated that the responsibilities that an adult mother faces are challenging, it is emphasized that the exciting aspect of adult femininity is the groomed, mature body. A similar pattern occurs in Kaye's text, even though it is published almost thirty years later.

Marilyn Kaye's *Happy Birthday, Dear Amy* (2001) is the sixteenth book in the *Replica* series that features Amy, a teenage girl who is one of a group of cloned girls created in a Project Crescent led by more or less evil scientists who have wanted to experiment with cloning to create a new master race. While the series gives scientific explanations for all the strange things that occur, the "science" in the explanations is vague. In the novel discussed here, Amy's sudden change from a thirteen-year-old girl into a twenty-five-year-old woman is said to be genetic but, as a fantastic trope, her transformation functions in a similar way as Sophie's spells in *Howl's Moving Castle* and the mother's spell in *Freaky Friday* since it is sudden, reversible and its cause is partly a mystery.

For Amy, this transformation first deconstructs her identity: she is not happy about losing her teenage years and does not know who she is while occupying the body of an adult without the experience of growing into it. Her transformation also deconstructs the idea presented by Amy's friend Tasha earlier, that "mature feelings" are in "your head."[69] What Amy finds out in her new body is that people do not judge her maturity by her thoughts but by the way she looks. Because she looks adult, her behavior is also interpreted as mature. Bodily adulthood thus also presents Amy with new, less regulated subjectivity that frees her from the restrictions put upon teenagers. This is only possible, however, because Amy is — quite amazingly, and most unlike Annabel in *Freaky Friday*— able to perform an adult identity without much trouble.

In the morning of her thirteenth birthday Amy wakes up and finds that she has aged twelve years overnight. Before she is aware of what has happened, her transformation is described as various, strange bodily sensations, "odd dizziness," "different perspective" and "a sense of heaviness."[70] While this shows Amy's initial challenges of getting used to her new body, at a special hospital the doctor announces her to be healthy, and soon she is able to move at ease in her new body. Moreover, while Amy thinks that losing her teenage years "wasn't fair," she actually enjoys her adult female body:

> She took a deep breath to steady her nerves and tried to look at the woman in the mirror objectively. Was she pretty? Yes ... not a supermodel or Miss Universe, but not bad. Her complexion was nice, with a peachy tone and no zits. Her hair seemed to be a little thicker, even a shade lighter. Her eyes looked larger. But it was in

the shape of her face that she could see a big difference ... it was narrow now, with higher cheekbones. Her nose was different too, longer, and it didn't turn up at the end anymore. Her ears were a little bigger, but not too big.

She smiled, opening her mouth. Her teeth were very white and straight. She turned her face from side to side. If she held her head at a certain angle, so that the sun shone on her hair, she was almost blond, and she thought that she looked a little bit like Rachel on *Friends*.[71]

Amy's self-examination goes on for another three paragraphs, where she imagines all the beauty technologies to enhance her femininity, make-up on her face and clothing on her "filled out" body. As seen in the above extract, she is also experimenting with various gestures, such as smiling and holding her head at a certain angle, that are performed to make her appear as good-looking as possible. The meticulous analysis of all her body parts suggests that, for Amy, femininity is related to beautiful, sexy appearance that concerns all aspects of one's body and an adult female body opens up new possibilities to do "proper" femininity, as her analysis of her curves especially suggests. Furthermore, appearance is important in a conventional heterosexual framework where the beautiful female body is the object of male gaze — a bit later Amy envisions herself "walking onto the beach in one of those bikinis" as a result of which her boyfriend's "eyes would pop out."[72]

The reason Amy thinks that adulthood might not be that awful has merely to do with her feminine body and the fact that she finds it good-looking, not only from her own but also from a male perspective. Interestingly, the text also shows that these discourses of femininity are familiar to Amy from certain cultural products, as she is comparing herself to a character in a television series and later plans to ask her mother to bring her issues of *Vogue* and *In Style* to the hospital. Since she is a pretty adult female, Amy's view of herself corresponds with the representations of femininity on television and magazines, and thus she feels comfortable in her new, mature body; in terms of corporeality, turning into an adult is an improvement for Amy.

Amy's new body also changes her agency. Amy is pleased to notice that her mother cannot stop her from experimenting with her appearance since "a woman in her twenties had the right to wear as much makeup as she wanted to."[73] What this implies is that a teenager's sexual appearance is controlled by her parents, a control that Amy is now freed from in her adult body. However, Amy's greater freedom is not only limited to the ways in which she grooms her body in her performance of heterosexuality. Feelings of boredom, frustration and loneliness — caused both by being treated like a child and the fact that Amy cannot show her new body to anyone — make Amy escape from the hospital and her mother and doctors who try to figure out ways how to reverse the bodily transformation.

Without any money, she ends up at Sanctuary, a shelter for runaway children, and is accepted there as a volunteer. No one suspects that there is anything mysterious about Amy's age or identity. She has no trouble in conversing with other adults or behaving in a mature way even in surprising, difficult situations where, due to her adult status, the runaway children are "looking up at her, as if expecting her do decide how to deal with this."[74] Amy is not afraid of this new, more responsible role and manages to sort out the emergency situations without betraying the trust of the runaway children. In sum, she seems to be able to perform her adulthood perfectly, including tasks that one usually needs to practice, such as driving a car. Apart from her appearance, not much time is spent in the text exploring the other potential challenges related to adulthood; instead, in an adult body Amy is able to fulfill the expectations associated with adult, mature, responsible behavior — that is, learning how to "do" adulthood is suggested to be easier than growing into an adult body through a process that normally takes years.

In the end, Amy's transformation is reversed because she is accidentally shot by a laser beam. When she is returned to the hospital she, again, examines her body that is now as it "used to be": "Five feet tall, about a hundred pounds. Plain brown eyes, straight brown hair. A figure that didn't look any different at the age of the thirteen than it had looked when she was twelve."[75] While Amy is happy to get to live through her teenage years, she is also worried that her young form is not as appealing to her boyfriend, who has described the adult Amy as a good-looking woman. In the closing paragraphs, Amy is still thinking about her adult appearance and is glad to have a photograph of her adult form, both for her boyfriend "to have something to remind him of how she had looked" as well as for herself to "see what she would look like in the future and remember those days when she'd managed to become an adult slightly ahead of schedule."[76] Thus, it seems that what Amy misses most from her short period of adulthood is her appearance as a pretty, sexy young woman — adult femininity is firmly defined by her looks and figure.

Whereas *Freaky Friday* employs situational irony to highlight the challenges that a teenager might have in performing the role and duties of an adult woman, Kaye's book represents adult subjectivity as something that one can easily perform as long as one is in an adult body; the former book thus takes a more critical approach to subjectivity. Yet, each text emphasizes appearance and looks at the moment of the bodily transformations and in each text beautiful, groomed appearance is associated with adult femininity. Be it one's mother's instructions or the magazines that one reads, it is suggested that young girls should be socialized into well-behaving, responsible, good-looking women and, moreover, that this is for everyone's benefit; the girls feel better themselves and others can appreciate their looks. Not all children's texts involving age-shifting females employ this discourse, however — especially when the transformation happens in the reverse direction, from adulthood back to girlhood.

Slipping Back in Time: Revisiting Girlhood

As suggested above, age-shifters who know that their bodies have transformed are in a disguise and thus their bodily change is linked to the notion of identity as performative, but also highlights the embodied aspects of identity — the physical appearance puts one's speech and behavior in a specific framework. The texts thus address the experiences of embodiment and the different ways of doing gender at different ages. However, in *Hexwood*, the age-shifting protagonists — only one of whom is a young woman — are not only transformed but also suffer from a loss of memory, exactly like Sally in *The Time of the Ghost*. Thus these characters are not aware of their identity performance but are doing their aged identities habitually. Because they have lost their memory, their identity narratives are disrupted and the characters are not fully aware who they are or should be; the memory loss therefore deconstructs their subjectivities. In Jones's *Hexwood*, the continuity between the protagonists' present and past selves is lost at the beginning but regained later with reconstructed memories of the past. The texts employ structural irony as a narrative strategy to expose conventional assumptions about gendered and aged subjectivities — while characters believe they are being their "true" selves, the moment that their disguise is revealed the behavior of the deluded heroes is recontextualized.

In *Hexwood* most of the characters age-shift when they slip in time, including the female protagonist Ann/Vierran, who is one of the main focalizers in the narrative. The time slips in *Hexwood* involve a partial memory loss, which enables the juxtaposition of the female protagonist's preteen identity and her young adult identity, because she initially believes she is younger than she truly is. As has been suggested in earlier readings of *Hexwood*, the time slips initially deconstruct the characters' subjectivities, but I will argue that the play with time and with subjectivity is represented as a problem to be solved.[77] The scene where Vierran remembers her "true" identity is marked as a key moment in terms of coming-of-age, and the mystery story structure in the narrative emphasizes the ending where Vierran and the rest of the characters have discovered not only what the true story was but effectively, their true identities.

While in Rodgers's and Kaye's books the protagonists do not forget their true identities (or their personal identity narratives are not disrupted), in *Hexwood* each of the three aspects of subjectivity — personal identity narrative, embodiment, discursive construction of subjectivity — is deconstructed at some point in the narrative. Vierran's transformation is similar to that of Sally in *The Time of the Ghost* in that at the beginning the characters and readers are unaware that a time slip has occurred. At the beginning, the girls' experiences of embodiment are manipulated and their personal identity narratives are disrupted.

In *Hexwood*, Vierran's transformation is based on a manipulations played by a computer game: placed in a distorted time- and spacefield created by a machine called the Bannus, Vierran believes she is a girl called Ann. The Bannus has been programmed to test alternative courses of action with a certain group of people. In the Bannus field, events occur in a non-chronological order and Ann's task is to discover what is happening both in the virtual time and in the real time outside the game. Ann has lost her memory and spends part of her time in bed due to an illness but, she is not aware of her memory loss. Instead, she believes that her virtual identity is all that there is. To solve the mystery of what is going on and escape confusion, Ann/Vierran needs to regain her memory.

Due to these manipulations Vierran believes she is young and behaves stereotypically like a preteen girl — her thoughts and behavior that are revealed through focalization and the narrator's descriptions of the character's actions are reflective of the discourses of girlhood that the young female character has internalized. These discourses that involve rather conventional notions about girlhood are only deconstructed later when Vierran regains her memory and becomes more aware about her past and present subjectivity.

Despite the disrupting time-shifts in the narrative, there exists a "true," that is, a verifiable and chronological version of Vierran's history. A moment of revelation occurs when Vierran listens to her own voice on tape and regains her memory and thus her 21-year-old identity. Her true narrative is based on a chronological sequence of events taking place in the real time outside the game. However, even in the game not all of Vierran's memories are erased. In fact, in terms of personality features she has a clear idea of who she is, as revealed through the narrative representation of Ann's speech and thought. Moreover, if one accepts that gender is habitually performed, it is possible to interpret the protagonists's unconscious actions (as described by the external narrator) as based on her habitual memory that is not deleted during the time slips; the character's behavior is indicative of internalized discourses of girlhood. Ann habitually follows the internalized regulations guiding the suitable behavior for girls — this is evident in her reactions to non-normative behavior. The return to girlhood means a limitation to agency, which is metaphorically represented through Ann's illness that partly restricts her detective work. However, negative aspects conventionally associated with young femininities — lack

3. Deconstructing and Reconstructing Female Subjectivity 131

of confidence, naivety, blind obedience, sense of embarrassment — are criticized in the text through the use of structural irony.

The 12-year-old Ann reflects a positive romance discourse of feisty heroines as a clever and adventurous girl who inspects the events taking place in the woods near her home. Ironically, to a certain extent Ann must be represented in stereotypical terms for readers to accept that she is twelve — playing with readers' expectations is a central part of Jones's narrative game. At the beginning there is nothing mysterious about the girl Ann's identity: she believes she inhabits a preteen body and her girl identity is supported by other characters who view her as a child. As any stereotypical preteen girl, Ann likes to pretend that she is older than she actually is and worries about her fingernails and nice jacket even while climbing into a tree to escape a potential killer. Although Ann challenges her parents, she is anxious about rule-breaking. For instance, she worries about getting back home in time for lunch, and later, her mother's warnings continue to ring inside her head. Ann is habitually behaving according to a preteen femininity and, due to her stereotypical qualities, readers are fooled into believing in her young identity.

Ann is satirized by the narrator, who describes her in awkward situations, thus highlighting the supposedly more ridiculous aspects of young femininity. Ann thinks that behavior that deviates from the norms is embarrassing if other people see what she is doing, and the incidents that Ann thinks are humiliating seem to reflect her supposed preteen identity. Since embarrassment is usually understood as an involuntary reaction, it reveals Ann's unconscious understanding of norms. In a passage where she has climbed into a tree to escape a threatening-looking man, Ann finds herself in an embarrassing situation:

> He looked up at Ann and croaked out a remark at her.
> She recoiled against the tree trunk. Oh my God! He knew I was there all along! And now she was the indecent one. Comes of climbing trees in a tight skirt. The skirt was rolled up round her waist. He must be looking straight up at her pants. And her long, helpless legs dangling down on either side of the branch.[78]

The "indecent" figure sitting in the tree in a tight miniskirt trying to hide from a man is a humorous image of a feminine girl — or a damsel in distress who has chosen to wear a tight skirt even during her outdoor activities. Ann is represented as silly and her feminine outfit as unsuitable for adventures; she is not in control of the situation and her way of doing femininity is ridiculed. Elsewhere Vierran/Ann is described as clumsy and not particularly beautiful, and while her attempts to do conventional femininity in a miniskirt are satirized, it is suggested that her greatest asset is her cleverness. As the narrative unfolds, Ann moves further away from the girl attempting to do femininity by wearing nice clothes and becomes more critical as she begins to resemble her adult self. For Ann, it is better to use her brains rather than aspire for a conventionally feminine appearance, and the more Ann uses her brains, the more aware she becomes of her adult subjectivity.

In her discussion of *Hexwood*, Kaplan argues that Vierran gains her self-knowledge "by recognizing that her younger self is a fiction,"[79] and while this is true to a certain extent — Vierran is indeed not the 12-year-old Ann Stavely living on Earth — I would argue quite the opposite: Vierran's younger self is not fiction but reflects her own experiences of girlhood, including those behaviors that are later criticized. It is crucially important that the similarities of the two are described to build continuity between Vierran's differently aged selves.

Vierran's identity and self-knowledge are based on the fact that she is now more conscious of her earlier identities that are not illusionary but based on her embodied memories. This is suggested in the novel when Vierran finds Ann similar to her preteen self when comparing them. In terms of characterization, then, the text suggests that the girl identity is not illusionary but indeed based on memories of embodied girlhood — otherwise it would make no sense for Vierran to compare her adult identity to her former selves when she regains her memory and contemplates her recent adventures as a "girl." The continuity between the young and old subjectivity is provided at the moment the time games are revealed — regaining memory is necessary for Vierran to know her personal identity and to become an agentive subject.

Initially, the time slips in the novel raise questions about the role of memory in subjectivity: the personal identity narratives are disrupted and the sense of embodiment is played with. However, the reconstruction of the real course of events in the narrative solves these problems by introducing causality, the links between the characters' past and present subjectivities and between their earlier choices and the consequences of those choices. Furthermore, when Vierran realizes her true age, she acquires a judgmental perspective in relation to her earlier behavior as a girl; thus discourses of girlhood are criticized. After Vierran regains her memory, the 21-year-old Vierran immediately dismisses Ann's typical preteen behaviors by calling her a "little idiot." In the same passage it becomes obvious that, in Vierran's view, to behave like a preteen girl when one is twenty-one is embarrassing: when she remembers herself in the tree, her face flushes hot and she hopes that "Mordion had seen her only as the girl of twelve she had thought she was then."[80]

In Vierran's view, girlhood as a period in a woman's life is portrayed negatively as it is something that one is glad to leave behind. Yet, the preteen Ann has not been represented as such an awful person as Vierran sees her. In fact, readers might be more sympathetic towards Vierran when they learn that she is the one formerly introduced as Ann — a brave, clever young woman. It is clearly suggested that the older Vierran is the same as the earlier Ann in the game — the active and brave romance heroine — because the game cannot make a person "do things which it is not in their natures to do."[81] While a person's "nature" seems to signal an essential identity, the word also indicates that the people and their subjectivities inside the game are not mere fictions. In the game, the setting and appearances are illusionary but the people in the game can — if they become conscious of the rules — act purposefully; whatever goes on inside the game may be based on disguised identities but those identities are no less real than the participants' identities outside the game. The continuity between Ann and Vierran is enforced in the representation of Vierran before the game as a brave, intelligent young woman who participates in a resistance movement against the Reigners, the rulers of the universe. However, the mature Vierran, the Vierran before the game, and Ann are not all exactly the same. When she remembers her real-time history, the mature Vierran dismisses not only the preteen Ann's behavior but also her own more recent actions as the rebellious young woman, "the Vierran of ten days ago," or the "high-class sheltered little deb" as dangerous, irresponsible and naive.[82] Vierran thus rejects the negative aspects of her young feminine identity, naiveté and irresponsibility and, by becoming critical of her own subjectivity, enters adulthood. As a reward, Vierran is made into one of the Reigners — her new role is based both on her identity narrative and on her unique, innate Reigner qualities.

From the perspective of the whole narrative, Vierran's age-shifting is empowering because the time slip allows (or forces) her to realize who she really is and leave her misconceived self-images behind. When Vierran returns to her adult body, her old ways of doing femininity are deconstructed as she becomes aware of their earlier behavior and wants to change. In this sense the fantastic time slips and transformations replace the psychological process of reconstructing a self through memory, or even through therapy where one re-experiences the past. As seen in *The Time of the Ghost*, the (re)construction of a coherent subjectivity at the close can be necessary in terms of trauma. However, if adulthood is understood as an identity connected with agency and responsibility, Sally's new-found identity may also be interpreted as a result of a maturation process. A similar process takes place for Vierran. Regaining her subjectivity after the time shifts is a liberating experience. The mysteries are solved, her personal identity narrative is reconstructed and she finds her "true" calling. This seems to echo discourses of liberal feminism that celebrate empowerment, individual agency and finding of one's unique identity. The mystery narrative structure in the novel supports the liberal-feminist discourse at the close: here the solution to the mysteries involves both the reconstructed identity narrative and the realization of the protagonist's unique talents.

Nevertheless, an agentive subjectivity is also necessary from the perspective of poststructuralist feminist theory. The amnesic Ann trapped in the nonchronological game might seem to be a perfect example of a fluid, postmodern subject, but from a feminist perspective this is not a particularly optimistic way to represent female subjective agency. As Braidotti writes, non-unitary, nomadic subjects inhabit "a time that is the active tense of continuous 'becoming'" and thus their identities will never be fixed to one thing. Nevertheless, Braidotti also maintains that "one cannot deconstruct a subjectivity one has never been fully granted control over."[83] A person who does not know who she is and has no agency is not a subject. Thus, Ann needs a personal identity narrative and a sense of her own material body to become an agentive subject — life narratives and bodies are not fixed, but constantly in the process of becoming. This is also supported by the fact that like Sally, Ann is dependent on others when building her new subjectivity. Individual agency is challenged also in *Hexwood* by emphasizing intersubjectivity: Vierran needs the "necessary others" to fill in her narrative and thus to participate in the interpersonal construction of her subjectivity. Vierran relies on the four voices in her head to fill in her narrative and, at the end, joins the actual people to whom the voices belong to form the new group of Reigners. Interdependency can here be seen as a positive factor rather than as a proof of Vierran's lack of independence, skills or potential.

In *Hexwood*, age-shifting functions as a narrative device that initially deconstructs the embodied and narrative aspects of the girl protagonist's subjectivity and causes readers to experience a level of uncertainty at the beginning of the narrative. However, while the time slips and age-shifting temporarily disrupt the natural aging process, there is one true narrative that results from putting the pieces together. The return to young adulthood at the end emphasizes the desirability of adult subjectivities in opposition to the irresponsible, naive girl subjectivities. The mystery narrative structure emphasizes the new identities at the ending as logical solutions to the uncertainty experienced by both the characters and readers earlier in the narrative. This is problematic, since girlhood is associated with naiveté, irresponsibility and embarrassment — a form of femininity that is satirized and deconstructed — and the passage to adulthood and agentive subjectivity is reached through feelings of guilt and self-accusation. Nevertheless, from a feminist perspective it is desirable that the girls' coming of age is represented as an empowering experience of acquiring an agentive adult subjectivity and leaving behind misconceived self-images based on conventional discourses of girlhood. Vierran's adult subjectivity seems to reflect a liberal feminist project of finding one's identity — yet, this does not necessarily imply that her identity becomes fixed. The time slips and age-shifting have deconstructed Vierran's earlier sense of self and have demonstrated that transformation is possible if one becomes aware of both one's past and one's present ways of performing identities.

Identities as Solutions to Mysteries

In the novels discussed in this chapter invisibility and age-shifting function as narrative devices that initially deconstruct the girl protagonists' subjectivities in the texts. The uncertainty experienced by the protagonists in relation to their identities may be interpreted as a postmodern moment in their subjectivity. Yet, in each narrative, the protagonist's new identities at the ending function as solutions to the mysteries or challenges posed by their bodily transformations. The endings could be seen as a betrayal of the deconstructive strategies in the novels, but in a feminist socio-political interpretation become necessary solutions: it is impossible to deconstruct a subjectivity that does not yet exist or has not existed before.

What is more striking is that in all of these novels about bodily transformations, appearance and beauty — in contrast to, say, strength or agility — are the key factors according to which young feminine/female bodies are described and evaluated. While in most of the texts the importance of looking beautiful is uncritically embraced, in Jones's novels the attempts to maintain a conventionally feminine appearance (and a passive status associated with it) are questioned. Yet, even when criticized, beauty and looks necessarily come up in the constructions of young female subjectivities. I will return to this topic in the following chapter on (in)visibility and gaze.

4

Discourses of Gender, Power and Desire: Invisibility and Female Gaze

IN THE TEXTS DISCUSSED in the previous chapter, invisibility and magic changes in age are represented as wholly or partly undesirable transformations that are necessary events in the identity narratives of the characters — the transformations enable the characters to realize aspects of their own powerlessness, immaturity and restricted subjectivity. However, invisibility in particular is an ambiguous trope that does not only function to communicate ideas of loss of self and powerlessness — moreover, it is not only invisible witches in fairy tales or second-world fantasy contexts for whom invisibility can be an empowering or liberating state. In this chapter, I will focus on the relations between invisibility, gaze, power and subjectivity: invisibility as a state where one escapes gaze and a state where the invisible person has power over people whom she or he observes.

While metaphorical invisibility is often associated with powerlessness stemming from being ignored, invisibility, as a form of hiding and secrecy, also prevents one from becoming the object of other people's gaze. Furthermore, invisibility grants the transformed person a peculiar position as the subject of the gaze, as one who secretly observes others. Both of these possibilities are explored in feminist discourses on (in)visibility and gaze, which I will briefly review before turning to analysis of Jones's *The Time of the Ghost*, Patrice Kindl's *The Woman in the Wall*, Hurley's *Ghostgirl*, Laura Whitcomb's *A Certain Slant of Light*, and Susan Price's *The Ghost Wife*. While the different feminist discourses on (in)visibility in relation to females and femininity may seem contradictory, they also illustrate the complexity of gendered discourses and representations in relation to notions of gaze.

The analysis first focuses on the problems of visibility in *The Time of the Ghost* and *The Woman in the Wall*. Although invisibility in these novels functions as a metaphor for powerlessness and is a state that the protagonists must leave behind to acquire agency, the texts also address girls' or women's visibility as potentially problematic. As I have suggested elsewhere, the complex and often contradictory discourses in *The Time of the Ghost* on the one hand present invisibility as problematic and on the other hand show that visibility can be a trap and invisibility a form of escape[1]; the same concerns *The Woman in the Wall*. The subsequent sections will focus on the invisible girls as subjects of gaze from two perspectives — gaze in relation to definition of other people's identities and gaze in relation to sexuality and desire. From the first perspective, among those who have considered issues of visibility and power, Warner and Haldane have noted that visibility and vision are linked to knowledge and human understanding in many discourses, including discourses of truth (seeing is believing, eye-witnesses); what is visible, and what can be known.[2] The one who sees, gazes — in a narrative, the focalizer — often defines the object of the gaze, what is known about the object. This involves defining other people's identities. Gaze in relation to sexuality functions in somewhat similar terms — in psychoanalytic notions of desire and gaze, gaze fixes its object as someone desirable. While both types of gaze are forms of power, they are distinctively different in the sense that the first, defining gaze is assumed to be based on rationality and "neutral" observation, whereas the desiring gaze is based on instincts and emotions. The final section will address the relationships between sexuality, desire and gaze in *A Certain Slant of Light*, *Ghostgirl* and *The Ghost Wife*, and analyze how the feminist psychoanalytical notions of male and female gaze are challenged in the novels.

Feminist Discourses of Gaze and (In)visibility

In contrast to notions of women's metaphoric invisibility in patriarchal orders, a female's status as an object of (the male) gaze, or the notion of women's visibility as a problem in relation to male sexuality, became popular during the early phases of second-wave feminism in the 1970s. Feminist film theories that appropriated the psychoanalytic concept of gaze, such as Laura Mulvey's (1975), contrasted with pragmatist feminist discourses that regarded cultural invisibility as an undesirable state for women. While the psychoanalytic concept of gaze was a new notion in terms of feminist theory, the associations between gender, sexuality and (in)visibility are ancient. As Teresa De Lauretis notes, "The representation of woman as image (spectacle, object to be looked at, vision of beauty — and the concurrent representation of the female body as the *locus* of sexuality, site of visual pleasure, or lure of the gaze) is ... pervasive in our culture."³ This pervasiveness is reflected in the ways *in*visibility is represented in association with sexuality and gender, as has already been seen with invisible girls and their performance of consumer femininity that focuses on maintaining a beautiful appearance.

In relation to the beastly behavior of invisible males, Haldane suggests that the "connection of invisibility with male invasion of female privacy occurs too often for this conflation to be mere coincidence." Here he introduces another story from Greek mythology, the story of Hermes and Lamia, later interpreted by John Keats in his poem "Lamia," in which Hermes arrives on an island secretly to pursue the beautiful nymph Lamia who has been made invisible to protect her from male desire (although she is not literally invisible but has been turned into a snake). According to Haldane, for Lamia invisibility means "freedom from the lustful male pursuit of beauty, from a predator — a freedom that is lost with the appearance of Hermes."⁴ Haldane seems to be suggesting a difference between an active male invisibility that enables one to pursue one's (sexual) desires and a passive female invisibility that enables the escape from another person's desire. This, of course, reflects the conventional representation of heterosexuality where a male is the active pursuer and a female is the passive object.

In feminist film theory, Mulvey's notions about the male gaze involved the idea of the male as the subject of the gaze and the female as the object of the male voyeurism and desire. Although theorists such as De Lauretis called for a new, feminist politics of representation and for attempts to challenge the gendered binary of gaze and (in)visibility, Mulvey's writings, based on Freudian psychoanalysis, remained popular for a long time. While early feminist theorists did not see invisibility as the solution, even at a theoretical level, in Peggy Phelan's poststructuralist feminism in the early 1990s invisibility is seen as a form of power: to remain invisible and "unmarked" is a powerful state in contrast to becoming visible and thus an object vulnerable to gaze and domination.⁵

Phelan, reflective of the mythological representations, sees invisibility as a liberating state — a sort of escape — but the original aspect of her interpretation is that invisibility is not understood as either a passive or an eternal state. Although Phelan partly relies on Lacanian psychoanalytic theory, she reinterprets invisibility as potentially empowering. This is in contrast to earlier feminist interpretations of Jacques Lacan, such as Julia Kristeva's (1974) *About Chinese Women* and her other writings in the mid-seventies, where the whole sign "woman" was interpreted as a gap, a silence, invisible and unheard, and clearly an undesired status.⁶ Phelan calls for a more critical stance towards the politics of visibility and representation and warns against connecting greater visibility automatically with enhanced (political) power. She does not suggest that continued invisibility could be "the 'proper' political agenda for the disenfranchised," but "rather that the binary between the power of visibility and the impotency of invisibility is falsifying."[7] Thus, while it is necessary to become temporarily visible — or temporarily represent some fixed identity — through a performance, afterwards one should return to the less vulnerable state of invisibility, or become "unmarked" again. In Phelan's framework being "unmarked" or invisible is not merely a theoretical position. As an example of "active vanishing" Phelan describes the Guerrilla Girls — a group of artists who make their thinking visible in their artwork but remain anonymous, making public appearances only in gorilla masks and mini-skirts and thus "resisting visible identities."[8] Strategic "invisibility," then, can become political action. While in the real world the Guerrilla Girls or any other artists might have difficulty turning literally invisible as an act of resistance, in a fantastic text the concerns with visible identities can be addressed by introducing literally invisible characters.

Another strand of feminist discussion has focused on the female gaze, that is, females as subjects of gaze. One strain of this discourse is based on psychoanalytical tradition — a framework in which the female gaze automatically begins to seem a subversive act because it is against the patriarchal norms/male gaze as the norm. The psychoanalytic-feminist film critic Linda Williams suggests in her 1984 article "When Woman Looks" that the female look is often punished in classical narrative cinema where "to see is to desire"— thus many good girls are not allowed to look (at males), whereas the powerful female look of screen vamps adds to their dubious moral status; the look implies the threatening female desire and sexuality.[9] Curiously, she suggests that the subversive female look occurs in horror films: it is the female's look at the monster, because the look not only involves fear but a sympathetic identification with the monster as an Other and an object of male gaze, recognizing "their similar status within patriarchal structures of seeing," although this look is usually punished as the monster attacks the woman.[10]

The discourse of the threatening female gaze was challenged by other feminist theorists mainly because — if the female gaze is always punished — it leaves little room for female subjectivity. A later psychoanalytic-feminist film theorist writing on horror movies, Barbara Creed offers a different kind of interpretation of the female gaze in her discussion of female monsters, or the "monstrous feminine." Creed suggests that the "femme castratrice" (here referring to violent females on screen) controls the sadistic gaze on the male victim.[11] Creed suggests that neither the violence and sadism in the gaze nor the switch of subject-object positions in relation to the gaze makes the gaze itself masculine or male (or, the gazing woman a "phallicized heroine") because that interpretation is based on the essentialist binary between violent, powerful males and non-violent, powerless females, a binary that Creed tries to challenge. Instead, Creed claims that the sadistic female gaze, reflective of female agency, is not punished in the films, and although it remains threatening, it is also a central part of female subjectivity.

In the late 1980s and 1990s feminist discourse relating to the female gaze begun to challenge psychoanalytical feminist theorizations altogether. In a collection of articles titled *The Female Gaze* (1988) by Lorraine Gamman and Margaret Marshment, the editors set out to challenge the orthodoxy of the notion of the male gaze and pose questions about women's gaze at both men and other women in contemporary media.[12] Although some articles in the collection, such as Suzanne Moore's text on female desire and sexualized representations of males deal with gaze and desire, others discuss gaze in different contexts. Gamman, for instance, examines the (mutual) female gaze in a television detective series as an act of solidarity and, on the other hand, as a potentially subversive vehicle of gender parody ("mockery of machismo").[13] Conventional notions of the male gaze and females as objects of gaze have also been challenged in recent studies on earlier historical periods. As Sharon Marcus (2007) argues in her study of various social relationships between women in the 19th century, unlike in later research on the Victorian period, femininity was not only understood in relation to masculinity and males by Victorians themselves. Part of Marcus's study discusses fashion literature and dolls as girls' playthings, and there she argues that, instead of objectifying women for men, "Victorian commodity culture incited an erotic appetite for femininity in women, framed spectacular images of women for a female gaze, and prompted women's fantasies about dominating a woman or submitting to one.... A reputable wife had to take an erotic interest in images of fashionable ladies; an engaged mother had to relish dressing and disciplining her daughters; and a proper girl had to worship at the altar of femininity by idolizing, caressing, or tormenting her female doll."[14]

The female gaze was thus also aimed at female bodies and could be associated with homoeroticism as well as heterosexuality. While Victorian period is usually understood as the source of conventional notions of femininity and masculinity, Marcus shows that even then notions of gaze, desire and sexuality were not as simple as has later been suggested. Marcus maintains that a more complex theorization of the (female) gaze can also be applied in contemporary contexts.

This kind of complex understanding of gaze occurs, for instance, in Caroline Evans's and Gamman's queer theory of gaze where identities of the object of gaze and the subject viewing positions are formulated as fluid categories, and, in Annamari Vänskä's call for the analysis of "the multiplicity and mobility of identification and desiring possibilities, for the *queerness* of *all* viewing positions."[15] In such more recent arguments, gaze is not fixed into the psychoanalytic heteronormative gender binary, but gaze can also be female, it can be directed towards any gender, and I would also argue that it is not necessarily sexualized. Gazes define people's identities, attitudes towards each other and relations between people, and regulate and create the space in which social interaction takes place. Although in early feminist psychoanalytic discourses — particularly those based on Freud — gaze is connected with sexuality, I will appropriate the concept for a more flexible use.[16]

It is worth noting, as Gamman and Marshment do, that it is not necessarily gender that defines gaze; other identity categories are at play as well.[17] Thus, as seen in *Ghost Dance*, the czar's "imperial gaze" is indexical of several different social identities and power relations. Yet, even though gaze is not always sexualized, gaze itself as well as reactions to gaze can be gendered. As Martina Löw writes in her study on gender and spatiality, the "genderdization" of modern spatiality occurs "through the organization of perceptions, and in particular of gazes and the body techniques that go along with them."[18]

There are all kinds of unwritten gendered rules and regulations about who can and does look at whom, in what way and where — these are reflected in people's reactions to each other's gaze. However, the rules and regulations about gaze and proper behavior are also reflected in unconscious routines that are reactions to gaze that might be there even though no one would be looking. This notion in feminist theory is based on Foucault's analyses of processes of surveillance as disciplinary technologies of power as well as his notions of power as both outside control and internalization and bodies as loci of social control.

Feminist adaptations of Foucault's theories, such as Evans and Gamman's (1995), appropriate Foucault's notions of panopticon — the ever-present monitoring gaze — and the idea of internalization of the surveying (and disciplining) gaze. The internalization of gendered discourses — and gaze, or surveillance — can happen through habitual memory and be reflected in fictional representations as descriptions of habitual actions, as seen in the previous chapter. Although at present the heightened sense of a controlling gaze is, as Warner suggests, enforced by the new technologies of surveillance and documentation,[19] the phenomenon itself is not modern — the sense or the lack of the sense of monitoring or moral gaze is addressed in the stories of invisibility by Plato and Cicero.

In my analysis, I will discuss gaze both in relation to sexuality as well as control, knowledge and subjectivity on a more general level. Thus, I am looking for several possible representations and discourses of the gaze in relation to the issue of (in)visibility. In literary representations, gaze is evident in focalization but can be represented in other ways as well: by describing processes of seeing, looking, and observing, and by reporting the characters' reactions to others' gaze.

Problems of Visibility

As discussed in the previous chapter, for many invisible girl protagonists gaining visibility is necessary to build an agentic subjectivity that is partly based on recognition by others. However, visibility is also problematic since it is frequently linked to the bodily appearance and the need to look pretty or beautiful — the connection between visibility and beauty emerges in many novels about invisible girls. I will consider how visibility is treated as a problem in *The Time of the Ghost* and *The Woman in the Wall* and explore the ways in which these texts represent invisibility as a welcomed form of escape from the gazes of others. While in each novel the representation of female beauty echoes the discourses of consumer femininity, good looks in these two novels are not achieved through consumerism, and, moreover, visibility is presented as more problematic as in Hurley's, Kaye's and Rodgers's novels discussed in the previous chapter.

Performing Femininity: Visibility and Beauty

As argued above, metaphorical (as well as literal) invisibility in *The Time of the Ghost* is, in general, an undesired state that Sally must leave behind to reach full subjectivity. Nevertheless, the novel does not simply celebrate visibility either. Sally's invisibility and inaudibility are, ironically, contrasted with her sister Imogen's visibility and "voice," or her musicality. Both Sally and Imogen are metaphorically invisible, Sally as the nice girl who has no sense of subjectivity, and Imogen invisible behind her visibility, her good looks and her musical talent. Although reflective of the feminist discourses of visibility as a problem — and "femininity" as a fake image controlled by the male gaze that does not capture "real" women — it is the female gaze that has trapped Imogen in her role as a pianist.

The mother, Phyllis, has fixed career plans for three of the four girls. Whether based on looks or talents, Phyllis's views of gendered roles are essentialist to the core: looks and talents are inborn and define who you will be. However, it seems that the mother is wrong about Imogen because in her view Imogen has been destined to be a pianist because she has the looks (a visible identity of a pianist) for it:

"Of course Imogen is going to go on with music. She has enormous talent. Every time I see her seated at the keyboard—"
"About once a year," muttered Fenella.
Phyllis shut her eyes in order not to hear this. It was one of Fenella's stupid remarks. "Every time," she repeated, "I'm impressed by the serenity and passion of her profile. It reminds me of Myra Hess. I know Imogen is cut out to be a concert pianist. Your father would be so disappointed if she gave up."[20]

The mother rarely listens to Imogen play and therefore cannot know much about her talents — she is only excited about the "serenity and passion" of Imogen's profile which reminds her of a famous pianist. Moreover, the mother does not mention how Imogen's playing sounds — a crucial aspect of a real musical talent — she is only referring to her own process of looking at Imogen at the piano. The mother sees but does not hear Imogen. Gaze is here linked to hearing and invisibility to inaudibility — the common notion of invisibility as a metaphorical state of people who are ignored on all levels is explicitly invoked. The mother's reaction to Fenella's remark emphasizes the link between invisibility and inaudibility: shutting her eyes metonymically functions as a sign that she is ignoring them.

It is curious that Phyllis refers to the father's disappointment rather than her own if Imogen ceased to play — a possible interpretation might be that she is therefore a representative of patriarchal control and her gaze is a vehicle of that control. However, because the father cannot even tell the sisters apart from each other, it is plausible to assume that it is namely the mother's own wishes that she is talking about. It is the mother's gaze that is here defining a conventionally feminine role for Imogen based on her appearance — the mother mistakes her good looks for her talent. Later in the novel, after leaving the music college as an attempt to make a sacrifice and save Sally from the goddess Monigan, Imogen states, "I was never any good anyway. I only took up the piano because Phyllis said I looked beautiful playing it."[21] Whether one interprets Phyllis as a representative of patriarchal control or as a liberal feminist (after all, she is rather ambitious about her daughters having careers of their own and herself focuses on her career in the school rather than on her family), it is indicated that the daughters will have to challenge the mother's control if they want to become subjects in their own terms.

The problems with (in)visibility/inaudibility are also addressed in a scene that immediately precedes the one above. The sisters try to make Imogen look like pantomime fairy and that represents Imogen's tragedy of attempting to perform a prescribed role in a minor scale. The invisible Sally's attempts to make herself heard during the scene are ironic in relation to Imogen's attempts. While Sally struggles to be heard, Imogen struggles to be seen (and look beautiful), but not heard, trying desperately to look graceful. Imogen's attempts towards dramatic grandeur are ironic in connection with the description of what she actually looks like from Sally's perspective: "majestic in her withered loopy pyjamas."[22] On the level of the whole scene, the image of a graceful pantomime fairy is contrasted with Cart's and Fenella's amusing yet horrifying attempts to heave Imogen into the air with the help of a skipping rope thrown over a roof beam and tied around her waist.

Towards the end, the scene turns into a complete mockery of the gracefulness of a pantomime fairy: Imogen is grinning in pain because the ropes are strangling her. Instead of a graceful, conventionally feminine image, Imogen ends up, from Sally's perspective, looking almost dead ("eyes had ... a bulging look," "face was a muddy mauve"), inhuman ("scarecrow," "Hallowe'en lantern") or even strangely masculine ("grinning wrestler") — all of these images contribute to Imogen's grotesqueness.[23] The scene almost ends up as a tragedy, when after being severely hurt Imogen wants to try again and is nearly killed because the skipping rope strangles her. The irony in the scene is associated with the juxtaposition of graceful and grotesque and the girls' innocent enthusiasm in aiming for the first and gaining the latter, and the connection between "suffering in the cause of Art" and performing a conventional role.

Both Sally's voicelessness and the pantomime fairy scene contribute to the liberal-feminist discourse working at the level of the whole novel. Without a voice a woman cannot really exist: the real problem is not merely visibility or invisibility but the lack of voice. In the pantomime scene Imogen is nearly killed by trying to play the role of conventional "perfect" female (or child); seen but not heard. This is a symbolic representations of both Imogen's and Sally's lifelong attempts to try to be something they can never achieve. Sally has also ended up almost dead by trying to perfectly perform the conventional feminine role by focusing on pleasing her father and her boyfriend. The deliberate misidentifying and identifying between Sally and Imogen — misidentifying because they are not the same person; identifying because they share similar features, feelings and fate — highlights the problems each girl has faced because of her conventionally feminine behavior.

However, a gendered discourse that emphasizes beauty as an admirable and desirable quality for females is not completely undermined. For Sally, female beauty is important, and since she is the main focalizer in the text, it is her views of others that readers will "see." Sally describes all her sisters, as well as herself and Phyllis as different types of angels and there is a pattern that associates the angel imagery with conventional femininity: angels are beautiful and able to protect other people; those girls who are ugly, depressed or do not manage to protect others are failed, or unsuccessful angels. Apart from the angel imagery, the bodily appearance of people is constantly commented upon by Sally, and in relation to her sisters and herself these comments are often related to beauty.

While Sally and Imogen have been pretty girls, the young Cart and Fenella are ugly ducklings that are represented as unfeminine, even grotesque. However, the flaws in Cart's and Fenella's young appearances have disappeared later when Sally sees them as young adults in the future: in the hospital Sally is quite shocked to realize that the grotesque girls have turned into beautiful, self-confident women. The transformation of both sisters is, from Sally's perspective, for the better.

From a feminist point of view there is a problem with Sally's dominating gaze: at the end when she describes her adult sisters as beautiful, the conventional discourse relating to femininity and appearance is once more emphasized. Arguably, Sally's appreciation of female beauty might suggest that Sally's gaze is, in fact, masculine; female beauty (linked to visibility as more desirable than audibility) has a central place in patriarchal discourses of femininity. However, relying on queer theorizations of gaze, I would argue that appreciation of female beauty is not tied to male gaze but to female gazes as well, whether sexualized (lesbian gazes) or not (heterosexual women admiring other women).

Obviously, Sally has internalized the discourse of female beauty as admirable, but this discourse itself can be viewed either as a conventional or a liberating one. There is, for instance, the suggestion that beauty might be the result of Cart's and Fenella's self-confidence and happiness — after all, Imogen, who has been pursuing the wrong career, is depressed and her depression has clearly destroyed her looks (her looks are also destroyed in the painful pantomime fairy scene). As earlier, the novel seems to reflect contradictory discourses in relation to women's visibility. Appearances clearly matter, but can prove to be dangerous. Yet, beauty may also be a result of self-confidence, in which case a beautiful appearance reflects female agency. While this kind of understanding may well be deemed postfeminist — contemporary consumer culture is constantly draws on assumptions about the connection between appearance and agency — it is, however, significant that the novel suggests that beauty is not enough in itself.

Escaping into Invisibility

Although invisibility serves as an indicator of a conventional, powerless female status in *The Time of the Ghost*, Sally finds her horrifying state partly liberating — not least because visibility is clearly portrayed as problematic. In her invisible state she is able to forget her past self and reinvent herself— during her visits in the past she tries to identify herself in different kinds of femininities represented by her sisters; a passionate and beautiful artist, and a noisy but brave, goblin-like sister. This idea of self-reinvention while invisible echoes Phelan's poststructuralist formulation of invisibility as a powerful state: to remain invisible is to be able to move fluidly between different identities. As Phelan suggests, while it is necessary to become temporarily visible — or temporarily represent some fixed identity — through a performance, afterwards one should return to the less vulnerable state of invisibility.

Furthermore, for Sally invisibility is a state where she can escape the male gaze, here defined as an aspect of patriarchal control. Not all the male characters are associated with this kind of gaze in the novel, but in certain passages involving Sally's and her sisters' thoughts it is indicated that they react to the imagined male gaze: they imagine themselves as objects of a masculine gaze that is controlling and either mocking or sexualized. Wandering in the schoolyard Sally remembers how she has been ashamed when boys looked and laughed at her, and she describes her new invisible condition as "the ideal state for not being noticed":

> *I think*, Sally said uncertainly, *I think I like watching cricket.*
> But it made you very shy, she remembered, being one girl out in the middle of a field full of boys. They stared and said to one another, "That's Slimy Semolina, that girl." Some said it to your face. And being boys, they were, of course, quite unable to tell you and your sisters apart and called all four of you Slimy Semolina impartially. But now, when she was in the ideal state of not being noticed, Sally somehow could not face all that wide green space.[24]

For Sally it is here easier to be without a body than in a girl's body — in the boys' gaze girls' bodies are amusing and all the same because the sisters cannot be told apart from each other; they are not perceived as individuals but as representatives of femininity. As an invisible person Sally can go where she wants, because she is free from her visible body and the shame of being looked at by the boys. Invisible, Sally avoids becoming an object of gaze and domination. Her condition represents a fantastic response to the problem of visibility introduced in the feminist discourses of the 1970s. Yet, as seen in the previous chapter, and in the above example, Sally is not completely free, even in her invisibility — she has internalized the negative experience of conventional, passive female subjectivity. Even though no one can see her, she imagines the boys mocking her. From the reader's perspective it is significant that the focalization through Sally shows not only her insecurity but that she is aware of her own fears and lack of self-confidence.

The issue of the male gaze is explicitly addressed in the novel also when Sally's sisters discuss bras — Cart says that she would like to have one but Fenella says that their father would think it too expensive. As a reply to this dilemma, Imogen suggests, "You don't need a bra ... if you intend to be a properly liberated woman" but when Cart does not think that she is "that liberated," Fenella interprets this as a concern about the male gaze: "Cart means, will it please boys?"[25] Appearance and femininity are, then, in this brief piece of dialogue addressed from both the conventional perspective ("will it please boys") as well as from a feminist one. In both of these scenes, Sally in the schoolyard and the girls discussing bras, the internalization of conventional gendered discourses is emphasized because in each case the male gaze is imagined rather than actually present.

The Time of the Ghost includes traces of both poststructuralist and liberal-feminist discourses of invisibility and femininity. While I have argued earlier that the gaze that Sally escapes is mainly the male gaze, I have here attempted to show that by focusing also on female gazes, the issue becomes more complex.[26] Although Sally does not experience the mother's gaze as fearsome — instead, she yearns for the mother's gaze, attention and recognition — her invisibility frees her from the mother's notions of what a female career means. In this sense, Sally's invisibility is a state of unrealized potential and fluid identity. By the end Sally escapes both her literal and metaphorical invisibility and finds her voice and agency, but we are left with the image of her still lying in the hospital bed, covered in bandages. It depends on the reader, whether one sees Sally as finding a stable role as an empowered female artist, or whether one sees a suggestion that she might remain invisible, becoming only temporarily visible through her paintings. Similar ideas are also present in Patrice Kindl's *The Woman in the Wall*, a novel about an invisible young woman whose return to visibility happens through a spectacular performance.

Kindl's novel is narrated in the first person by fourteen-year-old Anna, who describes herself as a very shy girl and suggests at the beginning that readers might not be interested in her story at all. When she, after the apologetic opening, starts her story, she explains that her shyness has made her to turn herself as invisible as possible:

> I have always been shy. The urge to hide came over me at a very early age. My mother says I was a good baby; I never fussed at all. Both of my sisters came out of the womb with mouths wide open, screaming their heads off, their hands outstretched to grasp at whatever life offered. I, on the other hand, never even whimpered as I entered the world. I just lay there quietly in my incubator and tried to fit in. I had no longings for power or domination. I didn't want to intrude in any way; I simply wanted to blend into the scenery with as little fuss as possible. In this I succeeded.[27]

Supposedly born prematurely (since she has been in an incubator), Anna is also a tiny child and her size makes it easier for her to disappear. The narrative is written in a magic realist mode and it openly plays with the distinction of literal and metaphorical invisibility — at the beginning it is never clear whether

Anna disappears completely or whether she is merely unnoticed by others. This is combined with other incredulous elements such as the seven-year-old Anna sewing clothes for her mother and her two sisters and, to escape starting school, building herself secret hiding places around their home.

The scene that triggers Anna's need to hide for good also slides from the hyperbole into the fantastic: when a school psychologist comes to their home to assess Anna, she does not see her at all and Anna accidentally falls into her purse and is carried out of the house. Terrified, Anna manages to jump out of the purse, get back into the house and hide. Here she turns into a ghost-like creature who hides in the walls for years, leaving her secret rooms only by night. In the eyes of her family, Anna continues to exist in spirit, if not in flesh. In Anna's view, her older sister treats her as "a half-remembered family myth, a strange story that mustn't be told," while her mother and younger sister only speak to her when they need something (new clothes, fixing things around the house) and think of her "as a kind of disembodied spirit, present and listening behind any wall of the house at any time."[28]

In Anna's disappearance in the walls, Kindl's novel echoes Charlotte Perkins Stetson's (Gilman) short story "The Yellow Wall-paper" (1892) in which the female protagonist suffers from nervous depression, according to her husband, who is a doctor, and is locked away in a room with decaying wallpaper to rest and recover from her condition. The protagonist begins to believe that the wallpaper hides women behind it and that she is one of those women; the closure where the wallpaper is torn mostly off and the women behind it are freed can be interpreted either as a descent to madness or a freedom from the restricted subjectivity imposed on the protagonist by her husband. Both in the short story and in Kindl's novel the protagonists live in huge houses — the key difference between the two is that Anna is not locked up by anyone else but builds herself secret passages and rooms in the house and withdraws willingly into the walls herself.

She is also different from the madwoman in the attic in Charlotte Brontë's *Jane Eyre*, another 19th century text explicitly referred to in the novel, when someone suspects that the hiding Anna might be "like the crazy wife in *Jane Eyre*? They kept her shut up because she liked to set fire to people in their beds."[29] Anna denies this and indeed bears little resemblance to the mad women that get locked up in the earlier narratives; instead, she emphasizes her normality and sensibility at several points and, in the end, her coming out of the wall is associated with her "normal" passage to blossoming adulthood, rather than any revelation of a hidden, wild or monstrous identity. The only time that Anna feels that she is losing control is when her body starts to change when she is twelve and she does not understand what the strange, monstrous transformations are about and believes they only concern her: "In punishment for my eccentric lifestyle, I was turning into some sort of fat, hairy, bleeding monster with skin eruptions."[30] Soon, however, she realizes that the changes are perfectly normal in the embodied passage from girlhood to womanhood.

At first Anna is, in fact, happily invisible in her hiding place — the house shelters her and has "no eyes to see me or ears to hear me or tongue to scold me."[31] Anna, who thinks that she is better with objects than people, ends up staying invisible from her family for seven years. Before and during her hiding Anna tells about herself as a girl who believes that she is not worth anything unless she makes herself useful by doing all kinds of tasks for other people. While Anna is proud of her handiwork and all the things that she does for her mother and sisters, her completely self-denying status is linked with conventional femininity in that she believes she should only exist to please and serve others. On the level of the whole narrative, this is a subjectivity that Anna needs to leave behind to be able to become a self-confident young woman in her own terms.

Towards the end, her coming out of the wall is strongly associated with coming of age, which here is about growing into a heterosexual female identity. When she is fourteen, Anna starts her contact with the outside world again with a boy, Francis, who has left a love letter in a crack in the wall — really addressed to Anna's older sister but Anna first believes and later pretends to be the "A" indicated in the letter since she has "fallen in love like a stone falling into a well. His letter had released something in me, and how there was no going back. I was changing, changing forever."[32]

Anna's strong heterosexual desire towards the writer whom she quite naturally assumes has to be a boy — "I was pretty sure that girls didn't usually send love letters to other girls"[33] — makes her seek contact with him by exchanging several letters before he finally finds starts searching her and finds her hiding inside the wall. With him, Francis also brings Anna's little sister, Kirsty, and soon Anna feels another strong gendered urge, the urge to identify with other females: "I looked at Kirsty and she giggled. I giggled too, experimentally. It felt nice, like soda fizzing inside of you. Female stuff, I thought happily. Kirsty and I were being women together, doing female stuff."[34] The key issue in Anna's new self-identification as a female is that everyone else treats her as such, and, moreover as a visible, beautiful female.

Anna leaves her hiding place when she learns that her mother is planning to sell the house; Francis and Kirsty persuade her to come out during a Halloween party at the house because she can then show herself in a costume and thus become only partly visible. At the party, Anna, whom Francis has earlier mockingly described as "an Olympic class wallflower,"[35] appears dressed up as a luna moth, in a spectacular dress made by herself that attracts the attention of a popular, older boy. He finds Anna's entrance "incredible.... Are you in

Drama Club or something?"[36] His comment is ironic, since Anna is playing a role that she is not familiar with, the role of a visible, sexualized young woman, although she pretends to know what she is doing while she dances with the older boy and Francis. Anna has metamorphosed from a creature hiding in a cocoon into a beautiful butterfly; yet she is still unsure about her new performance of a gendered, sexualized identity.

Although Anna has not been a ghost, as in ghost stories, the mystery surrounding her identity is solved at the end when it is revealed to her older sister and mother that she still exists and to her mother's new fiancée that Anna is the long-lost daughter of his beloved. In a sense, Anna's new identity is a mystery to herself since she knows that she has been away from social interaction for a very long time and not yet ready to become a woman, despite all the changes in her body that have occurred during her hiding. The closure ties an adult woman identity strongly with heterosexuality, and, furthermore, reproduction, since Anna also thinks that women's bodies are "houses for our children" and thus, before having children of her own, "I will build myself a house out of my own flesh and bones where my frightened child-self can find shelter."[37]

While the text here almost seems to reflect biological essentialism, the ending also leaves Anna's subjectivity as an open construct; she is in the process of becoming, rather than being, a woman, and it is indicated that since her self-confidence has already changed her behavior drastically before, her growing belief in herself will continue to change her also in the future. What also seems certain is that Anna will not return to invisibility anymore, after experimenting successfully with her new, visible feminine identity. Moreover, while Anna makes her appearance in a beautiful form that attracts both wanted and unwanted male attention, it is significant that she appears in a costume rather than as her recognizable, older self. Her entrance is treated as a spectacle, a performance. As with Sally in *The Time of the Ghost*, one might interpret the closure as an open one: Anna might continue to develop her self-confidence in privacy, invisible, while becoming only temporarily visible in her costumes during a conscious performance.

Gaze and Female Desire

In this section I will discuss texts where invisible female ghosts become subjects of desiring gaze — these include Laura Whitcomb's *A Certain Slant of Light* and Susan Price's *The Ghost Wife*, as well as Hurley's *Ghostgirl*. In these novels the invisible ghost's gaze is represented varyingly as loving, possessive, or dangerous and monstrous. Instead of fitting into any general pattern about ghostly female desire, these texts suggest that the figure of the ghost is a flexible trope to address issues related to gaze and female sexuality. As suggested earlier, the ghost narratives discussed here are unconventional in the sense that the ghost — or the invisible girl — gets to focalize aspects of the texts; unlike in *The Time of the Ghost*, the ghost-girls here are not the only focalizers, however. The invisible ghosts become complex because their motives and actions gain different meanings when contextualized in relation to other characters' actions and point of view.

Unlike in most of the novels discussed above and in the previous chapter, the main plot in *A Certain Slant of Light* and *The Ghost Wife* does not circle around the invisible girl's identity — although, as typical of ghost stories, their identity is at the beginning a mystery to some of the characters, and the ghost's narrative (who she is) is revealed gradually as the story unfolds. Instead of identity, desire in its different forms is a central issue in these two novels — not only as the desire for someone but as the desire to be something else. In both its forms, desire is connected with gaze. While *Ghostgirl* thematizes identity, it also examines aspects of female desire and is thus revisited here from the perspective of gaze and sexuality. I will argue that by employing multiple focalizations, these novels play with the conventional notions of gaze, but they subvert the conventional assumption that only male desire is connected with gaze and that only females can be objects of gaze.

Price's *The Ghost Wife* also addresses connections between social class and gendered behavior — particularly in notions of decency and sexuality. Instead of focusing on one character's subjectivity, the texts address issues of gender and class through a strategy that Rolf Romøren and John Stephens have termed "metonymic configuration": "Patterns of gendered behaviors are built up through the simple fictive practice of developing conflict and/or thematic implication through interactions amongst diverse and contrasting characters (often character stereotypes)."[38] By introducing a set of characters that are, to a certain extent, stereotypes and contrasting them, the novels juxtapose different discourses of gender and class. Yet, because all of the main characters are focalizers, their characterization as well as the conflicts between characters are made more complex.

The Desire to Gaze and to Be Gazed At

Laura Whitcomb's *In a Certain Slant of Light* features the ghost of a woman who has died in the 19th century at the age of twenty-seven and has since then, for one hundred and thirty years, been haunting various writers as their invisible muse. The ghost, Helen, is what she calls "Light"; she exists in spirit and thinks that her hosts — who are the "Quick," the living people — can hear and feel her, even though they cannot see her. For centuries, Helen's desire has been to escape her memories where she sees her child drowning together with her and, instead, to follow the writers and inspire them. However, the state where she can only invisibly witness others' lives is no longer enough for her when she one day notices that a teenaged boy can see her. The boy, James, is in fact another ghost who has possessed a living boy's body, and he also teaches Helen how to do this.

In borrowed bodies, the young-old couple — they inhabit teenage bodies but were both in their twenties when they died and their spirits have wandered around for decades — remembers and re-experiences the joys of tasting, smelling, feeling and desiring. While pondering the unethical aspect of possessing another person's body, Helen and James manage to change the two possessed teenagers' lives for the better and leave their bodies in the end. As Sally in *The Time of the Ghost*, Helen is amnesic at first and does not remember her life or her death. When Helen finally regains the memory of the last moments of her life, she remembers that her child has managed to escape and that she has blamed herself for the death of her child in vain; after this realization Helen moves to another place with James and all the other loved ones who have passed away. In the following, I will discuss Helen's desire to be gazed at and her own gaze on others in relation to the portrayal of her sexuality.

As the other invisible girls discussed so far, Helen wants to be seen and recognized by another human being, even though she does not realize this at first. Quite the contrary, as the opening of the novel indicates, Helen finds it uncomfortable to be noticed by another person: "Someone was looking at me, a disturbing sensation if you're dead."[39] While Helen has followed her hosts and whispered inspiration in their ears, she has not been seen or truly heard by anyone during her time as a ghost. She has had to stay close to her hosts, otherwise she is drawn into the painful scene of the moment of her death; thus she has so far been tied to her hosts until they die. Although her ghostly existence has prevented Helen from experiencing any mutual human contact, invisibility has also granted Helen with safety and privacy, and she is confused about her conflicting feelings triggered by the fact that she is suddenly visible to someone:

> I had two strong and seemingly contradictory sensations. One was a fear of being seen by a mortal — as if beheld naked when you know you are clothed. The other was an almost indescribable sense of attraction — the vine curling toward the sun's light in slow but single-minded longing. I wanted to see him again, to see whether he really was that rare human who saw what others could not. Nothing was more disturbing to me, and yet nothing compelled me more.[40]

The significant someone who sees Helen is James, another ghost in a teenage boy's body. Helen's contradictory sensations soon result in anger at the boy who dares to disturb her privacy, and then in humiliation, when the boy smiles at her and thus not only sees her but tries to communicate with her. While Helen's feelings of confusion, fear, humiliation and anger return when the boy talks to her and can also hear Helen, she soon cannot but seek the attention of the boy and is amazed that someone longs to speak with her. Helen has explained earlier that for ghosts it is only their emotions that can connect them to the world of the Quick. Indeed, it is an emotion that draws Helen back to the world of the living: she desires James, the boy who can now see her, and she desires to be in a body that can be touched by him. As Helen tells James, who is afraid of being too bold towards her, "The most compelling thing in my world, sir, is to be heard and seen by you."[41] Being really seen and heard by someone is indeed different to whispering to hosts that may or may not hear you and who, in any case, do not know that you exist; thus Helen leaves her current host, Mr. Brown, for James, who becomes her lover.

Helen desires to be seen and touched by James, but she also enjoys watching him. Meeting James changes Helen's earlier patterns of gazing at her hosts, towards whom she has behaved in a very modest way: "I would never follow a male host into the bath, for instance, or into the marriage bed, man or woman."[42] She has followed these patterns even though she has been in love with Mr. Brown, although this might have also been because she has felt jealous of his wife and thus maintained the rules to mainly follow him when he is alone at work. All of this changes during Helen's encounters with James, when she is completely enchanted by him: "I couldn't take my eyes off him. Like a desert wanderer afraid of mirages, I gazed at my oasis, but he was real. It pleased me that he seemed to take no notice of the young lady who now sat across the aisle from him."[43] Helen is drawn to James because he can see her, but, as can be seen, also because she feels attracted to him, here indicated by her pleasure in the fact that James does not notice the other girls when Helen is present. James later explains to Helen that he has only noticed Helen after entering a living, borrowed body; this has changed his vision completely, which he expresses through the biblical quote: "For once I saw through a glass darkly, but now I see the world clearly."[44] What has here changed James's vision is not faith but corporeality; a body of flesh also changes Helen's vision and subjectivity later. However, after meeting James, Helen starts to see differently already in her ghostly form, not in any biblical sense, but as a desiring female subject.

During the night that Helen attaches herself to James, she first watches James in his sleep and, in the following morning, modestly leaves the room when James dresses but secretly watches him from outside: "I did something then I'd never done. I watched my host dress. I didn't go back into the room, but, like a guilty thing, I stayed at the window sill, a peeping tom, watching James throw his towel onto the corner of the bed and pull a pair of grey shorts from the top dresser drawer. He stepped into them and I meant to stop, but it wasn't just the novelty of his nakedness that gripped me. It was all of him."[45]

Helen here becomes a voyeur, for the first time in her life, watching the young man that she desires. She feels that she should not be doing it — she feels guilty — but she gives in to her own desire and does not stop watching. Helen also finds a new sexual agency when she possesses a living body. After entering the teenage Jenny's body, she finds feeling and touching amazing, a new, bodily existence that culminates in her and James making love in their borrowed bodies. While Helen has lived in a nineteenth-century world where "the bride waits, seen but not heard, ready to open at his command," she now undresses James without shame: "Now I marvelled at my own boldness."[46] In her own view, she here completely subverts conventional ways of performing a modest, feminine subjectivity. Helen's desire is stirred when she is an invisible voyeur, but it is only fulfilled when she is in a living, feeling body; thus gazing at someone is only a small part of her sexuality but when later done without feelings of shame, gives her pleasure. For Helen, desire is both about being gazed at and gazing, or being recognized and recognizing the other; realizing this also increases Helen's self-confidence and makes her bolder. Helen is a ghost that finds her sexual subjectivity again in a living body, yet other ghost-girls are not as lucky.

As seen in the previous chapter, also for Charlotte in *Ghostgirl* it is necessary to become visible to (re)gain subjectivity — she desires the recognition of others. However, Charlotte also finds her invisible state as a liberating one in the sense that she is now free to gaze at desirable bodies without any interruptions apart from her own feelings of shame. Indeed, her invisibility makes her powerful and completely changes her subjectivity in relation to how she can experience her sexual desire through gazing at a young male: "Charlotte was feeling powerful in a way she never had before. She felt 'reborn.' In fact, the endless, albeit stalker-ish, possibilities were almost overwhelming, *almost* being the operative word. She beat back the momentary crisis of conscience over the creepiness of this invasion of his privacy, and decided selfishly, shamelessly, to work her plan as Damen turned the corner in the hallway."[47]

Charlotte realizes that she can follow Damen everywhere and this is what she does, observing him in public as well as private places, including a boys' dressing room and Damen's private bedroom. While clearly enjoying stalking Damen and thus turning into a voyeur, Charlotte is fairly modest, however: "She didn't necessarily want to see him naked, per se, but she did want to see more of him.... She wanted to see his arms, his shoulders, his chest, up close."[48] This is followed by a description of Damen undressing that extends several paragraphs, mostly describing Damen's body parts that together add up to his male beauty that fills Charlotte with delight but also Charlotte's conventional heterosexual female desire that views strong arms as "the kind you could feel safe and comfortable in."[49] It is also suggested that Charlotte's desire is representative of the young women's desire in general: "Any girl would die to be sitting where she was."[50]

Charlotte's appreciation of the different parts of the male body that all together make a beautiful whole reflects the type of analysis conventionally associated with the female body.[51] Charlotte is clearly the subject of the desiring gaze and the young male is the object; however, Charlotte is able to enjoy gazing a sexual object only because she is invisible. Later Charlotte modestly disappears from the scene when Damen has an intimate moment with his girlfriend. Her gazing activities are thus controlled by her modesty — thus the novel subverts the conventional discourse of male gaze by putting a young woman in the position of the desiring, gazing subject but, at the same time, reflects the conventional discourse of female sexuality where modesty is seen as a necessary (sometimes natural) feature that prevents young women in particular from expressing their desire in an inhibited, carefree manner.

This is emphasized in a later scene where Charlotte again spies on Damen and enters a boy's private room for the first time in her life. Her desire to be close to Damen results in shock and shame when Charlotte creeps into Damen's bed, wakes him up and leaves him terrified because her ghostly form has scared Damen. Charlotte realizes that she is Damen's nightmare and escapes from the scene feeling ashamed and hopeless. In the end, she has to learn how to let go of the object of her desire and accept her fate as an outsider as well as realize that her own identity should be based on her own personality, rather than attempts to become popular and be admired by popular people. Charlotte's desire is thus suppressed and in her case the closure curiously suggests that to become a strong subject, a young woman has to put her sexuality aside — this does not concern the Goth girl Scarlet, however. While Charlotte does find herself a dead boyfriend in the sequels, nowhere is her desire depicted in such a detailed way as in the above extracts where she invisibly gazes at the object of her desire. The possibilities of a desiring female gaze are thus explored in the novel but denied at the end: it seems that as soon as a female subject becomes visible, she turns into the object of others' gazes and loses her subjectivity as the one who directs her desiring gaze at others.

The Working-Class Female Desire

Susan Price's *The Ghost Wife* plays with the conventional elements of the late eighteenth and early nineteenth century female Gothic novel, including the scene (a haunted home) and the set of characters (innocent female victims and their male perpetrators). In terms of gender and sexuality the text can be seen as a reflection on the middle-class features and concerns of the female Gothic genre in general.[52] In addition to the external-narrator focalizer, all the main characters and many of the minor characters get to focalize in the narrative. Because of this configuration, I will focus on the invisible ghost-girl, Becca, but also briefly comment on the characters that are contrasted and paralleled with her. In *The Ghost Wife* the stereotypical roles for females and males are partly reversed.

Unlike the other novels in this and the previous chapter, *The Ghost Wife* is not situated in a modern setting but in nineteenth-century rural Britain, where working-class colliers and (lower) middle-class land-owning farmers form two different groups of people. In addition to occupation, wealth and different notions of cleanliness and tidiness associated with both people's appearances and their houses, a significant part of the class-divide is a difference in notions of decency, religion and sexuality.[53] These ideas can all be included in the notion of "respectability" that has been a marker of the middle-class since the nineteenth century, and these ideas are also reflected in the classic female Gothic novel.[54]

Kate Ferguson Ellis writes, borrowing the term from Nancy Cott, that the new discourse of respectable (middle-class) femininity emerging in classic female Gothic texts in the early 19th century was based on "the ideology of passionlessness." As opposed to the earlier notions of females as especially sexual, the middle-class women were now seen as innocent, moral, less sexual than males and thus apt to act as the guardians of morals. Diane Long Hoeveler has termed the same discourse as "professional femininity": a gendered set of behaviors performed by the females who controlled the home and who were responsible for the decency and respectability of themselves and their surroundings.[55]

Most of the characters in *The Ghost Wife* more or less deviate from the typical roles and gendered discourses in the female Gothic. Different notions of sexuality and decency — which are linked to gender and gaze — are reflected in the encounters between Becca, a vampire-like ghost, Rattle Nailer, a collier girl, and two middle-class males, Jonathan Turner, a farmer boy, and Amadeus Warley or the Dudleigh Devil, a male witch. In her earlier life Becca has also been a member of the working class, or even underclass, as a pauper girl. The decent, shy Jonathan is desired by both Rattle and Becca, neither of whom fits the middle-class ideal of a decent girl. Becca and Rattle represent a transgressive form of female sexuality that is perceived as disturbing from the point of view of the two middle-class males, although for very different reasons. While Amadeus Warley is a violent misogynist, Jonathan has adopted modest middle-class notions of decency and sexuality and thus reflects a milder version of discourse on indecent working-class female sexuality.

The invisible, undead Becca has a complete control her invisibility; her invisibility is not metaphorical, but strategic. Yet, her invisibility is connected with her undead state and as such is a source of terror, not least because she reminds the inhabitants of the farmhouse of her invisible existence by making noises around the house. Although at the beginning Becca is referred to as a ghost by Sophie, she is not really a ghost or a poltergeist — if these are understood as something immaterial — but rather a vampire-like living dead; a special type of ghost called "a Fetch or a Follower ... ghost that attached itself to a family for generation after generation."[56]

Becca shifts between visibility and invisibility as well as materiality and immateriality; at times she only makes noises, while in other instances she can clearly move material things and become material herself. In her visible form she can appear either as a rotting corpse or a pretty girl, depending on whether she wants to scare people or make herself more desirable in the eyes of Jonathan, who calls Becca his "wife." Although the sexual encounters between Becca and Jonathan are not explicitly described, they are indicated in scenes where naked Becca goes to bed with Jonathan and steals warmth from him. The encounters with Becca, a kind of vampire, slowly consume him. In terms of the female Gothic, the gendered roles of the two are reversed — Jonathan fills in the role of the Gothic heroine, the decent, innocent middle-class victim captured in a haunted home while the perpetrator Becca is an underclass girl rather than an aristocratic, decadent male.

As a vampire or a succubus, Becca can be seen as a representative of the monstrous feminine or dangerous female desire and sexuality. She is not represented in wholly negative terms, however. Originally Becca is a male creation and she sees her consumption of young men's lives as justified. Becca has been created by Jonathan's great-great-grandfather, Devil Turner, who has made the "Fetch" by drowning a beggar girl in a rainwater tub and then fetching her spirit back before her body has gone cold. The undead girl has then become a servant for the Devil; she spies and steals for him, and is an object of torment for the male witch. The morally dubious activities conventionally associated with invisibility are here linked with the Fetch, although it is not the ghost but the one commanding her that is ultimately responsible for the immoral deeds. Thus the real monster behind the created monster is a spiteful male.

As with the monster in Mary Shelley's (1831) *Frankenstein*, here the readers are invited to sympathize with the Gothic monster that is, in both cases, a middle-class male creation. Whether or not the torment has been partially sexual in nature is not stated in the text — it is obvious, however, that the respectable middle-class family has had to keep both the murder of the pauper girl and her ghost a secret. The murder itself is reflective not only of gender relations but of class relations: an ignorant pauper girl whom nobody misses is a dispensable person from the Devil's perspective. Against this background, Becca's claims for a married, sexual life that she should have had seem just. As a Fetch she has grown stronger and out of fear of her Devil Turner has had to give her one of his sons and, after his death, another. The pauper girl Becca's "revenge" is associated with her sexuality.

Moreover, Becca's desire and sexuality reflect her agency. In Creed's formulation, the "monstrous feminine" that is associated with the female body and female sexuality is threatening but also "challenges the notion that femininity, by definition, constitutes passivity."[57] At points Becca seems to be merely an essence of jealousy and dangerous desire — not only does her cold body touch and consume Jonathan but her attacks leave visible scars on him. However, through events that are focalized through her, Becca's motifs and character become more complex. She is strong and powerful; although she has been created to be a passive slave she is now able to control the Turners through fear, and Jonathan, in particular, partly through her gaze that is supernaturally enhanced. The novel opens with a small passage that is focalized through Becca where she is looking at "the warm ones" in their beds and focusing on "the little one, in the cradle."[58] The passage builds a contrast between Becca and the living ones and reflects her future desire for the baby who will eventually become her next lover. Becca's gaze is perceived as threatening by Sophie, who wakes up and takes the baby into her arms when she sees Becca standing beside his cradle watching him. Sophie is terrified because the ghost is "after the babby!" and she explicitly states that she "don't like it *looking at* the babby."[59] Sophie knows that the ghost has attached itself to Jonathan and controls him — here she associates the ghost's gaze with possible control and threat.

Becca's gaze is not restricted to a normal kind of looking, as at points she seems to exist in several places at once and observe different things happening almost at the same time. She can see in the dark, observe people in another room and look back in time and observe events that have taken place earlier when she has not been present. She is thus able to monitor Jonathan's actions almost perfectly, "catching him up in space and time,"[60] and seems to embody the idea of the panopticon: the ever-present gaze and the threat of punishment associated with it. Jonathan is wary of Becca even when she is not present, knowing that her supernatural gaze can reach him quickly wherever he is — he is a victim of both Becca's jealousy and the resulting supernatural domestic violence.

The love — and the control linked with it — that Becca offers is threatening from the living people's point of view, yet she herself views it as a form of utter devotion. Becca's love changes from nurturing and motherly kind of love into sexual desire; she attaches herself to the boys when they are still babies and stays with them until their premature death under the age of thirty. Jonathan has accepted and welcomed her love, first when he has still been a child in the form of nurturing, and later, after getting used to Becca's coldness and learning that she cannot do him any lasting harm, he has allowed Becca to be his wife. It is implied in Jonathan's thoughts that if she was not a supernatural wife, but a living one, he might be happy — Becca's desire may only be dangerous because she has been turned into an undead girl by a spiteful male witch. Jonathan loves her, and when his life is threatened, it is Becca whom he calls for help. He is miserable, however, because he knows that he will die young and can never have a living wife, and because Becca does not grow any older but seems to stay at the age she was murdered and is, in Jonathan's view, "hen-brained, and petty and jealous and childish."[61] The passages focalized through Becca do, to certain amount, reflect this: she is often angry, jealous, and childishly pleased when she manages to frighten people. She is thus a supernatural being also in terms of her aging. However, the eternal life is a punishment rather than an empowering factor, in particular because she seems to be made of negative features associated with adolescent girls.

However, the brief passages focalized through Becca and her dialogues with Jonathan reveal that her jealousy and obsession result from her unfortunate state. Becca is angry at Rattle not only because she is jealous of Jonathan but because Rattle is alive, unlike Becca. Becca consumes Jonathan, but she also needs him to escape her loneliness, because as a living dead she is separated from the living people. While Jonathan is a means of survival for her, she seems to care about him. At the end when Jonathan's spirit has been ousted from his body by the Dudleigh Devil, Becca recognizes Jonathan's invisible spirit because although it is Jonathan's body that gives her "warmth and strength," "it was the spirit she loved." Becca mistakenly believes that if she kills Jonathan's body, his spirit will remain with her and she would no longer be alone but could turn Jonathan into a fellow vampire by teaching him "how to draw strength and warmth" from living bodies, after which "he could be with her forever."[62] This romantic but desperate idea is not realized because Jonathan is sucked back into his living body when it dies. Moreover, the romanticized idea of two vampires living together happily ever after is undermined because Becca forgets Jonathan as soon as he has died and goes to Sophie's baby for another body to consume.

The text is firmly rooted in the Gothic conventions, although rewriting some aspects of them. Yet, the text does not only focus on the invisible female or her supernatural gaze as an indicator of her control and power, nor does it focus on her fate and relationship with the victimized Jonathan. Becca's gaze is paralleled in the gaze of the collier girl, Rattle, who also desires Jonathan. If the classic Gothic roles are reversed in the case of Jonathan and Becca, in the portrayal of the working-class Rattle, the class usually absent from the classic Gothic novel is represented in sympathetic terms. In contrast to Becca, the monstrous, invisible female, Rattle seems not only less threatening but also more flexible in her gendered roles and behaviors. Rattle, as her name might indicate, shakes the notions of conventional (middle-class) femininity, also in relation to gaze and sexuality. Rattle has been working in the coal pit since early childhood and at fifteen, she is a collier who has pride in her occupation and who likes to cross-dress. Rattle behaves like a stereotypical working-class male: she works hard, smokes, curses all the time and is rude. In relation to the female Gothic where sexuality is ever-present but repressed or decently controlled, Rattle is an unconventional character who openly shows her desire and for whom sexuality is not a source of anxiety, but of humor and play — albeit that the middle-class males do not perceive her sexuality in positive terms.

The passages focalized through Becca do not involve any detailed description of how she sees Jonathan's appearance — she watches his scars and observes his reactions but does not comment on his looks otherwise — but it is precisely Jonathan's good looks that attract Rattle's attention throughout the novel. The extended descriptions of Jonathan's appearance and figure subjected to Rattle's gaze clearly reflect her desire. She is not ashamed of her tastes nor her sexuality, both of which reflect her class-status. As with Charlotte in *Ghostgirl*, Rattle's appreciation of the different parts of the male body shows in the extended lists of items — "slim legs," "a small, tight waist," "a small round bum," "lovely face"[63] — that all together make a beautiful whole.

Unlike Charlotte, Rattle is not confined in any way by modesty; when her stalking activities are noticed by Jonathan, she directly offers a "snug" to him. While usually cross-dressing, Rattle is ready to show off her breasts if she is mistaken for a boy and is also prepared to dress up in a pretty dress for a date, since this is a part of her game for chasing men. All of this reflects her straightforward attitudes towards her own body, her gender play (cross-dressing) and sexuality. Rattle also tries to save Jonathan from the ghost-girl, although she fails and almost ends up dead herself. Rattle does not see Becca as a real competitor but as a ghost that has to be laid to set Jonathan free from his supernatural pursuer. Furthermore, whereas Becca is serious in her anger, Rattle considers the laying of the ghost as a game, as her thought "Come on, Madam, Madam Ghost. I'll give thee best"[64] indicates. This playfulness is very much her attitude towards sexuality, desire and attraction as well; it is a game or play where one has to do whatever it takes to attract the desired party but which one should never take too seriously.

Moreover, the views of Rattle's behavior as indecent are challenged in the text. When the Dudleigh Devil, Warley, thinks of Rattle in less flattering terms, his views are framed as suspicious and spiteful because he is represented as a violent character. Warley's views of the "ignorant" Rattle as "a tough and dirty little slut ... smelling of tobacco and sweat"[65] seem to reflect the same spite that is associated with the Devil who has made Becca — they also reflect the class differences. Towards the end of the novel, when Warley has possessed Jonathan's body and feels sexual arousal in the closeness of Rattle, his reaction is anger and an attempt to kill Rattle. Instead of agreeing to kiss "this dirty animal," Warley thinks he "would sooner strangle it."[66]

Warley's reaction is reflective of conventional violent male behavior towards sexually confident females — because he cannot control his desire, he attacks the object of that desire. The conflict here is also class-based: a working-class girl's relaxed attitudes towards sexuality are condemned by a middle-class male. Disturbingly, Warley seems to gain pleasure from violence and murder — as the typical Gothic male villain would. Warley's spite, violent pleasures, and misogynist discourse that associates Rattle and all working-class girls with animals are introduced to make the feminist (or humanist) implied reader to align strongly with the victims of violence — Rattle and Becca. Although readers might find it more difficult to sympathize with the violent, supernatural Becca than with Rattle, the text invites them to sympathize with Becca's fear and anguish that is caused by her murderer and the other Devil that resembles him.

According to ghost story conventions, Becca should disappear after her horrible fate has been brought into daylight, but she is not a conventional ghost — she is unstoppable, a spirit whose existence is based on desire. In this sense, female sexuality is not punished at the end — Becca cannot die and has to find another young male to consume; at the last scene she befriends Sophie's and Harry's baby. The Gothic circumstances are going to prevail in the house of Turner for yet another generation. However, it is perhaps even more significant that Rattle survives. Although it seems that Rattle's desire for Jonathan almost gets her killed when she approaches him at the end without knowing that Warley has taken over Jonathan's body, eventually Rattle escapes death and, in that sense, punishment because Becca kills Jonathan and Warley's spirit inside him. Although female sexuality is perceived as dangerous from the middle-class male perspective, it is the males who are destroyed at the end. Yet it is not the invisible female who is celebrated in the text (she is a victim and remains as a kind of monster at the end) but, particularly in contrast to the female monster, the living, working-class girl.

In terms of female gaze and sexuality the novel is not particularly radical at its time of publication in 1999 — as Moore suggests, sexualized images of males became commonplace in popular culture in the 1980s and thus the idea of women looking at males was hardly a new one in the following decade.[67] On the other hand, the female gaze on a male body still seems exceptional and potentially transgressive in the novels from the 21st century discussed above. In *A Certain Slant of Light* and *Ghostgirl*, females cannot openly gaze at males but have to do it while invisible. As regards *The Ghost Wife*, I would claim that the connections between female sexuality and class make the novel more radical than it first seems. By introducing the desiring working-class females, Becca and Rattle, as the survivors, and by representing the latter's sexuality in positive if somewhat provocative terms, the text challenges discourses of female sexuality and class. Becca and Rattle are the main contrasting pair of characters, the first fantastic or supernatural and the latter a girl depicted in realist terms: the contrast between the monstrous female and the living one also contributes to the subversion of conventional gendered discourses in the text.

Although reflecting and challenging conventional gendered discourses of the female Gothic, Price's novel is a commentary on contemporary rather than historical gendered discourses — the associations between class, gender and sexuality invoked in the novel are in circulation in contemporary British society. As Valerie Walkerdine, Helen Lucey and June Melody state in their ethnographic study on girlhood in contemporary Britain, "Class is a central parameter of the regulation of the sexuality and fecundity of young women in Britain today."[68] This is reflected particularly in British media discourses of working-class young female sexuality and misbehavior in relation to "ladettes." As Carolyn Jackson and Penny Tinkler suggest, these media discourses that have been in circulation in the British media since mid–1990s bear a striking resemblance to earlier discourses of young troublesome femininities.[69] Popular discourses that concern sexuality of working-class girls are usually not positive, even less celebratory — in contrast to these the representation of Rattle in *The Ghost Wife* seems subversive.

Gaze and Power

The novels discussed in this chapter involve complex representations of gaze in relation to gender and subjectivity, but each novel employs a different strategy to represent gaze. Invisibility and visibility in relation to female characters and femininity are shown to be ambiguous categories that are context-dependent — neither of them is exclusively associated with power, or powerlessness. All these texts juxtapose different discourses of (in)visibility, gaze, and sexuality; in this sense they are multivoiced in their representation of gendered and sexualized subjectivity. In novels that involve several character-focalizers, which allows readers to view the events from each of the protagonists' perspectives in turn, conventional gendered discourses are juxtaposed with radical ones, such as notions of invisibility as liberating and the working-class female perspective on sexuality, and gaze is linked to the subjective agency of the focalizing female characters. It is less obvious whether the gazing itself makes the protagonists empowered. Rather, the processes of gazing in the novels illustrate effectively that power is a relation, negotiated interpersonally, and not a position that can be gained — particularly because participating in human relations means that one becomes both the subject and the object of gaze.

5

Crossing Borders: Queer Aging

THIS CHAPTER EXAMINES characters that depart from conventional life trajectories due to their abnormal aging patterns, be it accelerated, arrested or reversed aging. Whereas some forms of age-shifting can be recurring and reversible, the focus here is on one-way transformations; thus I will here use the term magic aging in relation to the supernatural or abnormal forms of bodily change (or, in some cases, non-change) that occur in the texts discussed. In earlier chapters I have discussed age-shifting as a way of juxtaposing two or three differently aged bodies and identities and thus highlighting the social expectations that are related to being young, adult and old. Here characters are not shifting among differently aged identities but have to adapt to uncommon aging patterns that permanently change the ways in which they can foresee their lives and both present and future identities. The conventional social expectations associated with gendered and aged bodies are put into new frames by introducing characters who, for instance, skip over childhood, live for three hundred years, or age in a reverse direction. The characters discussed here go through various forms of queer aging in the sense that when they no longer age and grow old according to natural patterns, they are either free or forced to depart from the normative assumptions concerning mainstream human lives.

After briefly introducing queer theorizations about growing up and aging, the first half of the chapter discusses the shape-shifting figure of the shaman in Price's *Ghost World* novels and in Pullman's *His Dark Materials* trilogy and investigates how the shamanic ability to cross boundaries of worlds and different ages is connected with representation of gender and conceptualizations of queer temporalities and identities. The novels will be discussed in relation to representation of shamans in Nordic mythology and anthropological accounts. Magic aging symbolizes the exceptional ability of the shaman to cross borders and escape the limits of the material body, as well as the social expectations associated with gendered and aged bodies. I will argue that the shamanic ability to cross boundaries in several different ways and their liminal position outside ordinary people's organizations of time and space can be fruitfully interpreted from the perspective of queer theory because the symbolic character of the shaman allows the novels to challenge conventional ideas and discourses of gender.

The second half of the chapter will analyze the reversed aging of characters in Margaret Haddix's *Turnabout* (2000) and Gabrielle Zevin's *Elsewhere* (2005). In these novels characters are growing younger — either due to a medical injection or in their life after death — and have to adapt to going through earlier phases of their lives again. The queerness of the reversed aging patterns challenges heteronormative views because the characters are unable to envision their futures in relation to conventional views about growing up and growing old, including finding a job, getting married and having children.

Queer Temporalities and Marginal Identities

Judith Halberstam's recent work on transgender people offers useful theoretical concepts that can also be applied outside transgender contexts. Halberstam discusses transgenderism as a liminal identity but also draws attention to how transgendered bodies gain different meanings in relation to identity categories such as age, class, or ethnicity, and in different settings (e.g. urban, multicultural cities vs. rural, homogenous communities). While Halberstam's main focus is on transgender people, she also addresses various other ways of doing nonnormative identities and proposes the concept of "queer temporalities" to examine these. In Halberstam's framework, "queer" refers to "nonnormative logics and organizations of community, sexual identity, embodiment, and activity in space and time" while "'Queer time' is a term for those specific models of temporality that emerge within postmodernity once one leaves the temporal frames of bourgeois reproduction and family, longevity, risk/safety, and inheritance."[1] Halberstam associates "queer" with sexual identity but also with other issues — she lists, among others, homeless people as persons occupying queer time and space. In this framework, queer life trajectories challenge notions of normality and normativity in terms of gender and sexuality, but also in terms of age and social class.

Halberstam's notions about normativity in relation to growing up, aging, and maturing are of particular interest here. According to Halberstam, "queer temporalities" offer ways to rethink what is meant by maturity, a concept that is commonly tied to normative uses of time and normative life trajectories in conventional Western discourses of youth and adulthood where "youth" or "adolescence" is the unstable period preceding "adulthood" where persons settle on more stable identities.[2] Maturity is often measured according to certain gendered milestones — a typical (middle-class) life trajectory in Western world would involve landmarks such as completing education, finding a job and starting a family by around thirty as indications of achieving an adult status (in terms of maturity that is defined socially and culturally). All of these milestones belong to what Halberstam describes as "the temporal frames of bourgeois reproduction and family, longevity, risk/safety, and inheritance" all associated with notions of respectability and normality.

Individuals who do not follow the normative, middle-class life trajectories are often not only interpreted as deviant but also immature and irresponsible. In her study of constructions of adolescence in the genres of fantastic realism, Waller also summarizes the tendencies in developmental theories to interpret adolescence in terms of the concepts of transition and liminality that locate adolescence as an in-between phase between childhood and adulthood — a phase that one must, normally, develop out of. Waller argues that in teenage fantastic realism these ideas are reflected in fictional teenagers who are represented either as successes or failures in terms of the normal developmental patterns and thus "protagonists who do not succeed in completing a developmental task are represented as existing outside of usual adolescent discourses."[3] The way out of instable adolescence is understood as a development towards a stable, responsible, mature identity and way of living.

As characters who live outside ordinary people's organization of time and space, the magically aging girls and women in the novels discussed below fit into Halberstam's notions of queer. The shamans in Pullman's and Price's novels exist outside of usual discourses of adolescence — not least because they live in parallel universe that does not resemble modern urban settings — but, they still challenge normative ideas of development because for them liminality is the key marker of their subjectivity throughout their lives, not merely as adolescents. The women or girls who age in the reverse direction are different from shamans in that they do not — in the novels discussed below — blur any borders between conventional masculinity and femininity. Instead, they challenge the normative patterns of women's "normal" life trajectories. Since they are moving away from old age and adulthood, they have to plan their lives in new ways, which often means abandoning such quotidian dreams as getting a driver's license, a job, or a family. However, while being positioned in a queer time and place, these characters do not necessarily subvert discourses of normal, good lives — on the contrary, their exceptionality may only highlight what is conventionally viewed as a desirable way of living one's life.

Shamans, Liminality and Border Crossing

Two aspects of shamanism are particularly relevant from the perspective of feminist and queer theory: the position of the shamans as cultural others and the shamanic ability to cross and blend boundaries. As regards cultural otherness, Liza Potvin suggests that "primitive" religions such as shamanism appeal to feminists "because they are largely ritualistic, non-hierarchical structures of faith which are both democratic (having no seminars, but on oral transmission of power through mentoring) and populist. Their potency also appeals to women because they represent 'forbidden' or subversive beliefs which are opposed to officially sanctioned religions; they are invoked because of their nonconformity."[4]

For Potvin, shamanism is a non-hierarchical, democratic structure of faith — these aspects can make it empowering for women. In this respect, the appeal of shamanism is similar to the appeal of the radical-feminist myth of the witch. The key issue is Potvin's second point on nonconformity — after all, the witchcraft/shamanism represented in Pullman's and Price's novels is not simply empowering, nor are the women's communities completely non-hierarchical. The issue of nonconformity is of importance in the novels that do not thematically focus on female coming of age but on the use and abuse of power. Issues of maturation and empowerment are addressed, but any witch/shaman character's psychological growth is not tied within the main plot.

Earlier readings of Price's *The Ghost Drum* reflect a humanist understanding of maturation and coming of age: a process during which an individual finds her identity and agency and reaches an empowered position of an adult.[5] I will argue that although the process of becoming a shaman partly fits in this pattern, the novels also challenge normative discourses of gender and age because the shamans do not conform to ordinary people's norms. Even though the magic aging is a folktale element, it reflects Mircea Eliade's notion of shamans as "superhumans" or, in Joseph Campbell's view, as persons who because of their abilities "in a profound sense ... [stand] against the group."[6]

I view the nonconformity associated with shamanism as a critique of gender as a category rather than as a critique of femininity only. Introducing female shamans as such is not a radical form of rewriting in relation to the anthropological accounts of shamanism, although the influential studies by Eliade and Campbell treat female shamans as additional to the traditions.[7] Later studies, including those by Joan Halifax (1980) and Barbara Tedlock (2005), discuss female shamans at length — yet Tedlock suggests that the common notion of the majority of shamans as males prevails and that "the importance — no the primacy — of women in shamanic traditions has been obscured and denied."[8] Without attempting to decide on the primacy of any gender in actual shamanic traditions, it is important to note that in the Nordic mythology that Pullman's and Price's novels draw on, shamanism was perceived as a female practice.[9] Although the rewriting of earlier conventions in heroic fantasy includes the introduction of female characters in the conventional male position of the hero, in shamanic traditions the powerful positions have not only been a male preserve. In terms of rethinking gender, the more radical aspects of the portrayal of female shamans have to do with their nonconformity: their position as outsiders and their ability to cross boundaries.

As an example of both otherness and border crossing, in anthropological accounts of shamanism the transgender shaman occurs frequently. While Eliade mentions "androgynization," feminization or transvestism in relation to certain shamanic traditions, others suggest that the phenomenon has not been restricted to any local shamanic tradition.[10] In more recent reviews, Tedlock writes about the widespread phenomena of shamanic "gender switching, bending, blending or reversing," and Sami Raninen refers to the concept of "third gender" that has existed among the shamanic cultures of Eurasia, North America and the Arctic.[11] While in Nordic myths both gender-blending and female magic were treated as suspicious,[12] in some anthropological accounts the gender-blending is interpreted in a more positive manner. In *Shamanic Voices*, a brief study on shamans' own narratives of their experiences, Halifax writes that "assuming the role of the opposite sex gives the shaman the opportunity to recognize and understand the condition of femaleness or maleness and ultimately to become total."[13]

The idea of androgynous completeness of a human being is very much present in the early writings of second-wave feminism, such as Carolyn G. Heilbrun's (1964) thesis of androgyny as the ideal solution to gender polarization: males or females portray the conventional characteristics of the opposite gender and are thus liberated "from the confines of the appropriate."[14] A similar idea in relation to female heroes in literature is pursued by Carol Pearson and Katherine Pope, who discuss the hero's journey in a Jungian framework and suggest the journey is "a quest for wholeness and selfhood" which is completed, among other things, by reaching "accommodation with the best qualities associated with men and with women."[15] Potentially, then, androgynous shamans can challenge and transcend the boundaries of the binary gender system by performing the opposite sex, including sexuality. Whether the transgenderism makes them more complete human beings is, however, debatable.

From a queer theoretical perspective the key issue of androgyny or transgenderism is not related to an ideal view of a complete human being — transgenderism is not a "total" experience but a way to challenge normative gendered behavior and allow a pluralistic notion of gendered identities. Combining both feminine and masculine qualities but yet not being clearly either androgyny offers a kind of liminal subjectivity that challenges both conventional masculinity as well as femininity. This is what Flanagan suggests in relation to cross-dressing heroines in children's fiction. She maintains that a shift from the humanist notion of agency to Judith Butler's poststructuralist view of agency as "located in actions that disrupt and vary the normally reiterative nature of gender performance" enables one to focus on the cross-dressing performance itself rather than its outcomes (at the closure the cross-dressing heroines usually abandon their masculine attire).[16] This makes it possible to view this type of stories as transgressive because the girls challenge the limits of both conventional femininity and conventional masculinity in their successful performances of another gender. Cross-dressing is a motif that is often associated with shamanism, although shamanism as such can also be viewed as a form a transgenderism.

As suggested in Chapter 1, offers of unnaturally long or immortal life are usually refused in stories for children because the (child) protagonists must learn to accept change. Although the necessity and inevitability of change is also a central motif in Pullman's and Price's novels, the witches and shamans do acquire inhuman, or superhuman, qualities through their magic aging, and their unnatural longevity is not perceived as something undesirable, although it might seem suspicious to common people. While longevity is desired in the normative discourses that Halberstam discusses, I argue that the supernatural longevity of shamans is a way to challenge notions of normative life trajectories. The witches and shamans in Pullman's and Price's novels certainly seem to occupy queer time and space: they live for hundreds of years, have their own knowledge system and community, and they have deviant child rearing practices. Thus the witches and shamans are represented as others to ordinary people—not only because of their magic skills and longevity but also because they are represented as ethnically and culturally different from the urban people in the novels. The witches are situated in the Northern wilderness and associated with Sámi mythology; Pullman's novels involve "Lapland" witches while Price's shamans are "Lappish."[17] In terms of ethnicity, the otherness of the witch-shamans is problematic and difficult to interpret as symbolic of deviant identities, but shamanism and the character of the shaman remain appealing from feminist and queer perspectives.

In Price's novels queer time and space are also reflected in the shamanic ability to cross and blend boundaries between worlds and identities. The shaman-characters there are associated with various types of border-crossing: they can move between material and spirit worlds when they spirit-travel or dream, transform into animals and move into different bodies, and blend gender and age. Magic aging parallels the other features associated with the shamans: it sets them apart from ordinary people as (magic) others, but also enables them to cross and blend boundaries of identities. Their liminality, or their position in queer time and space, is what enables a challenge to normative identities and normative behaviors. In the following, I will discuss the magic aging of the witches and shamans in relation to both radical-feminist and queer discourses.

The Enchantresses of the Margins

The Northern witches in Pullman's *His Dark Materials* trilogy are not explicitly associated with shamanism, but their communities share several features with the communities of witch-shamans in Price's novels. The skills of the witches and shamans are also similar, including herbalism, spells that are sung, and spirit-traveling (in Pullman's novels the fact that the witches can send their daimons far away functions as a form of spirit-traveling). Each trilogy depicts witches/shamans living in matriarchal, democratic witch communities consisting of good, wise women. The difference to Nordic myths, as well as to real-life shamanic traditions, is that instead of being exceptional members of regular human communities, the witches here have separate, matriarchal communities of their own. Moreover, in Pullman's novels in particular it seems that the witches have moved into Lapland straight from the English-language traditions, where the witch often occurs in the form of a beautiful female enchantress; apart from the names of the witches and the references to Yambe-Akka, there are no references to Nordic myths.[18]

The witches certainly challenge common patterns of aging and organizing their family lives, in a way that strongly resembles radical-feminist visions of separatist communities of women. In Pullman's trilogy witchcraft is matrilineally inherited — witches have children with common men, and while female children are born as witches, male children do not inherit any magic abilities and are sent to live among common people. The witch clans have their own democratic government (a kind of witch parliament) and they do not use money or gather property but mutually help each other. What is more, the witch clans are said to have a special relationship to and knowledge about nature; this aspect, however, also involves representing the democratic, matriarchal witch societies as more primitive than the urban cultures in the novels.[19] In Pullman's novels, there is a rather familiar hierarchy between the civilized, urban Western Europeans and the more primitive people living in tundras and forests, including the witches. The witches' literacy, for instance, is associated with reading signs in nature: they can, for example, "track any animal, catch any fish, find the rarest berries" and "read the signs in the pine marten's entrails, or decipher the wisdom in the scales of a perch, or interpret the warnings in the crocus-pollen."[20] At another point Ruta Skadi's eating habits are represented as savage and uncivilized: "She ate like an animal, tearing at the remains of the roasted birds, and cramming handfuls of bread into her mouth, washing it down with deep gulps from the stream."[21] The witches are Others — or noble savages — who can be appreciated but who remain significantly different from the British main characters in the novels.

Apart from their knowledge system and societal structure, the abnormal, inherited aging pattern of the witches also sets them apart from common people. Significantly, the challenges of supernatural aging are mainly addressed in regard to sexuality and reproduction. Despite living in an all-female community, the witches are represented as strictly heterosexual. In their depiction of the witches' appearance, Pullman's novels circulate the stereotype of the beautiful sorceress: the witches are attractive women who stay young for several hundred years. The way in which they are depicted has strong associations with (hetero)sexuality. For instance, the first time Lyra meets Serafina Pekkala, she is amazed and can understand why a mortal man could love her, a woman who is "young ... and fair, with bright green eyes; and clad like all the witches in strips of black silk, but wearing no furs, no hood or mittens."[22] Amazingly to Lyra, Serafina does not seem to feel cold and thus can wear only strips of black silk in the middle of the winter — while it is later explained to readers that this is because she can sense things better with less clothes on, it is obvious that her clothing contributes to her image as a sexually attractive woman. Another witch queen, the Latvian Ruta Skadi, is also depicted as "vivid and passionate, with large black eyes ... beautiful, proud and pitiless,"[23] and during the same introductory depiction readers also learn whose lover this conventional femme fatale has been. Curiously, this happens from another witch's, Serafina's perspective; this suggests that witches also judge each other by their appearances, lovers and power.

Readers only learn to know a few witches by name in the novels and in almost every case they also learn whose lover the witch has or has not been; their heterosexuality is thus a key defining feature. Although it is stated that the witches live several hundreds of years, it is unclear whether they maintain their youthful appearance until the end; old-looking witches do not appear in the novels at all. Even when readers encounter a large group of fighting witches, they are all "young and ferocious, dressed in rags of black silk and riding pine-branches through the sky."[24] In terms of the witches' appearance, there are no signs of shamanic cross-dressing or gender blending here, unless one wants to interpret Serafina's daimon Kaisa as a gender-blender, since the goose is a "he" with a typical Finnish/Swedish female name.

Their heterosexuality is also what causes the witches pain, due to their peculiar aging pattern. Having a relationship with a witch that lives for hundreds of years is also challenging for a mortal man, as Lyra understands when he compares Farder Coram, a mortal man, and Serafina, who were once lovers: "Lyra could see why Farder Coram loved her, and why it was breaking his heart.... He was growing old; he was an old broken man; and she would be young for generations."[25] The sense of loss is, however, even worse for the ancient witches who witness the deaths of several loved ones during their lives, as Serafina explains to Lyra:

> Men pass in front of our eyes like butterflies, creatures of a brief season. We love them; they are brave, proud, beautiful, clever; and they die almost at once. They die so soon that our hearts are continually racked with pain. We bear their children, who are witches if they are female, human if not; and then in the blink of an eye they are gone, felled, slain, lost. Our sons, too. When a little boy is growing, he thinks he is immortal. His mother knows he isn't. Each time becomes more painful, until finally your heart is broken. Perhaps that is when Yambe-Akka comes for you.[26]

In another instance Serafina tells one of her witches to forget a man that she has loved, because "love makes us suffer."[27] It is men, then, that make witches suffer, both as lovers or husbands and as sons. Due to their magic aging, the witches are significantly and inherently different from human men and this is not something that they can change. Their embodied subjectivity prevents the witches from following conventional, heteronormative life trajectories where a woman and a man fall in love, start a family and stay a lifetime together, watching their children grow. Apparently the witches still have a strong desire for this kind of life since, instead of creating alternative, happy patterns of organization of sexuality and family life, they engage in relationships with human men even though they are fully aware that this results in suffering. What is more, the suffering only worsens in time; in Serafina's description the witches are presented as very emotional beings who, in the end, collapse under all the pain and suffering, rather than develop a thick skin to deal with the deaths that they witness during their lifetime spanning hundreds of years. Their magic aging is thus a curse as much as it is a source of power; longevity does not make the witches happy in the long run because it prevents them from taking part in conventional, heteronormative organizations of family life.

The Northern witches are here portrayed as women living in a strictly separatist society where biological sex completely determines which gender and culture a child will grow into. The witches live in a queer, or, should I say, radical-feminist time — as a female-only community they depart from the normal ways of organizing lives in the urban societies in the novels — yet they are depicted as conventionally feminine characters who go around charming mortal men. In contrast to this, in Price's novels the representations of the shamans — who, among other things, wear warm reindeer hide clothes instead of dressing up in straps of black silk — challenge conventional discourses of gender and age in a more profound way.

The Shaman's Path: Transforming into Superhuman

In Price's novels, magic aging is partly represented through figurative language, particularly metaphor, and it symbolizes the exceptional ability of the shaman to cross borders and escape the limits of material body as well as the social expectations associated with gendered and aged bodies. There are three types of magic changes in age in the novels: accelerated aging, prolonged aging, and a complete stop in aging, or, arrested aging. The first two are bodily changes whereas the last one is magic in the sense that it stops the natural process of aging altogether, thus what is embodied is non-change.[28]

In each of Price's novels the shaman grandmothers have adopted the girl protagonists to train them. The (foster) grandmothers as mentors who teach their granddaughters the secrets of magic echo the radical-feminist discourse of witchcraft as matrilineally inherited. The representation of the witch girls and their shaman grandmothers follows radical-feminist conventions: they all are sympathetic outsiders whose way of life offers an alternative to the totalitarian Russian czardom in the storyworld — the czardom representing any kind of totalitarian regime. Each grandmother, Baba Yaga, is a reworking of the ogre or the witch in Russian fairy tales. In Price's novels, Baba Yaga is actually replaced by a whole group of witches and shamans that live in huts on animal legs, and not all of them are grandmothers. In relation to the fairy tale tradition, Chingis and Shingebiss might also be regarded as rewritings of Baba Yaga not only because they are young but because they are witches who grow and age, or develop; the stock characters are turned into representations of more complex persons with histories.

To start with accelerated aging, *The Ghost Drum* includes a peculiar account of Chingis's childhood and early youth: her foster grandmother's song. The singing event can be interpreted metaphorically in two ways: the singing itself is an extended metaphor for nurturing, and Chingis's dreaming during the song serves as a metaphor for crossing borders, both in terms of identity and knowledge. Both nurturing and crossing borders are issues that are linked to radical-feminist and queer discourses in the novel. Chingis ages from a newborn child to a twenty-year-old apprentice in a year, during which the old shaman sings a song of life to her. The narrator explains that this is because "a witch has no time to waste in rearing babies," which seems to highlight the shaman grandmother's role as a tutor rather than a mother. Several years of nurturing are condensed in the old shaman's song of growth and development that lasts for a year: "Verse by verse the song went on: long verses; a long song. But at the end of the year, when the song was finished, there was no toddler lying wrapped in blankets on the witch's stove, but a young woman of twenty years, sleeping and dreaming."[29]

During the song Chingis transforms magically. She grows physically but also learns all the necessary skills that a child acquires during her development. There are two aspects of the song that have significant bearing on this version of female maturation: first, the power relations between the singer and the object of transformation and, second, the ability of a witch to develop both physically and mentally through a song. Power relations are central when the song is read as an extended metaphor for nurturing while the second aspect, the ability to develop magically, is linked to the metaphor of dreaming. While the emphasis on nurturing reflects the radical-feminist discourse of witches and female tradition, the dreaming can be interpreted as a symbolic representation of queer time and space.

As a nurturing metaphor, the song reflects the radical-feminist project of revising the conventional character of the fairy-tale witch as well as a radical-feminist discourse of the importance of motherhood. The singing of the song involves the same everydayness of feminine magic as the spells discussed in Chapter 2. The matter-of-fact description of the grandmother's daily routines and the growth of the child that she cannot ignore while singing puts the magic song in an everyday, domestic context. It is indicated that even though Chingis's development is an accelerated process, it requires an enormous effort from the grandmother to sing her foster daughter into womanhood.

Despite the notion that "a witch has no time to waste in rearing babies," the grandmother devotes herself completely to the task of (magic) mothering for a full year — a period of time not comparable to real-world child rearing practices but significant in relation to the pretexts of the novel: Russian wonder tales and accounts of real-world shamanic traditions. The Russian wonder tale formula that is expanded in the song is the description of magic aging of a hero who grows "not by days [or years] but by hours"— the grandmother certainly invests more time in rearing Chingis than the unnamed magic powers in the wonder tales. The grandmother's role as a nurturer is also different from the role of shaman-tutors in real-world traditions where their task begins only after the adolescent shaman-to-be has received the ecstatic or mystic initiation provided by spirits.[30] Chingis cannot be turned magically older with a swish of a wand but has to be sung carefully into young adulthood. Apart from her self-naming act — after Chingis wakes up she tells her name to the grandmother — Chingis seems to be her grandmother's creation. Yet, the song cannot include everything because the grandmother is not in a complete control of Chingis's experiences; Chingis's spirit goes traveling independently in different worlds.

Furthermore, the relationship between the two is based on mutual dependency. Chingis needs her foster-grandmother for her nurturing and training, whereas the old shaman must pass her knowledge to a new female candidate. The grandmother herself suggests that their relationship is different from ordinary (or biological) mother-daughter relationships: "'Mothers and daughters are strangers to each other,' she told Chingis, 'but you are my witch-daughter. You were my hard work, and are now my precious reward.'"[31] It is indicated here that the relationship between the tutor and the neophyte is closer than the familial relationship — the hard work binds the two together, because they are working towards the same aim. Female co-operation and interdependency are also emphasized later on when Chingis leaves the Ghost World with the help of her grandmother and two other women because she is not powerful enough to go back to the world of the living and to move her dead body on her own. However, although the text reflects the radical-feminist discourse of witches and female tradition, the hierarchical and normative aspects of the tradition are challenged by Chingis herself.

Although it seems that first-hand, embodied experiences are not emphasized in the song, Chingis has these experiences when she is sleeping and dreaming and, reflective of her shamanic features, spirit-traveling during the song. The experiences that the shamans have when they dream are real, and dreaming thus serves as a metaphor for crossing boundaries and acquiring experience and knowledge. Dreaming, or spirit-traveling, is central to Chingis's development — it is an ability that sets her apart from ordinary people but which has also enabled her to go wandering on her own in spirit-worlds during the song and thus escape the grandmother's control. Indeed, in relation to the dreaming, Chingis's magic aging seems to replace the shamanistic mystic initiation or vocation realized in initiatory sickness or dreams that precedes the traditional training of shamans in most cultures and, as the mystic initiation, sets the future-shaman apart from common people.[32] In terms of queer temporalities, Chingis's peculiar childhood is shown to be non-normative; her experiences are rather different from those of an ordinary child.

While the song in itself is already a queer representation of childhood, it can be also considered a part of the play with gender that has preceded and follows the song. The play with gendered representations begins at the very beginning of the novel when the old shaman comes to fetch Chingis from her biological parents. The grandmother is first represented as a figure that conventionally would be interpreted as a male and then an ancient woman who remains androgynous, made so by her age; she has a wrinkled face and a thin beard, and she is almost bald. Shingebiss's ancient shaman grandmother is represented in similar terms. The old foster-mothers of Chingis and Shingebiss are transgender, or queer figures that represent the shamanic tradition of blending gender. The play with gender continues after the aging song.

Chingis herself is a gendered human being; she grows from a baby girl into a woman of twenty. When she wakes up her body is female but the essential assumption that this leads to conventionally feminine behavior is immediately challenged. She eats and drinks for three whole days without stopping. Moreover, when she first speaks, she names herself, or perhaps remembers her "true" name as "Chingis," a male name.[33] Apart from her name, Chingis plays the conventional folktale hero's role in the narrative, even though she in several ways departs from the conventional hero's journey. The female who wakes up after the song is an extraordinary human being, able to cross boundaries by spirit-traveling, but also by challenging conventional gendered behaviors. Whether she is a male spirit in a female body or a female spirit in a female body with a male name is ambiguous — in any case she symbolically blends the boundaries of gender. The abilities to cross boundaries and blend gender and age are linked to the prolonged aging of the shamans.

Both Chingis and Shingebiss are promised three hundred years of life by their foster grandmothers after they visit the Ghost World and become shamans. Even though the shamans are not immortal, their longevity sets them apart from ordinary human beings. It is important that the prolonged aging is not an innate quality but a reward — it is achieved after the witch-girls have completed their training and confronted death during their visit to the Ghost World. Thus the empowered identity of the magic outsider is the result of personal effort. Age, as an amount of time, is necessary to gain experience that can increase one's power, but age does not automatically guarantee experience — prolonged age is a resource (amount of time) rather than power in itself.

In terms of queer theory, prolonged aging can be seen as a queer temporality — it challenges normative life trajectories and conventional, gendered notions of maturity. The shamans in the *Ghost World* novels are positioned outside these trajectories. Magic aging is a way to omit borders and, as such, a parallel phenomenon to the gender blending of the shamans. Neither of the girls gets to live her three hundred years of life in the stories, yet the idea is intriguing. Because of their longevity they seem to be regarded as girls even after they have reached the age where females are usually called women rather than girls[34] — or, each witch-shaman can be seen as a powerful, wise woman in a young person's body. Whereas Chingis challenges the boundaries between girlhood and womanhood, Shingebiss is a character that is ambiguous both in terms of age and gender.

Descriptions of female maturation in literature often focus on a certain moment — or a series of events — that can be regarded as signifying a coming of age, or a passage from youth to adulthood. *The Ghost Drum* involves several such moments: the moment when Chingis wakes after her grandmother's magic song as a woman of twenty, or when Chingis gains the status of a shaman, or when she adopts an apprentice of her own, or, possibly, when she returns from death after her dismemberment and (symbolic) rebirth.[35] It is not particularly relevant to try to pinpoint the exact moment of Chingis's coming of age or maturation: because the text emphasizes maturation as a process of gaining experience, there is no end to this process. I maintain that the ambiguity about positions of power and borderlines between different ages is not an issue to be solved but a textual strategy to challenge the fixed nature of identity tied to a particular social position.

Apart from the magic song, Chingis's training resembles the shaman's initiation and training process that is described in Eliade's study; briefly, this training consists of both ecstatic and traditional guidance, the first provided by spirits and the latter by an older shaman. After the song, in the biological sense, Chingis is a woman rather than a girl, but despite her swift sleep through childhood and youth, Chingis is not a mature, self-reliant shaman, and in that sense, adult when she wakes up. This interpretation obviously depends on how "adulthood" and "maturity" are defined; the novels themselves challenge fixed notions of maturity because the life of a shaman is a path of constant learning which continues in their next life as well. Moreover, their shape-shifting is not associated with youth, the period of instability and metamorphoses, but is an important part of their subjectivity throughout their lives.

As a witch's apprentice, the biologically adult Chingis is described as completely inexperienced, and she has to learn all the skills from the beginning before she can be declared a shaman. This is a challenging and long process, described in a summary by the cat narrator: "In a minute I can say: Chingis learned all the magics so well that the old witch declared her an apprentice no longer, but a witch.... In a minute I can say all this, but it took Chingis years to accomplish."[36] Here, again, the narrator uses the wonder tale formula to highlight the difficulty of the learning process by emphasizing the difference between telling about a process and actually completing it. It is Chingis' own efforts that are highlighted here — she is not completely the grandmother's "hard work" but reaches the empowering position of a shaman through years of dedicated study. At this point it certainly seems that she has reached adulthood, she is biologically grown-up and a fully trained, independent shaman.

However, when she goes to free Safa from the tower, the imprisoned prince thinks he is dreaming and sees "a sharp-faced girl with black hair and black eyes."[37] "A girl" seems to refer to Chingis's appearance rather than her experience; she is a wise woman in a young body. This is the point where counting Chingis's age makes no more sense because, as a shaman, she continues to age magically. What does count, however, is experience — each witch-shaman grows not by years, but by experience. Kuzma manages to kill Chingis because she is still a young shaman. However, it is also significant that it is Chingis's unconventional thinking, and not her fixedness in traditions, that enables her to come back from death and take revenge on Kuzma. Her inexperience may thus be an advantage — she is able to depart from traditions and think of new ways of action. Although a fully trained shaman, Chingis refuses to follow the expected path of a shaman — she subverts even the shamanic traditions by adopting Safa, an apprentice of the opposite sex. Curiously, Chingis's ambiguous age makes it possible to interpret the tutor and the apprentice either as lovers or as a parent/guardian and a child. Because Chingis is more feminine than androgynous — her femaleness is never in question, even though she wears the shaman's androgynous clothes — and, moreover, because she is young, it seems possible to interpret the relationship as a romantic one. This interpretation makes sense in the conventional fairy-tale framework in which the young rescuer marries the young rescued of the opposite gender.

Nevertheless, the unbalanced power relationship between the fully-trained shaman, whose knowledge of the world is immense, and her apprentice, who has spent his whole life in a tower and has an extremely restricted knowledge of the world, makes the depiction of the romantic relationship a rather curious one. This may, perhaps, be read as an ironic reversal of the fairy tale roles — a completely helpless prince whom an experienced, wise girl/woman rescues and then adopts (not marries). Furthermore, this interpretation requires the appropriation of normative heterosexuality or what Butler (1999) refers to as the "heterosexual matrix" because at no point does the text itself plainly indicate that there is a romantic or sexual relationship between the two.[38] Indeed, the shamans in general are represented as asexual; they live alone and do not reproduce but adopt children — in this they represent queer life trajectories, as opposed to the normative heterosexual life trajectory which is organized in terms of coupling and reproduction. It might also be possible to read the relationship between Chingis and her foster-grandmother as a sexual one. This, of course, would make no sense in the conventional framework of romance (and would be taboo not only because of being a same-sex relationship but in terms of sexuality of an old woman, the age difference and the foster-parent–child relationship), but would make more sense in relation to accounts of shamanic tradition which records same-sex relationships among shamans.[39] Since there are no explicit indications of any such relationship between Chingis and her grandmother in the text, I doubt that any reader unaware of the queerness of shamanic traditions would see their relationship as a sexual one.

While the relationship between Chingis and Safa may be interpreted as based on romantic love, the unbalanced power relations between the two also seem to point towards a parent-child relationship. Although biologically mature, Safa is mentally at the level of an inexperienced child after growing up in a prison room in a tower. As an apprentice, Safa proves to be unteachable, but Chingis never loses her patience: she is a tutor who learns from her adopted apprentice's behavior. Chingis, the girl, is here more like a mother, a wise woman — and this makes perfect sense in terms of her magic aging. She does not proceed from one role to another, but may occupy several roles at the same time. Chingis fits in the radical-feminist wise witch schema, yet the radical-feminist discourse is challenged because the matrilinearity is broken, which happens whether Chingis is interpreted as a lover or a foster-mother. The novel thus suggests that an exceptionally powerful person may move beyond gendered boundaries and traditions, also beyond female traditions.

In terms of maturation, *Ghost Dance* is not unquestionably a female quest for empowerment — it is unclear whether Shingebiss proceeds from a powerless position to a more powerful one. She does not manage to save the whole of the Northlands and at the end remains in the Ghost World in her falcon form. On the other hand, she does become a shaman, kills all her adversaries and restores a piece of the Northlands in the land of the dead. Is she, then, empowered or disempowered and, moreover, an adult or mature at this point? While one can certainly pose these questions, I do not think that it is possible to answer them, in particular because the novel deliberately questions notions of individual agency and power. Instead of any maturation pattern, I will focus on Shingebiss's blending of age and gender. Even though she also belongs to the female tradition of witches, she is, more obviously than Chingis, a queer character who does not fit into other people's categorizations. Whereas Chingis's magic transformation appears at the beginning of the narrative and her prolonged aging begins soon after that when she is declared a shaman, Shingebiss's magic changes in age occur at the end of *Ghost Dance*. Her transformation into an immortal being in the Ghost World is, I will argue, a kind of culmination of her representation as an ageless, transgender character that starts right at the beginning of the novel when she is first introduced.

Like Chingis, Shingebiss is a witch-girl with a male name, and she is represented as a threat to a great (male) ruler.[40] Shingebiss's transgendered appearance is addressed explicitly already in the first scene of the novel where Lappish hunters see her dropping from the sky and shape-shifting from a gyrfalcon to a human form: "The stranger came closer and, in the light reflected from the snow, they could see the face of one of their own people. But it could have been the face of a pretty boy or a handsome girl."[41] Whereas the hunters seem to easily recognize Shingebiss's ethnicity, they cannot decide on her gender. The use of gendered adjectives — that is, breaking of the common collocation of the words "pretty" plus "girl" and "handsome" plus "boy"— is particularly interesting because they emphasize her transgender qualities: she could be a feminine boy or a masculine girl. While gender is highlighted in the passage, it is worth noting that Shingebiss's transgenderism is not the only feature that puzzles and disturbs the hunters — they also recognize that she is not an ordinary human being because she is dressed too lightly for the freezing weather. The hunters fear that the stranger might be a "forest ghost" or an "ice-devil"[42]— like Chingis, Shingebiss is a magic other to the ordinary people.

For a while, Shingebiss's gender remains a mystery to readers as well until her grandmother refers to Shingebiss as her daughter. When Shingebiss leaves for the czar's palace, she is no longer interpreted by other characters as an ambiguous figure, but as a boy, because she is cross-dressing, or wearing the typical shaman clothing — yet because readers know she is actually a girl, she remains a transgender character. It is never revealed what Shingebiss herself thinks about her cross-dressing and gender blending, because the passages that are focalized through her do not involve any thoughts on her own identity. It is clear, however, that her gender-blending is emphasized from the reader's point of view.

The ultimate form of portraying a male identity occurs at the end when Shingebiss apparently changes her sex when she becomes the First Shaman, Loki — although this is uncertain, because in Nordic mythology Loki himself is a god that can change his sex.[43] Furthermore, this transformation also involves a change from a human into a giant otter, thus it is even more ambiguous what happens to her in terms of gender — she is referred to as a combination, "Loki-Shingebiss." Whether or not she changes her sex at this stage is not, however, important, because symbolically she crosses the borders of gender (and age as well, Loki is an immortal god). As a transgender character Shingebiss challenges the fixed, conventional notions of femininity and masculinity — she is not a "perfect," androgynous human being but an example that it is possible to blend the boundaries, or move along the gender continuum.

Like Chingis, Shingebiss challenges the female tradition by disobeying her grandmother. Both girls refuse to follow the norms even inside the marginal shaman community. While Chingis challenges the matrilinear tradition by adopting a male, possibly of romantic interest, in *Ghost Dance* there is no indication of Shingebiss's sexuality at all. Shingebiss's challenge to the tradition is, perhaps, more profound because she wants to save not merely an imprisoned prince but the whole of Northlands, and she initially refuses to become a shaman because in her grandmother's view shamanism involves disinterest in the events in the material world. Because Shingebiss is a youngster, it would be easy to associate her rebelliousness with adolescence, particularly because her views are juxtaposed with the old grandmother's views. Yet, her rebelliousness is not represented as something she should grow out of. Instead, in the case of the grandmother, it seems to be a sign of passivity rather than wisdom to grow out of the desire to have an impact on the world and society, particularly because the passivity she represents is dangerous in the framework of anti-colonialist and environmentalist discourses operating in the novel. While it may be impossible to stop change, it does not mean that all kinds of change should be accepted — nor is it necessarily a sign of maturity to accept change, or non-change, for that matter.

In the final chapters of *Ghost Dance*, Shingebiss remains in the Ghost World and ceases to age. This is a transformation in the sense that her normal aging process is stopped and, effectively, she turns from a mortal human being into an immortal one — both in body and spirit — as long as she stays in the Ghost World. This happens for the first time after Loki-Shingebiss has restored the peace of the Northlands in the Ghost World. After accomplishing her task, Shingebiss is tired and falls asleep for a long time and stops aging: "Shingebiss might have slept through twenty, or fifty, seedings, and still not have been one moment older when she woke."[44] This kind of non-change is, of course, a typical motif in stories about mortal humans' visits to fairylands or similar supernatural places or worlds — in the other reality, time stands still and the mortal visitor does not age.

Although time stands still in the Ghost World, this does not prevent all kinds of change — the forest goes on growing and flowering whereas Shingebiss stops aging completely. In a sense, she has been transformed from an unnaturally aging mortal human being into a being that does not age at all. While it is plausible to expect that her aging process would start again if she returned to the real world, she only does this for a moment before she returns to the Ghost World and remains there as a gyrfalcon who "has almost forgotten that it was once a mortal baby, and then a shaman's apprentice and a shaman, and a Czar's black angel."[45] The closure is a circular one — Shingebiss returns to the form of gyrfalcon that was her appearance when she was first introduced in the narrative. As at the beginning, where the hunters are not quite certain what they are looking at, at the end it is not completely clear what is left of the human girl Shingebiss inside the gyrfalcon. She is ageless — not dead, because as a shaman she is still, supposedly, able to leave the Ghost World if she wants to, she has not (yet) completely forgotten her earlier identities. The gyrfalcon is also genderless in the sense that its gender is not marked.

Chingis also blends boundaries of gender and humanity when she acquires a posthumous — or a posthuman — form as she returns from death and enters her own dead body with the help of other female spirits. The group of female spirits in a dead body manage to kill Kuzma and then enter his dead body (apart from the foster-grandmother's spirit who returns to the Ghost World to guard Kuzma's spirit). The body of Kuzma, moved by the female spirits, goes to save Safa from the Czaritsa Margaretta whom he/they eat in his/their bear form. The image of three female spirits in one dead male body seems to blend gender — as well as the boundaries of individual subjectivity — but the gender-blending is questionable, because Kuzma's body functions as a dress for the spirits and there is no indication that wearing his body would affect the spirits of Chingis or her two companions. While Shingebiss becomes Loki both in body and in spirit, what is emphasized here is the female cooperation.

The ending of *The Ghost Drum* is hopeful; Chingis and her helpers are reborn, and Chingis, her foster-grandmother and Safa are once again adopted by a shaman. In contrast, *Ghost Dance* does not offer a promise of a new beginning: Shingebiss remains in her animal form as a gyrfalcon in the Ghost World and she will — as far as the cat knows — remain in the land of the dead for ever after. Moreover, the piece of the Northlands that she manages to save for eternity only exists in the Ghost World where it always stays the same — in the real Northlands the new czar and his associates go on exploiting the land in the similar manner as the previous ones. From a liberal-humanist perspective, this is a dystopian ending: Shingebiss has ceased to exist in a human form. She also fails as a traditional hero because although she restores justice, she does not restore harmony or peace and thus departs from the Campbellian heroic pattern.

The ending is not exactly celebratory from a radical-feminist or queer perspective either. Shingebiss ends up in the land of dead and cannot think of ways to exist in the world of living. However, by the closure, the discourses of colonialism and environmentalism are emphasized and the gendered discourses become less significant. Furthermore, unlike Chingis, who manages to overcome death by relying on female cooperation, Shingebiss has been acting alone and fails in her task, or succeeds only partially. The novel can be read as a criticism of the liberal-humanist belief in an individual's agency; an individual cannot save the world alone. While this makes sense in the light of radical-feminist theories of female community and intersubjectivity, it also reflects the criticism of early environmentalist movements that, according to Kevin Michael DeLuca, "revolve around the achievements of heroic individuals who fight against corporate industrialism and save wilderness."[46] Shingebiss's failure can be interpreted as a criticism of society: it is not the individual who should change but the society, here characterized by colonialism, greed and abuse.

Because change is perceived as necessary in the novels, there is no stable, empowered position where one could stay at the end. Both novels involve criticism of individual heroism and the hero's linear quest that leads to empowerment, and, instead, reflect radical-feminist emphasis on the role of (female) community. Each novel addresses the limits of individual agency: *The Ghost Drum* shows how remarkable results can be achieved through female cooperation while *Ghost Dance* demonstrates how a hero who acts alone fails in her task. Although Chingis and Shingebiss restore justice, they do not restore harmony or peace, because the new rulers that replace the previous ones are also cruel—the dystopian sense of the impossibility of restoring peace and stability is a breach in the Campbellian heroic narrative pattern. Change is all that matters, there is no happily ever after because nothing can stay the same forever. Yet, this is what includes the promise of hope—even death is not the end for the shamans and, in rebirth, they once again challenge the normative, linear life trajectories.

Reversed Aging: Regaining and Losing Agency

As suggested in Chapter 1, rejuvenation and immortality are usually treated as suspicious in literature for young audiences. The following examples suggest, however, that when rejuvenation, or, more specifically, reversed aging, is not combined with physical immortality, it can become an efficient narrative strategy to challenge normative views of normal life trajectories. While each of the following texts does invoke the idea immortality—in *Turnabout* the scientific experiment is aimed to introduce immortality together with rejuvenation, but this fails, and in *Elsewhere* people are immortal in the sense that they are reborn after growing young in the afterlife—the focus is on the challenges of envisioning a future where one eventually turns into a child again. Both examples demonstrate how the old fantastic tropes of rejuvenation and immortality continue to have relevance in contemporary children's literature speculating about what forms human life and death can take.

Escaping Old Age: The Queerness of Living Backwards

Margaret Peterson Haddix's *Turnabout* (2000) tells about two women who participate in a scientific project aptly called "Turnabout" where a group of old people have been subjected to a treatment that restarts the renewal process of cells and thus makes their bodies "unage." Amelia and Anny Beth are both over a hundred years old when the process starts but most of the narrative deals with their experiences as teenagers for the second time in their lives. The story shifts between the start of the project and the end of it; shifting between the viewpoints of Amelia in two differently aged bodies (her lived number of years is, of course, adding up; when her body reaches sixteen, Amelia is actually 184 years old).

The project has not been a great success for most of the participants, many of them have disappeared, committed suicide or died when they have taken the second injection that was supposed to stop the unaging process at a selected point. Since the second injection does not work and also because all the unaging people have been isolated from their families and relatives to secure the secrecy of the project, most of them do not find the process of unaging into childhood appealing. Moreover, the subjects gradually lose their memories from their earlier lives, which is why Amelia and Anny Beth keep diaries where they record all the significant events from their earlier lives as long as they can remember it. Amelia and Anny Beth are the only ones who have reached adolescence — at the beginning of the book Amelia is sixteen and Anny Beth eighteen — and thus face new challenges, as they know that soon they will be no longer able or allowed to take care of themselves; a large part of the narrative consists of their search for surrogate parents.

The portrayal of very old women in teenage bodies allows the text to highlight several expectations that are associated with young and old subjects. While questioning discourses about what counts as normal behavior at a specific age, the text also emphasizes the effects of embodiment, since, in Amelia's view, she and Anny Beth are behaving more and more like young people as their bodies turn younger. However, the novel mostly focuses on the expectations that people have about their lives in general since the unaging process makes it impossible to follow a "normal" life trajectory. Despite their shared experience of unaging, Amelia and Anny Beth are represented as two women with completely different attitudes towards and emotions about their second lives.

Amelia, the main focalizer in the novel, constantly misses things from her earlier, normal life that she remembers as a good one. The novel opens up with a section from Amelia's diary, written on her sixteenth birthday when she feels sad about growing younger:

> My sixteenth birthday. Sad, sad day. What I mind most — what I've been dreading most — is losing my license.... My body feels good. Healthy. Teeming with life and possibility. I remember this feeling from the last time. I had such hope for the future then.
>
> It's not the same when my body feels hopeful and my mind knows that the

future is only sixteen more years of loss.[47]

The bodily sense of rejuvenation does not console Amelia, who views her second life as consisting of "years of loss." The remaining number of her years is fixed and will consist of gradually losing her agency and independence; a vision that saddens her particularly because she later understands that she has already experienced the loss of agency and memory once already: "She'd never realized how much being young and being old were alike."[48] The beginning of the process of unaging has been empowering for Amelia, who has enjoyed the regained ability to see, hear and move without assistance but, in the long run, she finds losing her memories of her earlier life almost unbearable and the process of growing younger painful, since she is not able to be the same person as in her previous life. She also does not find herself the type of woman who would wholly enjoy getting her youthful looks back: "She had never lied about her age, never fought the advances of gray hair or crow's-feet or the march of time. She thought birthdays meant something: an additional year of life and, hopefully, wisdom gained."[49] In a teenager's body she knows very well that whatever wisdom she may have gained, adults unaware of her real age are unlikely to pay any attention, since adulthood is — by law — defined by a number and not by gained experience; a sixteen-year-old who does not reveal her life history is treated as an immature child.

Apart from the sense of losing her agency and being treated as someone who she feels she is not, Amelia has not found it easy to imagine a new way of life during her years of growing younger. Amelia has maintained a fairly conventional view of what a normal woman's life should be like. Her earlier life as a married mother of six children who has spent most of her time taking care of others has been a happy one and since the possibility of setting up a new family with children is not an option when one ages backwards, Amelia has had a hard time coming up with new meanings for her existence. To keep her unaging a secret in her new life, she has changed names, identities and jobs (all of them in women-dominated fields, including teaching at preschool and nursing). In her queer backwards life she is no longer certain of what she is, which is in contrast to her more stable identity in her earlier life: "I've had so many identities in my lifetime I hardly remember them all. The first time around I was always pretty much the same person. I just got older."[50] Even though she later recognizes that even in her "dead ordinary" earlier life she has had many identities, "daughter, sister, wife, mother, grandmother, great-grandmother," all of which, of course, fit in a conventional pattern of a woman's life, these are in sharp contrast to Amelia's new life where "she'd been a virtual change artist."[51] At sixteen for the second time in her existence, Amelia has no idea what her next identity will be. For Amelia, her queer life of living backwards is characterized by anxiety and sadness because it does not make sense in regard to the norms of a good life that she knows from before. However, at the very end, Amelia shifts her views.

In contrast to the sad Amelia, Anny Beth is perfectly content with their choice of not trying the second injection and views the rest of their unaging years optimistically, reminding Amelia that she has a new life waiting for her. Curiously, it has been Amelia who has suggested that they leave the agency managing the project Turnabout and live their lives surrounded by normal people, even if this means plenty of challenges; yet it is Anny Beth who is thankful to Amelia for this decision and has no regrets about it. Anny Beth's previous life has consisted of a childhood characterized by her stepfather's violence and three unhappy marriages. Unlike Amelia, she is not nostalgic about her old life at all. In her new life she has studied new occupations, got a Ph.D. in psychology and even been married for a short while, before faking her death to avoid revealing her peculiar aging pattern to her husband. Anny Beth has also had less trouble with changing her social identities.

After turning teenagers again, both women find reading psychology books about adolescence hilarious because they or anyone else that they know have never behaved as described in the books and they make fun of the conventional assumptions. Anny Beth treats the stereotypes as a great possibility to play with her identity: "Imitations are my specialty.... You should see my teenager impression."[52] It is Amelia, however, who tells Anny Beth that there is no difference between what is imitation and what is real when Anny Beth is worried about confusing the two — identity is thus viewed as profoundly based on performance. Moreover, there is no difference between the two because every single moment — whether part of a conscious performance or not — is part of one's life narrative and thus becomes a part of one's personal identity.

For both women their personal identity narratives matter even more in their new life — while they have not kept diaries in their earlier lives, both of them do so now. When they escape once again to avoid being put into a childcare institution, their diaries are among the few things that they take with them. When explaining to Amelia why she has also kept her diaries, Anny Beth states, "Under this stunning physique, I'm just a sentimental old lady."[53] Yet it is clear that keeping the diaries is not only about sentimentality but about remembering who one has been and is. The talk about changing identities in the novel thus refers to changing one's social identities, rather than forgetting one's past life trajectory. What makes one a unique human being is one's life narrative, which is here more important than the normative or non-normative social roles and identity positions that one adopts and abandons during life.

The importance of life narratives is highlighted at the end, when the text again focuses on Amelia's sense of purposelessness; after finding someone to care for them as they grow into babies, she feels that she is now ready to prepare for death again. She needs a clear purpose in life — unlike Anny Beth, whose prospect for the rest of her life is to have more fun. Their new caretaker suggests that they do still have a purpose in life, which is to tell their stories to the public so that scientists and society can make a more enlightened decision about whether to offer the unaging treatment to everyone. This is still presented as a possibility, even though the scientists at the agency have concluded that humans are not made for longevity, even if Amelia and Anny Beth seem to be exceptions since they have survived for so long. Indeed, what makes the ending ambiguous is that Amelia explains the scientists that — despite her mourning for her earlier life — she has in her second life wanted to "prove I could meet the challenge" since in her first life she has "just done what people told me to do, been who they expected me to be."[54] The ending is ambiguous, since while Amelia embraces the new purpose that gives meaning to her life, the "clear path ahead of her" is only clear "until the next bend in the road."[55] Change is thus presented as necessary and preplanning one's life as impossible; yet it is clear that accepting change is not easy as long as one also holds specific ideals about what a good life consists of. Moreover, by portraying two characters, one of whom has enjoyed a conventional life and another one who is perfectly content with the abnormal life of unaging, the novel shows that there is not single ideal life trajectory for everyone.

The Circle of Life: Getting Younger After Death

In Gabrielle Zevin's *Elsewhere*, the almost sixteen-year-old Liz dies in a traffic accident and ends up in Elsewhere, a place that closely resembles Earth with its modern, urban setting but that is inhabited by dead people growing young. The concept of death is relative here, however. As one nurse in Elsewhere puts it, "It's all life, isn't it," pointing out the fact that as long as one remembers one's past life and continues to exist in a bodily form, even though this happens in a parallel world where one grows younger, "death" is only another phase in one's life.[56] The process of reversed aging goes on until one turns into a baby and is put into a river that carries the baby back to Earth to be reborn again as a new person, since babies have lost their memories of their earlier lives. As in *Turnabout*, the process of aging backwards challenges conventional assumptions about what it means to grow up and age, and, moreover, what is the meaning of one's life.

Most of the novel is focalized through Liz, and the whole novel is written in the present tense, which emphasizes the immediateness of Liz's new form of existence where she has no idea of what to expect from the future, even though she knows the exact number of years that she has left in her backwards life. At the beginning, Liz does not remember her death and does not accept it even after remembering; during her first months in Elsewhere she spends her time mostly using the magic binoculars to watch people back on Earth. Since the process of reversed aging does not involve losing one's memories until the very end when one becomes a toddler and a baby, people continue to gain new experiences and their identity narratives get longer, even though their bodies get younger. Potentially life in Elsewhere could thus offer Liz a chance to go on living and gaining new experiences but, at the beginning, she refuses to grasp this chance.

Liz's refusal to accept her new form of existence is clearly connected with her disappointment in the fact that she will never live a "normal," good life as she views it. When her grandmother, Betty (who has aged back to thirty-five during her time in Elsewhere), tries to console Liz after her arrival, Liz explodes in a rant that contains many of the conventional markers of adulthood that are no longer in her reach: "I'll never go to college or get married or get big boobs or live on my own or fall in love or get my driver's license or anything! I can't believe this!"[57] A bit later she also feels that everything that she has done on Earth to reach these aims has been in vain: "On Earth, Liz was constantly occupied with studying and finding a college and a career and all those other things that the adults in her life deemed terribly important. Since she had died, everything she was doing on Earth had seemed entirely meaningless."[58] Here Liz's thoughts reveal also where her ideas for a good, normal life come from: these are ideas deemed important by adults. All of these ideas are, in nutshell, what Halberstam describes as the normative, middle-class life trajectories; a trajectory that has been in Liz's reach due to her family background as well as intelligence, or good grades in school.

Like Amelia in *Turnabout*, Liz mourns for her earlier, happy life that has been without major obstacles and does not want to accept her new form of existence in a queer time where none of her earlier life plans no longer make sense. Moreover, similarly to Anny Beth in *Turnabout*, those characters in *Elsewhere* who have had difficult lives before are quicker to accept their new form of existence and explore the possibilities it offers, rather than mourning for their earlier lives. With her fixed ideas about a normal, good life, Liz has, at first, difficulties understanding why others are happy to focus on their present lives, doing things that they have not done before and trying new "avocations" that they do for pleasure, not for money, or deciding that after plenty of romance and excitement in their previous lives, they are now happy to spend their time fishing or walking their dogs in a park. She simply cannot envision any meaningful way of living that does not follow the normal life trajectory as she understands it. However, after mourning over her death and past life for a few months while witnessing the happiness of others in Elsewhere, Liz realizes her death has not been the end, but actually a start of a learning process — or, perhaps, an unlearning process, as Liz has to abandon her earlier views of what good life consists of to be happy in Elsewhere. While all her life plans do not work out, Liz does, in fact, get a driver's license, a job and also falls in love, which leads to both happiness and disappointment.

After one year in Elsewhere Liz is offered the opportunity to use the "Sneaker Clause" that allows someone who has died very young to go back to Earth before unaging back to zero. Liz plans to use the clause because has just been disappointed in love and wants to be reborn. Significantly, Liz decides in the last moment to go back to Elsewhere, not only because there are people that she loves but also because she does not want to let go of her identity as Liz — when the babies reach Earth, they will have lost their memory and thus will grow into completely new persons.

Since Liz still remembers her past and knows who she is, she is curious to find out who she will become since she still has years left: "If I interrupt this life, I will never know how my life was supposed to turn out. A life is a good story, Liz realizes, even a crazy, backward life like hers.... This backward life was her forward life when she really thought about it."[59] As in *Turnabout*, here the emphasis is on one's personal identity that is based on one's life story — it is this story that provides one with a sense of meaning, rather than one's social roles, even, or, perhaps, especially in circumstances where one is unable to live one's life as she has planned it. Since life is a good story, Liz wants it to go on. In the end, the process of reversed aging will make it easy to let go of one's old identity and be completely reborn since people start to lose their memories when they become toddlers, thus already before floating away in the river.

Towards the end of the novel, when Liz is four and has just unlearned her ability to read, Liz'z friend reads passages from Babbitt's *Tuck Everlasting* to her. The juxtaposition of Babbitt's book where the Tuck family remains eternally the same and the girl who is growing younger highlights the main theme of each novel, which is the acceptance of life as a process of continual change. At the end, when Liz the baby is traveling back to Earth, she thinks that "there is no difference in quality between a life lived forward and a life lived backward."[60] In both forms of lives one needs to learn to accept change to be able to be happy. Moreover, in both forms of lives one progresses towards a loss of agency in the end, due to the aging or reversed aging that finally turns one's material body weak and makes one dependent on others. There is a difference in the way Liz's two lives have been represented, however, and that is in the queerness of living in the present tense that Liz has only discovered in her afterlife, where she has learned how to focus on being content without planning the future and, yet, always anticipating change. For Liz, her afterlife has hardly been what she has earlier considered a "normal" life, yet she finds that it has been a good life. While the text is not particularly queer in terms of gender and sexuality, it is queer in terms of age; the present tense of the novel is a queer time where one can be free from conventional assumptions regarding aged identity and normal life trajectories and, thus, happy.

Blurring Age Boundaries and Learning

The novels discussed in this chapter portray female characters that symbolically challenge normative notions of life trajectories — these novels clearly illustrate the potential of the fantastic as an allegorical or metaphorical mode. Although the shamans in Pullman's and Price's novels do not overturn the gendered structure in the ordinary people's world — they are located outside modern, urban societies — they do provide alternative models of how to do gender differently.[61] Similarly, the characters who age in the reverse direction in Haddix's and Zevin's novels do not change the ordinary societies around them but live in a queer time that challenges normal patterns of life — a challenge that is, of course, directed at readers rather than all the "normal" people in the fictional societies. In terms of age, the texts blur the boundaries between childhood, adulthood and old age and emphasize life-long learning instead of age-tags.

While the idea of maturation as a continuous and never-ending process is hardly a revolutionary notion — most contemporary educational and developmental theories emphasize the significance of life-long learning — it is significant that in any of these novels there is no longer a particular moment of coming of age.

Conclusion

THE MAIN AIM OF THIS STUDY has been to analyze the textual and narrative representations of fantastic bodily transformations — invisibility and age-shifting — in contemporary children's and young adult fantasy novels and examine the ways in which the fictional transformations are connected with representations of girlhood and womanhood. In terms of gender, the transforming female characters have been discussed both in relation to conventional discourses of gender in earlier fantasy, fairy tales and myths, as well as in relation to non-fictional feminist discourses of gender. The starting point was to investigate the transformation types as intertextual devices that point towards earlier stories and representations of invisibility and magic aging, but also towards contemporary feminist discourses of cultural invisibility, aging and gender. By comparing the transforming characters in the studied novels to earlier invisible and magically aging fictional females and to the types of young women featuring in non-fictional gendered discourses — including nice, empowered, transgendered, invisible, and sexually transgressive girls — the purpose has been to examine whether the transformations can function as textual means to address, rewrite and rethink conventional gendered discourses.

The invisible girls and age-shifting young women in the examined works are complex characters that invoke various gendered discourses circulating both in and outside children's fantasy fiction. In most of the books examined in this study, the transforming girls and young women are not simply replications of conventional invisible or age-shifting characters, but, instead, the transformations — whether used as motifs or tropes — are explicitly employed to address issues of gendered identity and subjectivity and experiences of embodiment. Invisibility can be associated with either power or powerlessness and is tied to problematics of gendered visibility, while magic changes in age can be restrictive curses, or ways to perform and play with various gendered identities at different ages, or even a means to challenge normative gendered patterns of growing up. While exploring these possibilities, the novels point towards and comment on contemporary discourses of girlhood and young womanhood, often juxtaposing conventional discourses of passive, nice, obedient girls with feminist discourses of active, empowered, transgressive girls and young women. The analyzes show that the novels are not either thoroughly conventional or radically subversive but multivoiced: the novels involve a multiplicity of gendered discourses, some of them conventional, others varying from liberal-feminism to radical-feminism and queer critique. The implications are that in terms of gender, children's fantasy novels can be more complex than they are often interpreted as and that a third-wave feminist theory that views gender as a fluid category enables an intricate reading of gendered representations.

In regard to gender, there has been a great deal of discussion about whether children's fantasy as a genre is conventional or subversive — fantasy contains both imaginative, possibly subversive elements but is also based on traditional genres including folktale, romance and legend that involve various gendered conventions. This study suggests that fantasy is neither a thoroughly conventional nor radically subversive genre but involves a multiplicity of gendered discourses, some of them conventional, while others are feminist or subversive. The novels studied here are, in Bakhtin's terms, multivoiced or heteroglot: a single text can include different, even contradictory, voices and discourses — thus a text may rewrite some traditional elements while keeping others. While in Bakhtin's definition the multivoicedness is a feature of the modern novel as a genre, the multiplicity of discourses is particularly obvious in fantastic texts that explicitly rewrite generic conventions or retell earlier stories. Moreover, as suggested in the introduction, feminist rewritings are always "double-voiced" because they necessarily refer to conventions while reworking them. This does not mean, however, that feminist texts involve only two voices, or discourses — one conventional and conservative and one feminist and radical. Instead, a text may include traces from a variety of both conventional and feminist discourses. These various discourses have been addressed in the analyzes above, but I will here comment on some general tendencies.

In most of the studied novels the transformations have a central place in the protagonists' identity narratives and their processes of developing agentic subjectivity. Because the transforming young women are focalizers in the texts, the bodily transformations are a way to address differences between a young woman's own embodied sense of self and her positions in interpersonal networks where gendered subjectivity is negotiated in relation to others.

Several novels address the boundaries between different femininities, that is, explore different subject positions in discourses of femininity, rather than discourses of gender in general. In *Howl's Moving Castle*, for instance, Sophie's exclamation "How one's point of view does alter!"[1] is linked to a change in perspective inside discourses of femininity: she moves from one female position into another female position while the text addresses the connections between age and femininity.

Many of these novels focus on empowerment of the female protagonists and offer "happy endings" in regard to the protagonists' subjectivity and agency; the texts reflect a liberal-feminist discourse where "nice" or "invisible" girls must realize their powerless position and find ways to develop a (more mature) agentic female subjectivity. In novels that depict young women whose identities and subjectivities at the beginning are not fully realized, the endings that involve a sense of empowerment and realization of one's own identity narrative and subjectivity are important from a feminist perspective.

While some novels question the limitations set on certain femininities (such as a "nice girl," an "old crone"), other texts depict characters that blend gender and age on a more profound level. Some of the studied novels do not focus strictly on individual protagonists but are more concerned with groups of people and relations between the groups and individuals, particularly the relations between non-normative or exceptional individuals or groups and "normal" groups of people. The exceptional individuals in Price's Ghost World novels, for instance, are those who go through bodily transformations, all of them active shape-shifters who occupy liminal social positions by blending age, moving between visibility and invisibility, and cross-dressing. The novels also address the intersections between gender and other identity categories, not only age, but also ethnicity and class. These intersections make questions concerning empowerment and agency more difficult to answer. For instance, is it necessary to grow up and turn into a stable, respectable adult to gain agency and if so, can or should magically aging, transgender shamans ever reach respectable adulthood? Are shamans, immortal people or humans growing younger who choose to live outside society empowered? What about someone who is dead — can she even symbolically represent empowerment? Indeed, some of the texts reflect contemporary queer critique in the sense that they focus on questioning and challenging conventional and normative structures and, even at the close of the novels, do not offer a single, unambiguous solution to the questions they raise.

In terms of the findings in earlier research on fantastic realism and retellings for children cited in the introduction,[2] it seems that several of the studied novels reflect the general humanist tendencies: many of the texts can be characterized as liberal-feminist in the sense that they are based on a humanist understanding of agency, identity and empowerment. However, other novels are better characterized as radical-feminist and queer because they question the notion of agency and limits of gender. It may be that these differences are partly the result of different narrative strategies. In some of the novels examined here, the focus is on individual characters, and the novels build up an argument for the necessity of knowing one's identity narrative and becoming an agentic subject. In other texts the focus is on groups of girls or women, and they often question notions of individual agency and depict non-normative gendered identities. Yet powerful females feature in both types of works. One could argue that the novels discussed in this study are not comparable because they focus on different aspects of gender, yet I would claim that comparisons between these texts help to bring out exactly the point that gender means various things in different contexts.

The double-voicedness may be obvious in terms of feminist rewritings. However, any radical gendered discourses are, in fact, double-voiced because readers' ability to recognize something as gendered means that they are making associations with conventionally gendered aspects. That is, a character's radical behavior is only radical because readers are aware of the more conventional possibilities. Furthermore, what may seem radical in terms of earlier gendered discourses in children's literature is not necessarily radical in relation to gendered discourses circulating elsewhere, such as contemporary subcultures. The boundaries between radical and conventional are even more difficult to draw because empowered girls themselves have become a convention already — there are plenty of red-headed, clever young witches as well as brave cross-dressing girl heroes in children's fantasy. Yet, these conventions may not be familiar to everyone; even the most stereotypical cross-dressing, sword-heaving hero in drag may seem radical to a reader who has only encountered representations of femininity in popular discourses circulating in different media.

During the last decade, popular gendered discourses have often been reflecting "postfeminist" tendencies. Angela McRobbie, among others, is concerned about "the undoing or dismantling of feminism, not in favor of re-traditionalization ... but instead there is a process which says feminism is no longer needed, it is now common sense, and as such it is something that young women can do without."[3] What often follows is that whatever girls and women do is viewed as something based on their own choice because gender equality has been achieved — yet this is hardly the case. When it comes to fantasy fiction, the last decade has also witnessed the fame of *The Lord of the Rings* raise its peak after Peter Jackson's (2001–2003) film adaptation of the trilogy. The heroic (male) quest thus remains as popular as ever, alongside the conventional women's genre, romance, now increasingly popular also in its fantastic or paranormal forms — although, from women readers' and writers' perspective, romance narratives may be empowering and subversive even in their conventionality.[4]

If it was difficult for a gender-conscious author to introduce female heroes in fantasy in the 1980s and 1990s, the situation may not be less controversial today. Because both conventionalism and radicalism are relational issues, I am not promoting any specific rewriting strategy or feminist discourse as superior to any other — different strategies of rewriting are needed to challenge stereotypical or conventional discourses of gender in children's fantasy fiction. Because of these complexities, I am reluctant to put a single label on any of the books. Drawing distinctions between "conservative" and "feminist" texts is not enough.

In the course of the research it has become apparent that either one of the transformation types — invisibility or age-shifting — could have been examined more closely also in relation to other identity categories, such as ethnicity and social class that have not been systematically examined in this study. (In)visibility in particular is a category that could be employed in various ways in further studies, judging by recent developments in sociology, where the "basic" categories, including gender, class, and ethnicity are complemented by new analytical categories, such as visibility.[5] Moreover, this study has demonstrated that the concepts of empowerment and agency that are central to feminist theory remain problematic. The concept of empowerment is especially ambiguous, because it has been appropriated in contemporary marketing discourses. As Banet-Weiser notes, "Empowerment became the buzzword of the 1990s — not only in marginalized political communities, but squarely within mainstream commercial culture."[6]

McRobbie also maintains that female empowerment today seems to be mostly about consumerism; girls and women make their own choices and purchases to express, indulge, or recreate themselves.[7] In feminist criticism, a possible move might be to focus on agency instead of empowerment — agency is, in any case, a necessary concept to address issues of gender, power, and subjectivity. Recent discussions in related fields acknowledge the challenges with these concepts. For instance, in research on politics, Lois McNay has drafted new ways to understand agency and gendered subjectivity that move beyond both humanist approaches that involve an optimistic belief in an individual's agency and those poststructuralist/constructivist approaches where subjective agency is minimal because structures and discourses produce subjects.[8] Feminist theory and feminist children's literature criticism need to critically rethink the use of these concepts in future research — an ongoing project that will never be completed but must always be in progress.

Chapter Notes

Preface

1. Hopkinson (2002, 1).
2. On feminist criticism of science fiction and feminist science fiction, see Attebery (2002); Barr (2000); Donawerth (1997); Larbalestier (2002); Roberts (1993). On feminist fairy tale scholarship, see Bacchilega (1997); Haase (2004); Warner (1995); Zipes (1986). On studies on gender and Gothic fiction, see DeLamotte (1990); Ellis (1989); Halberstam (1995); Heiland (2004); Hoeveler (1998); and on gender and horror films, Berenstein (1996); Creed (1993); Williams (1996). I should note that my discussion here concerns the English-language contexts mainly in Britain and North America — the developments, theories, criticism and literature elsewhere and in other languages may be significantly different.
3. In her article on the separation of children's literature from serious adult forms in Britain at the turn of the twentieth century, Felicity Hughes (1990) offers a plausible explanation for this: writers who have wanted to write in the fantastic mode have had no other options than to write for children — or to realize that their fantastic writing is perceived as writing for children because of the widespread notion of fantasy as a particularly suitable genre for young readers. This is, Hughes (1990, 73) suggests, because the British theorizations of the novel as a genre by Henry James and others at the end of the nineteenth century maintained that to be a serious form of literature (rather than idle family entertainment for the bourgeoisie), the novel — which subsequently became the most important genre in adult mainstream literature — should incorporate challenging textual devices and objective realism and be aimed at an elite audience, that is, educated adult males. The result was that "fantasy was immediately déclassé ... as the antithesis of realism ... also the opposite of serious, i.e., trivial or frivolous" (Hughes 1990, 81–82) and, what is more, as such suitable for audiences whose intelligence was perceived as limited: women and children.
4. There are exceptions, however. Several works, for instance, consider feminist fantasy fiction or fantasy written by women writers. See Armitt (2000); Sellers (2001); Spivack (1987).
5. Clark (1999, 4). See also Clark (1993).
6. Clark (1999, 2–3); Paul (2005, 116).
7. Clark (1999, 5).
8. See, for instance, Clark (2002, 285); Marshall (2004, 256); Sunderland (2004, 60).
9. Brown and St. Clair (2002, 26).
10. Adler (1993, 114).
11. See Mack-Canty (2004, 158–159).
12. See Braithwaite (2002, 336); McRobbie (2009, 8).
13. See Abate (2008); Butler (2009); Flanagan (2008); Mallan (2010); Österlund (2005); Pennell (2002); Pugh (2008); Rabinowitz (2004); Stephens (2002); Wilkie-Stibbs (2002).

Introduction

1. See, for instance, Krasniewicz (2000, 43); Mikkonen (1997, 2).
2. For studies about older women and invisibility, see Bell (2012); Cruikshank (2003).
3. See Hunt (1990, 2); Reynolds (2007, 2); Stephens (1992, 3).
4. Reynolds (2007, 3). On conservatism see, for instance, Hunt (2001, 9). On radicalism, see Lurie (1990, x–xi); Warner (2005, 26).
5. See, for instance, Grant (2000, 21–27); Hunt and Lenz (2001; 21–22); Manlove (1999, 184–188).

6. Attebery (1992, 87).
7. Stephens and McCallum (1998, 201).
8. Cf. Cranny-Francis (1990, 205–206); Stephens (1996, 29); Talbot (1995, 155).
9. I am aware of the drawbacks of the term "postmodernism." Most importantly, postmodernist texts might not actually involve techniques that are truly *post* modernist; all the textual strategies listed above are not novel inventions. In fact, postmodernist aesthetics might be connected with the new poststructuralist or deconstructionist ways to read texts rather than any new narrative strategies. Brian McHale (1992, 6) suggests that contemporary critical theory "'helps' us to 'recognize' postmodern texts — it often seems that anything that is not a pure, linear, realist narrative with a clear beginning, middle and end can be titled as a 'postmodern' text"; among other texts, Homer's *Iliad* would meet this criteria. However, although there are differences in emphases and interpretations, the notion of what are postmodernist strategies is fairly established and I find postmodernism a convenient concept to refer to the group of textual strategies listed above.
10. Butler (1993, 182).
11. See Mills (1995).
12. Cf. Foucault (1979) and (2006) on "docile bodies." For feminist interpretations of Foucault's theories of body, see also Bordo (1990, 14).
13. Braidotti (2005, 26). Although Braidotti uses the terms "sex" and "sexual difference" for the reason that gender cannot be separated from notions of biological sex, I will use the terms gender and gender difference mainly because these terms are commonly used in Anglo-American feminist criticism. Both Butler and Braidotti note that gender and sex cannot be separated in the way that Anglo-American feminists traditionally have done (biological sex vs. social gender), although each emphasizes different aspects of the sex-gender continuum, Butler the discursive and Braidotti the material. Butler sees sex as an aspect of gender because of the socially imposed meanings on biological sex (that is, biological sex becomes gendered because the meanings that are attached to it are not natural but social), whereas Braidotti emphasizes the embodied sexual difference and maintains that gender is always based on and affected by biological sex.
14. Butler (1999, 199).
15. Butler (1999, 33).
16. Bal (1999, vii–viii).
17. Butler (1993, x).
18. Butler (1999, 32).
19. Braidotti (2005, 27).
20. Braidotti (2005, 21–22); Braidotti 1991.
21. Halberstam (2005, 5).
22. Cavarero (2000, 33–34).
23. Cavarero (2000, 39). As Susan J. Brison (1999, 41) points out, the notion of personal identity based on one's life story or narrative goes at least as far as John Locke.
24. Braidotti (2005, 7).
25. See, for instance, James and James (2004); Jenks (1996); Cruikshank (2003).
26. Cruikshank (2003, 173–174).
27. On "nice girls," see Fox (1977), Reay (2001, 158), Walkerdine (1990, 76), Walkerdine, Lucey and Melody (2001). Halberstam (1998) and (2005) discusses female masculinity and transgenderism. The discourse of "girl power" has been examined, among others, by Banet-Weiser (2004).
28. Mills (1996, 7).
29. Mills (1996, 17–18).
30. Foucault (1972, 49).
31. See Mills (1995, 2); Weedon (1997, 97). For a review of sociological and ethnographic studies that have addressed the strategies of resistance in relation to institutional discourses, see Smith (1990).
32. In narrative theory and narratology, "discourse" is often used in opposition to the term "story" or "plot" to refer to the manner the elements (events, characters, setting) are organized into a narrative text which consists of the actual words appearing on a page (see Herman 2004, 13; Stephens 1992, 11–12). I will refer to "discourse" in this sense as "text" or "narrative discourse."
33. Bakhtin (1981, 279).
34. Other scholars, such as Gérard Genette (1997), reserve the term "intertextuality" only for such cases where references to earlier texts can be clearly traced in the new texts as allusions, quotations, or other direct references. Genette (1997, 1–7) uses the term "transtextuality" of the wider phenomenon which can be divided into five subcategories, including "paratextuality" (various elements surrounding texts, such as framing texts and book covers), "metatextuality" (criticism of literary texts), "architextuality" (taxonomical relationships between texts; genres), "hypertextuality" (texts rewriting other texts, such as parodies and translations), and "intertextuality." In a similar manner, Bal (1997, 65) makes a differentiation between "intertextuality" (a study of "traceable" pretexts) and "interdiscursivity," the latter term referring to the "mix of different discourses" or the interaction between different discourses and genres within particular texts. While Genette's and Bal's narratological frameworks offer valuable concepts to separating between different levels of intertextual relations, I have chosen to position myself in the Bakhtinian paradigm.
35. Bakhtin (1981, 263).

36. Bakhtin (1981, 262–263).
37. Bakhtin (1981, 291–292).
38. Bakhtin (1981, 262–263).
39. See Sunderland (2004, 81).
40. Bakhtin (1981, 296–299). While Bakhtin here discusses the differences between poetry and novelistic discourse, in *Problems of Dostoevsky's Poetics* (Bakhtin 1984), he contrasts the "dialogic" prose style of Dostoyevsky to the "monologic" prose style of Tolstoy. The first allows the interplay of different characters' voices, whereas the latter subordinates other voices in the text to the single voice and viewpoint of the author. For a more detailed account on monologism in relation to standardization and unification of language in general, see Bakhtin (1981, 270–272).
41. McCallum (1999, 17).
42. Bauer (1988, xiv).
43. Bacchilega (1997, 22).
44. Hutcheon (1989, 4).
45. Cranny-Francis (1990, 206).
46. Trites (1997, 6).
47. Dale M. Bauer (1988, xvi) notes in relation to women writers' novels, texts "beginning in polyphone can be subsumed by a larger cultural imperative to order and sameness and hence, into monologism," and Cranny-Francis (1990, 20) holds a similar view by stating that a conventional text "often presents a resolution to the conflict [of voices/discourses] in which the oppositional [female/feminist] voice is shown to be invalid or incorrect or unnatural." As suggested above, McCallum has noted a similar pattern in children's texts that tend to be monologic because one discourse is emphasized at the end of each text.
48. Mills (1995, 93–94); Lehtonen and Varis (2009).
49. Mills (1995, 28).
50. See Blommaert (2001).
51. Mills (1995). See also Fairclough (1989, 24–25).
52. I will adopt Bal's (1997, 8) formulation of Gérard Genette's concept of "focalization" where "focalization, the relation between 'who perceives' and what is perceived 'colors' the story with subjectivity." Thus, perceptions are never objective but "colored" by the perceiver's worldview. While the focalizing characters "will have an advantage over the other characters" because readers watch "with the character's eyes and will, in principle, be inclined to accept the vision presented by that character" (Bal 1997, 146), the narrator, as the external focalizer, will similarly have an advantage over the characters.
53. Cranny-Francis (1990, 11).
54. Stephens (1992, 41–42).
55. See McCallum (1999, 266); Stephens (1992, 42).
56. See Bal (1997, 94–95) on "anticipations."

57. See, for instance, Nikolajeva (1988, 12). The purpose here is not to provide a broad general discussion of children's fantasy as a literary category nor outline its historical developments — both areas of research are covered in earlier studies. For general discussions on children's fantasy as a literary category and historical developments and subgenres in children's fantasy, see Manlove (2003), Nikolajeva (1988), Smith (1993), Sullivan (1992). For discussions on fantasy in general — rather than children's fantasy — as a literary category, see Attebery (1992), Hume (1984), Jackson (1981), Mendlesohn (2008), Swinfen (1984). Furthermore, I will not provide any kind of "defense" of fantasy as a genre — this has also been done before; see Hunt and Lenz (2001), Jackson (1981), Manlove (2003), Swinfen (1984). I maintain that fantasy, as any form of fiction, is capable of functioning as a form of social critique but does not necessarily do so.
58. Attebery (1992, 12–14).
59. See Bakhtin (1981, 288–289); Todorov (1990, 18–19).
60. For listings of various subtypes of children's fantasy, see, for instance, Nadelman Lynn (2005); Sullivan (1992, 104–105).
61. Here I draw on Kathryn Hume (1984, 20) who in her often-cited book divides between fantasy and mimesis as techniques or impulses: "literature is the product of two impulses. These are *mimesis*, felt as the desire to imitate, to describe events, people, situations, and objects with such verisimilitude that others can share your experience; and *fantasy*, the desire to change givens and alter reality." However, instead of referring to "fantasy" and "mimesis" as "impulses," I will use the terms "fantastic" and "realist" modes.

Chapter 1

1. See Mikkonen (1997, 272). As Warner (2005, 26) writes, thinkers such as David Hume at the end of the eighteenth century and Samuel Butler at the end of the nineteenth century challenged the ideas of unified, essential selves and personal identities, which they considered to be illusions. Furthermore, Mikkonen (1997, 2) and Kinder (2000, 67–68) associated the popularity of ideas of transformations and metamorphoses with earlier periods when societies were radically changing, including European Renaissance and the nineteenth century after the Industrial Revolution.
2. Creed (1993, 3).
3. Sobchack (2000, xi–xiv).
4. The concept of metamorphosis is commonly used in physical, bodily transformations in studies of fiction, and several writers use the terms "metamorphosis" and "transformation" in-

terchangeably; see, for example, Kuznets (1994), Lassén-Seger (2006), Mikkonen (1997), Warner (2002). However, I find it difficult to put aside the meaning of "metamorphosis" in biology as an irreversible alteration in shape and will thus use the concept of transformation of all kinds of physical changes, be they irreversible or reversible, single or repeated events.

5. Lassén-Seger (2006, 22).
6. See Chappell (2007), Easun (1994), Lassén-Seger (2006), Mikkonen (1997), Propp (2005).
7. Mikkonen (1997, 77).
8. Babbitt (1988, 585); Easun (1994, 40).
9. See, for instance, Reynolds (1994, 4) on the origins of the contemporary discourses of adolescence.
10. Waller (2009, 196).
11. See Lassén-Seger (2006, 23). On the Ovidian influences, see Bynum (2001), Clarke (1995), Mikkonen (1997), Warner (2002).
12. Kuznets (1994, 7–8).
13. Lassén-Seger (2006, 263).
14. Chappell (2007, 235).
15. Thompson (1955).
16. See Haldane (2006b, 262–263). As Haldane notes, the word *Nibelung* refers to someone surrounded by mist—invisibility is a central motif in the epic. There are also other items in Germanic mythology that enable the wearer to walk unseen, such as the *Wunschmantel* ("wishing cloak") and the *Vogelnest* ("bird's nest"), while Swedish legends involve mentions of Odin's *uddehatt* (a pointed, wedge-shaped hat which is at the same time a cap of darkness, a wishing-hat, and Mercury's hat); see Dickens (1992), Haldane (2006a).
17. Colum (1983, 596); a variant of the "Twelve Dancing Princesses" tale type.
18. Colum (1983, 425).
19. In Lang (1889b).
20. Haldane (2006a, 2006b). In the English language literature, Andrew Lang's *The Grey Fairy Book* (1900) involves a version of this story, titled "Fortunatus and his Purse," but the wishing hat in this version does not turn its wearer invisible but transports the person wherever she or he wishes.
21. Haldane (2006b, 266).
22. Foucault (2006, 73–79).
23. Foucault (1979, 138).
24. Foucault, (2006, 55).
25. Haldane (2006b, 268).
26. Haldane (2006b, 267).
27. *The Invisible Man*, 43; 103.
28. Haldane (2006b, 264).
29. See Raudvere (1996).
30. See, for instance, Myhill and Jones (2004), Working Group on Girls (2006). Examples of realist children's books discussing the cultural invisibility of specific child characters include Kerstin Johansson's *Som om jag inte fanns* [As if I Wasn't There] (1978), Natalie Honeycutt's *Invisible Lissa* (1985), and Hazel Townson's *The Invisible Boy* (2002).
31. Stone (1999, 328).
32. Banet-Weiser (2004, 121).
33. *The Enchanted Castle*, 77.
34. *The Enchanted Castle*, 70.
35. This happens in the books by Brown (1995), Gardner (2002), Houghton (1993), Yorinks and Cushman (2011).
36. *The Ogre Downstairs*, 168–169.
37. *Charlie Bone and the Blue Boa*, 325.
38. Another famous example of this type of invisible girl is Tove Jansson's "Story of the Invisible Child" (1962, Swedish orig. "*Berättelsen om det osynliga barnet*"). In Jansson's story, the girl becomes invisible under the cold and sarcastic treatment of her guardian.
39. While the stories listed here are focalized through the invisible characters, there are also narratives where invisibility is presented from another person's point of view but which in other ways are similar to the above texts. In Beatrice Colin's and Sara Pinto's (2010) *My Invisible Sister*, the protagonist is a young boy whose sister, Elizabeth, has a genetic condition that makes her invisible. Her invisibility enables her to play all kinds of pranks on other people but she is also unhappy in her extraordinary condition that prevents her from doing normal teenage things— and has prevented her from doing normal childhood things in the past, which has made her angry enough to force her family move houses and cities whenever she becomes fed up with her new surroundings. Things change only when Elizabeth manages to make friends with a boy whose grandmother is also suffering from invisibility; the boy accepts her condition and, at the end of the book, she begins to show some signs of visibility. Since the invisible girl in *My Invisible Sister* is not the focalizer and readers are offered her experiences mediated by the little brother, I have left the novel outside a more detailed discussion.
40. Waller (2009, 85–86). This type of an invisible male hero has also featured in a novel for adults. Thomas Berger's comic fantasy novel *Being Invisible* (1987) features a man who one morning finds out that he can turn invisible at will; his literal invisibility is clearly an aspect of his earlier metaphorical invisibility as a divorced man who does not have a proper career. While the protagonist is an anti-hero, he does not face corruption or death in the end; the ironic tone in the book subverts the conventional tropes of invisibility. For a discussion of Berger's novel, see Chapman (1992).
41. Colum (1983, 98).

42. Colum (1983, 449).
43. Colum (1983, 640).
44. Tatar (1992, 168–169). Tatar also suggests that in Grimms' stories it is namely old women who often are the victims of this type of violence — whether motivated or not — and explains that "the more hair-raising an event in these stories, the more comical its effect, hence my use of the term festive violence."
45. Wheeler (1912, 11; 259).
46. Colum (1983, 254).
47. Ross (1973, 146).
48. Pratt (1982, 172).
49. Butler (1993, x; 1996, 111–112).
50. Miller (1996, 77).
51. See, for instance, the articles by Fischer and Curl (1996), and Lee (1996) in Slusser, et al., *Immortal Engines: Life Extension and Immortality in Science Fiction and Fantasy*. In the same volume, other writers suggest, however, that adult science fiction and fantasy tend to treat immortality in negative terms; see the articles by Miller (1996) and Rosen (1996) in the same volume.
52. Lundquist (1996, 201–202).
53. See, for instance, Zipes (2004).
54. *The People in Pineapple Place*, 159.
55. *Immortal Beloved*, 25; *Darkness Falls*, 150.
56. The final book in Tiernan's *Immortal Beloved* trilogy, *Eternally Yours*, had not yet come out by the time of writing this chapter (the expected publication date was November 6, 2012).
57. See, for instance, Case (1991), Gelder (1994), Palmer (1999).

Chapter 2

1. Nikolajeva (1988, 13).
2. Turning earlier motifs into more complex tropes is, of course, a typical strategy in extending short folktales or fairy tales into fairy tale novelizations or fantasy novels in general. See, for instance, Stephens and McCallum (1998, 221); Nikolajeva (2003).
3. Waugh (1989, 22).
4. Weedon (1997, 77–78).
5. Paul (1987, 199); Trites (1997, 5).
6. As Lefanu (1988, 90) points out, the radical-feminist discourses were also reflected in feminist science fiction, particularly in feminist utopias in the 1970s that portrayed communal, classless, ecology-minded, almost non-violent and sexually permissive female-only societies. See also Russ (1981).
7. Pratt (1982, 178).
8. Radical feminism and eco-feminism share certain features and, at times, overlap, which is why it is not feasible to always differentiate between the two. Radical-feminist and eco-feminist discourses were both in circulation in the 1980s. Although Victoria Davion (1994, 17) differentiates between *ecofeminine* and *ecofeminist* positions — the first reflecting radical-feminist ideas in that they "uncritically embrace unified or one-stance views of feminine sides of gender dichotomies" and the latter employing a more critical stance towards gender and ecological concerns — making clear-cut differences is impossible, because there are not only different feminisms but various eco-feminisms. See also Warren (1994, 2).
9. Felski (2000, 202); Purkiss (1996, 8).
10. Sempruch (2004, 116). Sempruch associates these figurations with North American radical feminists Mary Daly and Andrea Dworkin, but also with French poststructuralist feminists, such as Hélène Cixous, Catherine Clément and Luce Irigaray.
11. See Stewig (1995), Stephens (2003).
12. See Purkiss (1996).
13. Stephens (2003, 198).
14. Trites (1997, 3–5).
15. Trites (1997, 6–7).
16. Trites (1997, 8); French (1985, 507–512).
17. For a more detailed analysis of the metafictional strategies in Price, see Lehtonen (2010a).
18. The Lapland witches live in the Lake Enara area — the fictional name is a modification of the name of a lake in Northern Finland, called *Anár* in Sámi, *Inari* in Finnish. Also the names of the witches have associations with the North. The queen of the Lake Enara witch clan is called Serafina Pekkala (the last name is a common Finnish surname) and her daimon — a kind of a soul that exists outside one's body — is called Kaisa (common Finnish or Swedish name). One of the Lappish witches, Lena Feldt, has a Swedish name, while the queen of Latvian witches, Ruta Skadi, is named after the goddess Skaði in Norse mythology.
19. *Ghost Song* is not examined in this study, because the protagonist in the story is a young boy and the story does not involve invisibility.
20. Chingis in *The Ghost Drum* is clearly named after the famous Mongolian khan, while Shingebiss's name in *Ghost Dance* comes from an Ojibwe legend.
21. Raudvere (1996, 47).
22. *The Subtle Knife*, 33.
23. *The Ghost Drum*, 66–67.
24. *The Subtle Knife*, 310.
25. *Ghost Dance*, 15.
26. *Ghost Dance*, 90–91.
27. *Ghost Dance*, 98.
28. That is, persuasion is a conventionally feminine strategy in patriarchal contexts where women are not in powerful positions and have to persuade someone else to act on their behalf.
29. Lehtonen (2010a).
30. Pratchett's Tiffany Aching novels include

Wee Free Men (2003), *A Hat Full of Sky* (2004), *Wintersmith* (2006), and *I Shall Wear Midnight* (2010).
31. *I Shall Wear Midnight*, 12.
32. *A Hat Full of Sky*, 18.
33. *A Hat Full of Sky*, 19.
34. *A Hat Full of Sky*, 57.
35. Brennan Croft (2008), 161–162.
36. *A Hat Full of Sky*, 19.
37. Stephens (2003, 201).
38. *Goddess of the Night*, 15.
39. *Goddess of the Night*, 80.
40. *Goddess of the Night*, 87–88.
41. *Goddess of the Night*, 191.
42. *Goddess of the Night*, 294.
43. Pratt (1982, 30–31).
44. *The Wall and the Wing*, 165.
45. *Visibility*, 14.
46. *The Wall and the Wing*, 16.
47. *Visibility*, 11.
48. *The Wall and the Wing*, 87.
49. *The Wall and the Wing*, 77.
50. *The Wall and the Wing*, 66–67.
51. *The Chaos King*, 246–247.
52. The term "carnivalesque" comes from Bakhtin (1984), who uses it in relation to renaissance adult literature to describe a narrative pattern drawing on role reversal between the powerful and the powerless, all the rulers and the servants. In his discussion of Bakhtin's notion of carnivalesque in relation to children's literature, John Stephens (1992, 132–139) uses the term "time-out."
53. *The Chaos King*, 313.
54. *Visibility*, 16.
55. *Visibility*, 164.
56. *The Earth Witch*, 22.
57. White (1998, 127).
58. See Sullivan (1999).
59. *The Earth Witch*, 72.
60. *The Earth Witch*, 105.
61. *The Earth Witch*, 214.
62. *The Earth Witch*, 134.
63. *The Earth Witch*, 196.
64. *The Earth Witch*, 189.
65. Kaplan (2010, 197).
66. *Howl's Moving Castle*, 1. Jones's novel has plenty of similarities with Andrew Lang's *Prince Prigio* (1889a) that explicitly comments on and parodies the convention of the eldest child being a failure.
67. *Howl's Moving Castle*, 13.
68. *Howl's Moving Castle*, 27–28.
69. Cruikshank (2003, 174).
70. See Tatar (1999, 148–156).
71. *Howl's Moving Castle*, 57.
72. For a more detailed analysis of Sophie's speech acts, see Lehtonen (2009).
73. See Comoletti and Drout (2001) on the notion of magic as performative language use, usually acquired in institutional settings such as wizarding schools in fantasy. Stephens (1992, 270–271) has briefly analyzed Sophie's use of words in *Castle in the Air* (1990), the sequel to *Howl's Moving Castle*, and argues that her conversational discourse with its use of randomly selected signifiers "is a comic reversal of the usual convention that a spell must be precise in its wording"; a convention based on the "assumption of a particularly close relation between sign and thing in a specialized example of how 'true' or 'secret' names of things command phenomena by expressing essences." One could also argue the opposite: that Sophie's spells are very precise; whatever she says to try to change the reality seems to come literally true, and the words she uses are not randomly selected, but chosen according to the rules of regular conversation.
74. *Howl's Moving Castle*, 64.
75. This is also one reason I find Sophie's character in the sequels, *Castle in the Air* (1990) and *The House of Many Ways* (2008), less subversive. Without the crone's disguise, her nagging and fussing, which are conventional forms of irritating feminine behavior, are no longer viewed in a parodic frame and Sophie's character is diminished into a conventional representation of femininity.
76. See Tatar (1992, 111); Warner (1995, 243).
77. See, for instance, the texts that Bacchilega (1997, 107; 113) describes.
78. See Stephens and McCallum (1998, 19).
79. Sempruch (2004, 123).

Chapter 3

1. Braidotti (1991, 122); Waugh (1989, 2).
2. Flax (1990, 41).
3. Weedon (1997, 171). See also Felski (2000, 195); Owens (1985, 70).
4. See Braidotti (1996, 2005); Haraway (1991); Phelan (1993).
5. Waugh (1989, 32).
6. Waugh (1989, 14).
7. Waugh's female postmodernism resembles what Hans Bertens (1991, 135) calls "poststructuralist postmodernism." This form of postmodernism overlaps with poststructuralist theory: it has a strong socio-political commitment and it focuses on questioning meaning and subjectivity. It thus differs from "avant-gardist" and "aesthetic, neoconservative" postmodernisms that have little interest in socio-political issues.
8. Wilkie-Stibbs (2002, 124–125).
9. On definitions of personal trauma, see Brison (1999), Etherington (2003).
10. Armstrong (1980, 117).
11. Armstrong (1978, 59).
12. Armstrong (1978, 64).

13. According to the conventions, the ghost is always represented as the other, from the outside — typically the stories are not focalized through the ghosts, which is such a strong convention that contemporary viewers continue to be surprised by the reversal of perspective in films such as Alejandro Amenábar's (dir.) *The Others* (2001) and M. Night Shyamalan's (dir.) *The Sixth Sense* (1999).
14. Armstrong (1980, 120).
15. Curti (1998, 159). The play between unfamiliar and familiar, inexplicable and known, or the uncanny and canny is also the starting point of Anna Jackson's (2008) analysis of *The Time of the Ghost*. The ghost in Jones's novel shifts between moments of familiarity and defamiliarity, between belonging and being an outcast — or, as Jackson (2008, 167) notes, between the familiarity of her surroundings and her own uncanny status as a ghost.
16. See Attebery (1992, 75–78), Jackson (2008, 164–169), Mendlesohn (2005, 34–35) and Waterhouse (1991).
17. The Swedish author Mats Wahl's young adult crime novel *Den Osynlige* (*The Invisible*) (2003) also employs a ghost as a focalizer at the beginning of the book — an invisible boy is floating around his school where no one notices him and he does not know, at first, what has happened to him. He has also been in an accident and is spirit-traveling while his body lies hidden in the back yard of an abandoned house. Unlike Sally, who survives her accident, the boy in *Den Osynlige* dies at the end and his ghost disappears soon afterward. In both novels, the invisible character's distress and powerlessness that is represented in the focalized sections highlights the horridness of the events they have been through — events that are revealed gradually, partly through their own memories and partly through the scenes that they invisibly witness.
18. *The Time of the Ghost* differs from other time-slip stories also in terms of the protagonist's memory loss. While it is typical that a character from a different time appears in the present time as a ghost — as in Philippa Pearce's *Tom's Midnight Garden* (1958), Elisabeth Beresford's *Invisible Magic* (1974) or Gene Kemp's *Jason Bodger and the Priory Ghost* (1985) — the characters have not lost their memory (although they might be puzzled about their displacement). Also in Lindbergh's *The People in Pineapple Place* (1982), the non-aging characters who live in the special traveling time-space consisting of their own small community are invisible to most other people.
19. *The Time of the Ghost*, 13.
20. *The Time of the Ghost*, 89.
21. Bal (1999, ix).
22. Bal (1999, ix).
23. Brison (1999, 44).

24. Brison (1999, 40). See also Etherington (2003, 25–26).
25. Etherington (2003, 24).
26. *The Time of the Ghost*, 8–9.
27. Brison (1999, 44).
28. *The Time of the Ghost*, 97.
29. *The Time of the Ghost*, 112.
30. *The Time of the Ghost*, 175.
31. *The Time of the Ghost*, 27.
32. *The Time of the Ghost*, 109–110.
33. *The Time of the Ghost*, 140.
34. *The Time of the Ghost*, 140.
35. *The Time of the Ghost*, 113.
36. Trites (1997, 83).
37. Brison (1999, 40).
38. *Ghostgirl*, 1.
39. *Ghostgirl*, 6.
40. *Ghostgirl*, 41.
41. The bands referred to include The Cure, Dead Can Dance, Depeche Mode, My Bloody Valentine, The Smiths, Radiohead, and Evanescence; while some of the writers that are quoted are Percy Bysshe Shelley, William Blake, Edgar Allan Poe, Emily Dickinson, Virginia Woolf and Sylvia Plath. None of these artists or writers — apart, perhaps, from The Cure or Edgar Allan Poe — alone can be considered as an epitome of the Gothic. Rather, these references in combination create a fairly stereotypical image of the Goth subculture that is in the novel represented by Scarlet, as well as the dead ghost-girl Charlotte whose last name, Usher, is a reference to Poe's short story, "The Fall of the House of Usher" (1839).
42. *Ghostgirl*, 186.
43. *Ghostgirl*, 317.
44. *Ghostgirl*, 165.
45. *Ghostgirl*, 226.
46. *Now You See Me*, 213.
47. *Out of Mind, Out of Sight*, 23.
48. *Out of Mind, Out of Sight*, 1–2.
49. *Out of Mind, Out of Sight*, 75–76.
50. *Out of Mind, Out of Sight*, 73–74.
51. *Out of Mind, Out of Sight*, 156.
52. *Out of Mind, Out of Sight*, 219.
53. *Now You See Me*, 2.
54. *Now You See Me*, 8.
55. *Now You See Me*, 15.
56. Talbot (2010, 139).
57. Gill (2008, 436).
58. Cronin (2000, 279).
59. McRobbie (2009, 19).
60. See Lehtonen (2011).
61. There are also three film adaptations of the novel, all of the same name, *Freaky Friday*. The first, for which Rodgers wrote the screenplay herself, appeared in 1976 (dir. Gary Nelson) and was later followed by a remake for television in 1995 (dir. Melanie Mayron). Another adaptation for the silver screen occurred in 2003 (dir.

Mark Waters, screenplay by Heather Hach and Leslie Dixon).
62. *Freaky Friday*, 85; 87.
63. *Freaky Friday*, 89.
64. *Freaky Friday*, 33.
65. *Freaky Friday*, 91.
66. *Freaky Friday*, 15.
67. *Freaky Friday*, 143.
68. *Freaky Friday*, 146.
69. *Happy Birthday, Dear Amy*, 3.
70. *Happy Birthday, Dear Amy*, 11.
71. *Happy Birthday, Dear Amy*, 19–20.
72. *Happy Birthday, Dear Amy*, 25.
73. *Happy Birthday, Dear Amy*, 20.
74. *Happy Birthday, Dear Amy*, 76.
75. *Happy Birthday, Dear Amy*, 154.
76. *Happy Birthday, Dear Amy*, 159.
77. Charles Butler (2006, 68) and Margaret Rumbold (1997, 23–26) both argue that in Jones's texts the play with time challenges the conventional notion of subjectivity as unique and continuous. As Linda Hall (2001, 46) writes, postwar British time-slip narratives have been keen to explore identity in relation to continuity in time; personal and cultural inheritance and identities are based on the relationship between the past and the present. However, unlike many British time-slip stories, where cultural and national inheritance is addressed alongside characters' personal experiences of the past and the present (see Hall 2001; Cosslett 2002), in Jones's text the protagonists visit their own pasts and the focus is on the construction of their subjectivity in relation to their identity narratives.
78. *Hexwood*, 45.
79. Kaplan (2010, 200).
80. *Hexwood*, 262.
81. *Hexwood*, 86–87.
82. *Hexwood*, 261–262.
83. Braidotti (2005, 62; 82).

Chapter 4

1. Lehtonen (2008, 222–223).
2. Warner (2008, 123); Haldane (2006a, 172).
3. De Lauretis (1984, 37).
4. Haldane (2006b, 263).
5. Phelan (1993, 6–7).
6. See Millard, Mills and Pearce (1996, 156–157); Stone (1999, 333).
7. Phelan (1993, 6).
8. Phelan (1993, 19).
9. Williams (1996, 15–17). Williams uses the terms "look" and "gaze" interchangeably.
10. Williams (1996, 17–18).
11. Creed (1993, 153).
12. Gamman and Marshment (1988, 4–5).
13. Gamman (1988).
14. Marcus (2007, 113).
15. Evans and Gamman (1995, 41); Vänskä (2005, 70).
16. I have chosen not to use the term "look" to refer to different ways of looking and gazing, mainly because the term is ambiguous and may also refer to someone's look(s) (appearance).
17. Gamman and Marshment (1988, 7).
18. Löw (2006, 121).
19. Warner (2008, 323).
20. *The Time of the Ghost*, 77–78.
21. *The Time of the Ghost*, 190.
22. *The Time of the Ghost*, 71.
23. *The Time of the Ghost*, 73–74.
24. *The Time of the Ghost*, 26–27, italics original.
25. *The Time of the Ghost*, 68.
26. See Lehtonen (2008).
27. *The Woman in the Wall*, 2.
28. *The Woman in the Wall*, 36; 38.
29. *The Woman in the Wall*, 106.
30. *The Woman in the Wall*, 42.
31. *The Woman in the Wall*, 20.
32. *The Woman in the Wall*, 59.
33. *The Woman in the Wall*, 54.
34. *The Woman in the Wall*, 117.
35. *The Woman in the Wall*, 107.
36. *The Woman in the Wall*, 149.
37. *The Woman in the Wall*, 182.
38. Romøren and Stephens (2002, 220).
39. *A Certain Slant of Light*, 1.
40. *A Certain Slant of Light*, 14.
41. *A Certain Slant of Light*, 60.
42. *A Certain Slant of Light*, 4.
43. *A Certain Slant of Light*, 21.
44. *A Certain Slant of Light*, 25. This is a reference to 1 Corinthians 13:12 in *King James Version*: "For now we see through a glass, darkly; but then face to face: now I know in part; but then shall I know even as also I am known."
45. *A Certain Slant of Light*, 72.
46. *A Certain Slant of Light*, 139–140.
47. *Ghostgirl*, 90.
48. *Ghostgirl*, 90–91.
49. *Ghostgirl*, 91.
50. *Ghostgirl*, 93.
51. See Mills (1995, 124–125).
52. For summaries of typical features of female Gothic, see Ellis (1989, ix) and Hoeveler (1998, 1–2). Albeit similar elements — particularly the set of characters and portrayals of excessive emotions and violence — are also present in other nineteenth-century fictions, most notably in later realist domestic melodramas (see Vicinus 1981), I will here focus on the genre of female Gothic because *The Ghost Wife* involves the quintessential trademark of the Gothic, the haunted home. The affinities between melodrama and the (female) Gothic are not surprising, since the genres developed during the same time in the late eighteenth and early nineteenth

centuries (see Brooks 1995) and, as John Cawelti (1977, 45) suggests, in terms of narrative and textual strategies, the Gothic romance can be treated as a subgenre of melodrama.

53. Throughout the novel, the two classes are also associated with different literary genres; the middle-class haunted home is depicted through the Gothic tradition, while the working-class colliers are introduced through a completely realist discourse of the daily life of the workers at the coal-pit. For a more detailed discussion of these differences, see Lehtonen (2010b).

54. On the concept of respectability in regard to gender and class, see Walkerdine, Lucey and Melody (2001, 45); Skeggs (1997, 2–4). As Ellis (1989, xi–xii) suggests, the "feminine Gothic" (her preferred term) explored the recently emerged middle class idea of home as the feminine sphere, a secure and controlled place. The security of the home is threatened in the novels but always restored at the end. Moreover, the restoration of the home as a secure, respectable and decent place was the task of the Gothic heroines who reflected the new discourse of middle class femininity.

55. Ellis (1989, 11); Hoeveler (1998, 5). This is also argued by Beverly Skeggs, who in her discussion of Lynette' Finch's concept of the "classing gaze," notes that by the end of the nineteenth century conceptualizations of the working class were based on moral categories rather than economic references and that "[o]bservation and interpretation of the sexual behaviour of working-class women on the basis of their appearance was central to the production of middle-class conceptualisations" (Skeggs 1997, 5). Skeggs's own study demonstrates that working-class women continue to be judged — or continue to feel that they are judged — on the basis of their appearance in contemporary British society where they are the objects of the classing gaze.

56. *The Ghost Wife*, 105.
57. Creed (1993, 151).
58. *The Ghost Wife*, 1.
59. *The Ghost Wife*, 4.
60. *The Ghost Wife*, 51–52.
61. *The Ghost Wife*, 89.
62. *The Ghost Wife*, 167.
63. *The Ghost Wife*, 23.
64. *The Ghost Wife*, 76.
65. *The Ghost Wife*, 167.
66. *The Ghost Wife*, 161.
67. Moore (1988, 47). Moore notes that although images of males became more popular in the 1980s, the male body has been presented as an object of desire also earlier; "from the silent movie stars to Smash Hits there is a long if uneasy history of male pin-ups" (Moore 1988, 47), and the fascination in the male body in works of art is, of course, an ancient phenomenon, even though it has commonly been associated with homoeroticism rather than female gaze.

68. Walkerdine, Lucey and Melody (2001, 209).
69. See Jackson and Tinkler (2007).

Chapter 5

1. Halberstam (2005, 6).
2. Halberstam (2005, 2).
3. Waller (2009, 34).
4. Potvin (2003, 636).
5. The notion of shamanism as a form of female empowerment is central to Peter Bramwell's (2005) Jungian-feminist reading of *The Ghost Drum*. Invoking a typical heroic pattern of quest that he interprets as a process of coming of age, Bramwell (2005, 150) suggests that becoming a shaman is an empowering journey for the female hero. John Warren Stewig (1995) also interprets the novel as a female character's successful quest for agency, although he reads Chingis as a fairy tale witch rather than a shaman.
6. Eliade (1972, 168); Campbell (1976, 254).
7. See, for instance, Eliade's remark on certain North Eurasian traditions where "shamanism is hereditary and is also transmitted in the female line" (1972, 15) or Campbell's statement that "Women too became shamans" (1976, 244). Eliade (1972, 39; 69) also uses the term "shamaness" of females.
8. Tedlock (2005, 4). Tedlock also points out that the body in the recently found shaman grave in Czech Republic — considered to be the oldest shaman grave that has been found — was a female body.
9. Raninen (2008, 26) writes that in Icelandic mythological texts the ritual complex called *seiðr* is associated with shamanic practices that were perceived mainly as a female domain — in these sources male practitioners are thus considered *ragr*, unmanly. Ironically, the war-god Oðinn is also a master of *seiðr* and, moreover, a god that changes his sex.
10. Eliade (1972, 168; 351–352).
11. Tedlock (2005, 250); Raninen (2008, 26). Most transgender shamans have been males — particularly so in places where shamanism has been perceived as a female domain, including Korea (see Harvey 1979, 3) and Nordic countries. A curious detail in Raninen's (2008, 26) article is the mention of a 12th century burial place in Vivallen, Jämtland, in Sweden that contains a male buried in female dress; details about the place suggest that the male was of Sámi ethno-cultural background.
12. See Raninen (2008); Raudvere (1996).
13. Halifax (1980, 23).
14. Heilbrun (1982, x).

15. Pearson and Pope (1981, 15).
16. Flanagan (2008, 42–43).
17. While "Lappish" as a name of an ethnic group is now a derogatory term in the countries where Sámi people live, the terms "Lappish" and "Lapps" were earlier commonly used of Sámi people and therefore appear both in studies of shamanism and in studies of Nordic myths and legends which involve references to Lappish witches or shamans (see Eliade 1972, 15; Ellis Davidson 1973, 30–31; Simpson 1973, 170–171). The Lappishness of the shamans in the novel is presumably a reflection of the Nordic mythology. In Price's novels the term "Lappish" seems to be appropriated as a sort of general reference to any group of Northern hunter-gatherers rather than to a specific ethnic group of people. The main function of naming the witch-shamans as ethnically others is to represent a group that is ethnically and culturally different from the imperialist rulers or oppressors. After all, the title of *Ghost Dance* may not refer only to visits to the land of the dead in Siberian shamanic traditions (see Eliade 1972, 311), but also connote the nineteenth-century pan–Indian spiritual and prophetic resistance movement, particularly because Shingebiss's name comes from an Ojibwe legend. On the Ghost-Dance movement as a religion of resistance, see Smoak (2006, 1–3).
18. However, another possible reference to Finnish mythology is the fact that Serafina's healing spell follows the so-called Kalevala measure; that is, a four trochaic feet that is used throughout the Finnish epic *Kalevala* (see *The Subtle Knife*, 254–256).
19. In his article on representations of Eastern Europe in Pullman's, J.K. Rowling's and Jonathan Stroud's fantasy series, Marek Oziewicz (2010) argues that in all these texts the people living in Eastern and Northern parts of Europe—including Pullman's witches—are depicted as primitive and subordinate to the British.
20. *The Subtle Knife*, 41.
21. *The Subtle Knife*, 269.
22. *Northern Lights*, 302.
23. *The Subtle Knife*, 49.
24. *The Subtle Knife*, 132.
25. *Northern Lights*, 303.
26. *Northern Lights*, 314.
27. *The Subtle Knife*, 54.
28. The shamans also live eternally in the sense that although they die, they will be reborn later, but this is not so much a magic change in age as a (non–Western) understanding of a human being's (or soul's) cycle of existence.
29. *The Ghost Drum*, 30–31.
30. See Eliade (1972, 110).
31. *The Ghost Drum*, 62.
32. See Eliade (1972, 33–35).

33. As Bramwell (2005, 143) points out, the name indicates Chingis's potential threat to the czardom (as an allusion to the Mongolian conqueror Genghis Khan), but from the gender perspective, it is also significant that it is a male name.
34. "Girl" denotes a female child, but in certain contexts adult women are commonly referred to as girls. "Girl" may be pejorative but it may also, depending on the context, indicate solidarity among women.
35. The last event is the one that Bramwell (2005, 148) regards as "the turning point in Chingis's maturation as an individual subject and as an agent in the community." In contrast, Stewig (1995, 123) interprets the same incident as a sort of failure: although Chingis is a very strong woman, she cannot save her (physical) self.
36. *The Ghost Drum*, 41.
37. *The Ghost Drum*, 69.
38. There are a couple of instances where Chingis holds Safa's hand and kisses him for goodbye—these, however, might also indicate a child-mother relationship.
39. See Halifax (1980, 23–25). Halifax (1980, 23) writes that the "androgyny" of shamans may involve "an actual change in a sex role" and that in Siberian traditions male shamans occasionally marry men. She also cites a Manelaq story where an old wizard woman turns herself into a man and marries her adopted daughter.
40. "Shingebiss" is the name of a duck in an Ojibwe legend. In an early published version of this legend that appeared in Henry R. Schoolcraft's *Hiawatha and Other Oral Legends, Mythologic and Allegoric, of the North American Indians* (1856), the duck is referred to as a "he," which in itself might be the (now sexist) non-gendered use of the pronoun, but together with the description of the duck as a hunter suggests that the duck is male ("Shingebiss" in Schoolcraft 1856, 113–115). The theme of Schoolcraft's version of the Shingebiss tale is expressed in its subtitle, "An Allegory of Self-Reliance" (Schoolcraft 1856, 113) and Price's novel reflects this theme. The textual similarities between Schoolcraft and Price suggest that the latter may be a retelling of Schoolcraft's tale—a retelling that changes the gender of the protagonist and modifies the ending. The duck in Schoolcraft's version of the tale survives winter and manages to beat Kabebonicca (the personification of the Northwest winds), but the shaman Shingebiss's perseverance does not lead to unquestionably positive outcomes.
41. *Ghost Dance*, 3–4.
42. *Ghost Dance*, 5.
43. In the famous myth discussed by Turville-Petre (1964, 125) Loki changes into a mare to lure away a stallion that is helping a giant to

build a wall to secure the gods from attacks — the gods, however, want to stop the building process because the giant wants the goddess Freyja as a reward. The mare–Loki lures away the stallion, breeds with it and afterward gives birth to the foal Sleipnir, gray with eight legs.
44. *Ghost Dance*, 204.
45. *Ghost Dance*, 217.
46. DeLuca (2001, 634).
47. *Turnabout*, 3, italics original.
48. *Turnabout*, 97–98.
49. *Turnabout*, 80–81.
50. *Turnabout*, 74.
51. *Turnabout*, 119.
52. *Turnabout*, 59.
53. *Turnabout*, 143.
54. *Turnabout*, 214.
55. *Turnabout*, 223.
56. *Elsewhere*, 213.
57. *Elsewhere*, 48–49.
58. *Elsewhere*, 57.
59. *Elsewhere*, 215.
60. *Elsewhere*, 268.
61. While the representations of the witch-shamans as outsiders who blend and cross boundaries may have radical potential in terms of gender, in relation to ethnicity they are more problematic. I have addressed some of these issues in an earlier article on Price's *Ghost Dance* (Lehtonen 2010a).

Conclusion

1. *Howl's Moving Castle*, 32.
2. See Waller (2009), Stephens and McCallum (1998).
3. McRobbie (2009, 8).
4. See Lee (2008), Radway (1987).
5. See Brighenti (2007).
6. Banet-Weiser (2004, 124).
7. McRobbie (2009, 2–3).
8. See McNay (2000, 2008).

Bibliography

Primary Sources
Alexander, Lloyd. 1964–1973 (2011). *The Chronicles of Prydain*. New York: Square Fish.
Anstey, F. (Thomas Anstey Guthrie). 1881 (1981). *Vice Versa*. Harmondsworth: Puffin Books.
Babbitt, Natalie. 1975 (2003). *Tuck Everlasting*. London: Bloomsbury.
Barrie, James Matthew. 1902/1911 (2004). *Peter Pan: Peter and Wendy; Peter Pan in Kensington Gardens*. London: Penguin.
Benton, Jim. 2004 (2005). *The Invisible Fran* (*Franny K. Stein, Mad Scientist* 3). New York: Aladdin Paperbacks.
Beresford, Elisabeth. 1974. *Invisible Magic*. London: Hart-Davis.
Berger, Thomas. 1987 (1988). *Being Invisible*. New York: Penguin Books.
Brown, Jeff. 1995 (2003). *Invisible Stanley*. London: Egmont.
Browne, Anthony. 1993. *The Big Baby: A Little Joke*. New York: Alfred A. Knopf.
Chaucer, Geoffrey. 1958. *The Canterbury Tales*. Translated into modern English by R.M. Lumiansky. New York: Holt, Rinehart and Winston.
Child, Francis James (ed.). 1957. *The English and Scottish Popular Ballads, Vol. I*. New York: Folklore Press and Pageant Book Co.
Clements, Andrew. 2002 (2004). *Things Not Seen*. New York: Puffin Books.
Colin, Beatrice, and Sara Pinto. 2010. *My Invisible Sister*. New York: Bloomsbury.
Colum, Padraic (ed.). 1983. *The Complete Grimm's Fairy Tales*. London: Routledge and Kegan Paul.
Cormier, Robert. 1988 (1990). *Fade*. London: Lions Tracks.
Cresswell, Helen, and Judy Brown. 1990 (1992). *Almost Goodbye, Guzzler!* London: HarperCollins.
Duncan, Lois. 1985 (1991). *Locked in Time*. New York: Bantam Doubleday Dell.
Eager, Edward. 1954 (2000). *Half Magic*. Oxford: Oxford University Press.
Ewing, Lynne. 2000. *Goddess of the Night: Daughters of the Moon 1*. New York: Hyperion.
Farmer, Penelope. 1972 (1992). *A Castle of Bone*. Revised edition. London: Bodley Head.
Gaiman, Neil. 2008. *The Graveyard Book*. London: Bloomsbury.
Gardner, Sally. 2002. *The Invisible Boy*. London: Orion Children's Books.
Greenburg, Dan. 1998. *Now You See Me ... Now You Don't* (*The Zack Files* 12). New York: Grosset and Dunlap.
Haddix, Margaret Peterson. 2000. *Turnabout*. New York: Simon and Schuster.
Hoffmann, Mary. 1996 (1997). *A Vanishing Tail*. London: Orchard Books.
Honeycutt, Natalie. 1985. *Invisible Lissa*. New York: Bradbury Press.
Houghton, Eric. 1993. *Vincent the Invisible*. London: Macmillan Children's Books.
Hurley, Tonya. 2008 (2009). *Ghostgirl*. London: Headline.

_____. 2009 (2010). *Ghostgirl: Homecoming*. London: Headline.
_____. 2010 (2011). *Ghostgirl: Lovesick*. London: Headline.
Irving, Washington. 1819 (1934). "Rip Van Winkle." In Henry A. Pochmann (ed.), *Washington Irving: Representative Selections, with Introduction, Bibliography, and Notes*. New York: American Book Co., 79–96. (Originally published in *The Sketch Book*, 1819.)
Jansson, Tove. 1962 (1981). *Det osynliga barnet och andra berättelser* (*The Invisible Child and Other Stories*). Stockholm: Almqvist and Wiksell.
Jocelyn, Marthe. 1997. *The Invisible Day*. Toronto, Ontario: Tundra.
Johansson, Kerstin. 1978. *Som om jag inte fanns* (*As if I Wasn't There*). Stockholm: Almqvist and Wiksell.
Jones, Diana Wynne. 1974 (1977). *The Ogre Downstairs*. Harmondsworth: Puffin.
_____. 1981. *The Time of the Ghost*. London: MacMillan's Children's Books.
_____. 1984. *Archer's Goon*. London: Methuen.
_____. 1985 (2002). *Fire and Hemlock*. New York: HarperCollins.
_____. 1986 (2001). *Howl's Moving Castle*. New York: Harper Trophy.
_____. 1990 (2001). *Castle in the Air*. New York: HarperCollins.
_____. 1993 (2000). *Hexwood*. London: HarperCollins.
_____. 2008. *House of Many Ways*. London: HarperCollins.
Kaye, Marilyn. 2001. *Happy Birthday, Dear Amy (Replica 16)*. New York: Bantam.
_____. 2009. *Out of Sight Out of Mind (Gifted 1)*. London: Macmillan Children's Books.
_____. 2010. *Now You See Me* (*Gifted 5*). London: Macmillan.
Kemp, Gene. 1985. *Jason Bodger and the Priory Ghost*. London: Faber and Faber.
Kernaghan, Eileen. 2000. *The Snow Queen*. Saskatoon: Thistledown.
Kindl, Patrice. 1997. *The Woman in the Wall*. Boston: Houghton Mifflin.
Lanagan, Margo. 2008 (2010). *Tender Morsels*. London: Vintage.
Lang, Andrew. 1889a. *Prince Prigio*. London: J.W. Arrowsmith.
_____. 1889b. *The Blue Fairy Book*. London: Longmans, Green.
_____. 1900. *The Grey Fairy Book*. London: Longmans, Green.
Lawrence, Louise. 1982. *The Earth Witch*. London: William Collins.
Lee, Stan, and Jack Kirby. 1961. *The Fantastic Four*. Vol. 1, No. 1. New York: Marvel Comics.
Levine, Gail Carson. 2008. *Ever*. New York: HarperCollins.
Lewis, C.S. 1950 (2001). *The Lion, the Witch and the Wardrobe*. In *The Chronicles of Narnia*. London: Collins.
Lindbergh, Anne. 1982 (2003). *The People in Pineapple Place*. Cambridge, Mass.: Candlewick Press.
Malley, Gemma. 2007 (2008). *The Declaration*. London: Bloomsbury.
_____. 2008 (2009). *The Resistance*. London: Bloomsbury.
_____. 2010 (2011). *The Legacy*. London: Bloomsbury.
Meacham, Margaret. 2001. *Quiet! You're Invisible*. New York: Holiday House.
Meyer, Stephenie. 2005–2008. *The Twilight Saga*. New York: Little, Brown.
Nesbit, Edith. 1907 (1956). *The Enchanted Castle*. London: Ernest Benn Limited.
Neufeld, Sarah. 2004. *Visibility*. Lincoln, Neb.: iUniverse.
Nimmo, Jenny. 2004. *Charlie Bone and the Blue Boa*. London: Egmont.
Noël, Alyson. 2009–2011. *The Immortals* series. New York: St. Martin's Press.
Pearce, Philippa. 1958. *Tom's Midnight Garden*. Oxford: Oxford University Press.
Plato. 2004. *The Republic*. Translated by Benjamin Jowett. Retrieved from http://ebooks.adelaide.edu.au/p/plato/p71r/index.html.
Pratchett, Terry. 2003. *The Wee Free Men*. London: Doubleday.
_____. 2004. *A Hat Full of Sky*. London: Doubleday.
_____. 2006. *Wintersmith*. London: Doubleday.
_____. 2010. *I Shall Wear Midnight*. London: Doubleday.
Price, Susan. 1987 (1989). *The Ghost Drum*. London: Faber and Faber.
_____. 1992 (1994). *Ghost Song*. London: Faber and Faber.
_____. 1994 (1995). *Ghost Dance*. London: Faber and Faber.
_____. 1999. *The Ghost Wife*. London: Scholastic Children's Books.
Pullman, Philip. 1995 (1998). *His Dark Materials 1: Northern Lights*. London: Scholastic.

_____. 1997 (2007). *His Dark Materials 2: The Subtle Knife*. London: Scholastic.
_____. 2000 (2001). *His Dark Materials 3: The Amber Spyglass*. London: Scholastic.
Rodgers, Mary. 1972 (1976). *Freaky Friday*. Harmondsworth: Puffin Books.
_____. 1982 (1984). *Summer Switch*. Harmondsworth: Puffin Books.
Rowling, J.K. 1997–2007. *Harry Potter* series. London: Bloomsbury.
Ruby, Laura. 2006 (2007). *The Wall and the Wing*. New York: HarperCollins.
_____. 2007. *The Chaos King*. New York: HarperCollins.
Say, Allen. 1995. *Stranger in the Mirror*. New York: Houghton Mifflin.
Schoolcraft, Henry R. (ed.) 1856. *Hiawatha, and Other Oral Legends, Mythologic and Allegoric, of the North American Indians*. Philadelphia: J.B. Lippincott.
Shelley, Mary. 1831 (1996). *Frankenstein, or The Modern Prometheus*. Ware: Wordsworth.
Shusterman, Neal. 2004 (2010). *The Schwa Was Here*. New York: Puffin.
Stetson, Charlotte Perkins. 1892. "The Yellow Wallpaper." *The New England Magazine* 11 (5), 647–657. Retrieved from http://digital.library.cornell.edu/n/newe/.
Stine, R.L. 1993 (1994). *Let's Get Invisible* (*Goosebumps* 6). London: Scholastic.
Swindells, Robert. 1999 (2000). *Invisible!* London: Corgi Yearling Books.
Taylor, Cora. 2005. *Adventure in Istanbul*. Regina, Saskatchewan: Coteau.
Tiernan, Cate. 2010 (2011). *Immortal Beloved*. London: Hodder and Stoughton.
_____. 2012. *Darkness Falls (Immortal Beloved 2)*. London: Hodder and Stoughton.
Tolkien, John Ronald Ruel. 1937 (1999). *The Hobbit, or There and Back Again*. London: HarperCollins.
_____. 1954–1955. *The Lord of the Rings*. London: Allen and Unwin.
Townson, Hazel. 2002. *The Invisible Boy*. London: Andersen Press.
Wahl, Mats. 2003. *Den osynlige* (*The Invisible*). Stockholm: Brombergs.
Wells, Herbert George. 1897 (1992). *The Invisible Man: A Grotesque Romance*. New York: Tom Doherty.
Wheeler, Post (ed.). 1912. *Russian Wonder Tales*. London: Adam and Charles Black.
Whitcomb, Laura. 2005. *A Certain Slant of Light*. Boston: Houghton Mifflin.
Winterson, Jeanette. 2006 (2008). *Tanglewreck*. London: A&C.
Yorinks, Arthur, and Doug Cushman. 2011. *The Invisible Man*. New York: Harper Collins.
Zevin, Gabrielle. 2005. *Elsewhere*. London: Bloomsbury.

Secondary Sources

Abate, Michelle Ann. 2008. "Trans/Forming Girlhood: Transgenderism, the Tomboy Formula, and Gender Identity Disorder in Sharon Dennis Wyeth's *Tomboy Trouble*." *The Lion and the Unicorn*, 32 (1), 40–60.
Adler, Sue. 1993. "Aprons and Attitudes: A Consideration of Feminism in Children's Books." In H. Claire, J. Maybin, and J. Swann (eds.), *Equality Matters: Case Studies from the Primary School*. Clevedon: Multilingual Matters, 111–123.
Armitt, Lucie. 2000. *Contemporary Women's Fiction and the Fantastic*. New York: St. Martin's Press.
Armstrong, Judith. 1978. "Ghosts as Rhetorical Devices in Children's Fiction." *Children's Literature in Education*, 9 (2), 59–66.
_____. 1980. "Ghost Stories: Exploiting the Convention." *Children's Literature in Education*, 11 (3), 117–123.
Attebery, Brian. 1992. *Strategies of Fantasy*. Bloomington: Indiana University Press.
_____. 2002. *Decoding Gender in Science Fiction*. New York: Routledge.
Babbitt, Natalie. 1988. "Metamorphosis." *The Horn Book Magazine*, 64 (5, September-October 1988), 582–589.
Bacchilega, Cristina. 1997. *Postmodern Fairy Tales: Gender and Narrative Strategies*. Philadelphia: University of Pennsylvania Press.
Bakhtin, Mikhail. 1981. *The Dialogic Imagination*. Austin: University of Texas Press.
_____. 1984. *Problems of Dostoevsky's Poetics*. Minneapolis: University of Minnesota Press.
Bal, Mieke. 1997. *Narratology: Introduction to the Theory of Narrative*. Second edition. Toronto: University of Toronto Press.

_____. 1999. Introduction. In M. Bal, J. Crewe, and L. Spitzer (ed.). *Acts of Memory: Cultural Recall in the Present*. Hanover: University Press of New England, vii–xvii.
Banet-Weiser, Sarah. 2004. "Girls Rule! Gender, Feminism and Nickelodeon." *Critical Studies in Media Communication*, 21 (2), 119–139.
Barr, Marleen S. (ed.). 2000. *Future Females, The Next Generation: New Voices and Velocities in Feminist Science Fiction Criticism*. Lanham: Rowman and Littlefield.
Bauer, Dale M. 1988. *Feminist Dialogics: A Theory of Failed Community*. Albany: State University of New York Press.
Bell, Christine. 2012. *Visible Women: Tales of Age, Gender and In/Visibility*. Newcastle upon Tyne: Cambridge Scholars Publishing.
Berenstein, Rhona J. 1996. *Attack of the Leading Ladies: Gender, Sexuality, and Spectatorship in Classic Horror Cinema*. New York: Columbia University Press.
Bertens, Hans. 1991. "Postmodern Cultures." In E.J. Smyth (ed.). *Postmodernism and Contemporary Fiction*, London: Batsford, 123–137.
Blommaert, Jan. 2001. "Context is/as Critique." *Critique of Anthropology*, 21 (1), 13–32.
Bordo, Susan M. 1990. "The Body and the Reproduction of Femininity: A Feminist Appropriation of Foucault." In A.M. Jaggar and S.R. Bordo (eds.). *Gender/Body/Knowledge: Feminist Reconstructions of Being and Knowing*. New Brunswick: Rutgers University Press, 13–33.
Braidotti, Rosi. 1991. *Patterns of Dissonance*. Cambridge: Polity Press.
_____. 1996. "Cyberfeminism with a Difference." Retrieved from http://www.let.uu.nl/womens_studies/rosi/cyberfem-htm.
_____. 2005. *Metamorphoses: Towards a Materialist Theory of Becoming*. Cambridge: Polity Press.
Braithwaite, Ann. 2002. "The Personal, the Political, Third-wave and Postfeminisms." *Feminist Theory*, 3 (3), 335–344.
Bramwell, Peter. 2005. "Fantasy, Psychoanalysis and Adolescence: Magic and Maturation in Fantasy." In K. Reynolds (ed.), *Modern Children's Literature: An Introduction*. Basingstoke: Palgrave Macmillan, 141–155.
Brennan Croft, Janet. 2008. "Nice, Good, or Right: Faces of the Wise Woman in Terry Pratchett's 'Witches' Novels." *Mythlore* 26 (3–4), 151–164.
Brighenti, Andrea. 2007. "Visibility: A Category for the Social Sciences." *Current Sociology*, 55 (3), 323–342.
Brison, Susan J. 1999. "Trauma Narratives and the Remaking of the Self." In M. Bal, J. Crewe, and L. Spitzer (eds.), *Acts of Memory: Cultural Recall in the Present*. Hanover: University Press of New England, 39–54.
Brooks, Peter. 1995. *The Melodramatic Imagination: Balzac, Henry James, Melodrama, and the Mode of Excess*. New Haven: Yale University Press.
Brown, Joanne, and Nancy St. Clair. 2002. *Declarations of Independence: Empowered Girls in Young Adult Literature, 1990–2001*. Lanham: Scarecrow Press.
Butler, Charles. 2006. *Four British Fantasists: Place and Culture in the Children's Fantasies of Penelope Lively, Alan Garner, Diana Wynne Jones, and Susan Cooper*. London: Scarecrow Press.
_____. 2009. "Experimental Girls: Feminist and Transgender Discourses in Bill's New Frock and Marvin Redpost: Is He a Girl?" *Children's Literature Association Quarterly*, 34 (1), 3–20.
Butler, Judith. 1993. *Bodies That Matter: On the Discursive Limits of "Sex."* New York: Routledge.
_____. 1996. "Gender as Performance." In P. Osborne (ed.), *A Critical Sense: Interviews with Intellectuals*. London: Routledge, 109–125.
_____. 1999. *Gender Trouble: Feminism and the Subversion of Identity*. Second edition. New York: Routledge.
Bynum, Caroline Walker. 2001. *Metamorphosis and Identity*. New York: Zone Books.
Campbell, Joseph. 1976. *The Masks of God (Vol. 1): Primitive Mythology*. Harmondsworth: Penguin.
_____. 1949 (1993). *The Hero with a Thousand Faces*. London: Fontana Press.
Case, Sue-Ellen. 1991. "Tracking the Vampire." *Differences: A Journal of Feminist Cultural Studies*, 3 (2), 1–20.

Cavarero, Adriana. 2000. *Relating Narratives: Storytelling and Selfhood*. London: Routledge.
Cawelti, John G. 1977. *Adventure, Mystery, and Romance: Formula Stories as Art and Popular Culture*. Chicago: University of Chicago Press.
Chapman, Edgar L. 1992. "'Seeing' Invisibility: Or Invisibility as Metaphor in Thomas Berger's Being Invisible." *Journal of the Fantastic in the Arts*, 4 (2), 65–93.
Chappell, Shelley. 2007. *Werewolves, Wings, and Other Weird Transformations: Fantastic Metamorphosis in Children's and Young Adult Fantasy Literature*. Sydney: Macquarie University.
Clark, Beverly Lyon. 1993. "Fairy Godmothers or Wicked Stepmothers? The Uneasy Relationship of Feminist Theory and Children's Criticism." *Children's Literature Association Quarterly*, 18 (4), 171–176.
_____. 1999. Introduction. In B.L. Clark and M.R. Higonnet (eds.), *Girls, Boys, Books, Toys: Gender in Children's Literature and Culture*. Baltimore: Johns Hopkins University Press, 1–8.
Clark, Roger. 2002. "Why All the Counting? Feminist Social Science Research on Children's Literature." *Children's Literature in Education*, 33 (4), 285–295.
Clarke, Bruce. 1995. *Allegories of Writing: The Subject of Metamorphosis*. Albany: State University of New York Press.
Comoletti, Laura B., and Michael D.C. Drout. 2001. "How They Do Things with Words: Language, Power, Gender, and the Priestly Wizards of Ursula K. LeGuin's Earthsea Books." *Children's Literature*, 29, 113–141.
Cosslett, T. 2002. "'History from Below': Time-slip Narratives and National Identity." *The Lion and the Unicorn*, 26 (2), 243–253.
Cranny-Francis, Anne. 1990. *Feminist Fiction: Feminist Uses of Generic Fiction*. Cambridge: Polity Press.
Creed, Barbara. 1993. *The Monstrous-feminine: Film, Feminism, Psycho-Analysis*. New York: Routledge.
Cronin, Anne. M. 2000. "Consumerism and 'Compulsory Individuality': Women, Will and Potential." In S. Ahmed, J. Kilby, C. Lury, M. McNeil, and B. Skeggs (eds.), *Transformations: Thinking Through Feminism*. London: Routledge, 273–287.
Cruikshank, Margaret. 2003. *Learning to be Old: Gender, Culture, and Aging*. Lanham: Rowman and Littlefield.
Curti, Lidia. 1998. *Female Stories, Female Bodies: Narrative, Identity and Representation*. London: Macmillan Press.
Davion, Victoria. 1994. "Is Ecofeminism Feminist?" In K.J. Warren (ed.), *Ecological Feminism*. London: Routledge, 8–28.
DeLamotte, Eugenia C. 1990. *Perils of the Night: A Feminist Study of Nineteenth-century Gothic*. New York: Oxford University Press.
De Lauretis, Teresa. 1984. *Alice Doesn't: Feminism, Semiotics, Cinema*. Bloomington: Indiana University Press.
DeLuca, Kevin Michael. 2001. "Trains in the Wilderness: The Corporate Roots of Environmentalism." *Rhetoric and Public Affairs*, 4 (4), 633–652.
Dickens, David B. 1992. "Rings, Belts, and a Bird's Nest: Invisibility in German Literature." *Journal of the Fantastic in the Arts*, 4 (2), 29–48.
Donawerth, Jane. 1997. *Frankenstein's Daughters: Women Writing Science Fiction*. Syracuse: Syracuse University Press.
Easun, Sue. 1994. "From Metaphor to Metamorphosis." *Canadian Children's Literature*, 20 (1), 40–47.
Eliade, Mircea. 1972. *Shamanism: Archaic Techniques of Ecstasy*. Princeton: Princeton University Press.
Ellis Davidson, H.R. 1973. "Hostile Magic in the Icelandic Sagas." In V. Newall (ed.), *The Witch Figure*. London: Routledge and Kegan Paul, 20–41.
Ellis, Kate Ferguson. 1989. *The Contested Castle: Gothic Novels and the Subversion of Domestic Ideology*. Chicago: University of Illinois Press.
Etherington, Kim. 2003. "Trauma, the Body and Transformation." In K. Etherington (ed.), *Trauma, the Body and Transformation: A Narrative Inquiry*. London: Jessica Kingsley Publishers, 22–39.

Evans, Caroline, and Lorraine Gamman. 1995. "The Gaze Revisited, or Reviewing Queer Viewing." In P. Burston and C. Richardson (ed.), *A Queer Romance: Lesbians, Gay Men and Popular Culture*. London: Routledge, 12–61.
Fairclough, Norman. 1989. *Language and Power*. London: Longman.
Felski, Rita. 2000. *Doing Time: Feminist Theory and Postmodern Culture*. New York: New York University Press.
Fischer, John Martin, and Ruth Curl. 1996. "Philosophical Models of Immortality in Science Fiction." In George Slusser, Gary Westfahl, and Eric S. Rabkin (eds.). *Immortal Engines: Life Extension and Immortality in Science Fiction and Fantasy*. Athens: University of Georgia Press, 3–12.
Flanagan, Victoria. 2008. *Into the Closet: Cross-dressing and the Gendered Body in Children's Literature and Film*. New York: Routledge.
Flax, Jane. 1990. "Postmodernism and Gender Relations in Feminist Theory." In L.J. Nicholson (ed.), *Feminism/Postmodernism*, New York: Routledge, 39–62.
Foucault, Michel. 1972. *The Archeology of Knowledge*. London: Tavistock.
_____. 1978. *The History of Sexuality, Vol. 1*. London: Allen Lane.
_____. 1979. *Discipline and Punish: The Birth of the Prison*. Harmondsworth: Penguin Books.
_____. 2006. *Psychiatric Power: Lectures at the Collège de France 1973–1974*. New York: Picador.
Fox, Greer Litton. 1977. "'Nice Girl': Social Control of Women through a Value Construct." *Signs*, 2.4, 805–817.
French, Marilyn. 1985. *Beyond Power: On Women, Men, and Morals*. London: Jonathan Cape.
Gamman, Lorraine. 1988. "Watching the Detectives: The Enigma of the Female Gaze." In L. Gamman and M. Marshment (eds.), *The Female Gaze: Women as Viewers of Popular Culture*. London: Women's Press, 8–26.
_____, and Margaret Marshment. 1988. Introduction. In L. Gamman and M. Marshment (eds.), *The Female Gaze: Women as Viewers of Popular Culture*. London: Women's Press, 1–7.
Gelder, Ken. 1994. *Reading the Vampire*. London: Routledge.
Genette, Gérard. 1997. *Palimpsests: Literature in the Second Degree*. Lincoln: University of Nebraska Press.
Gill, Rosalind. 2008. "Culture and Subjectivity in Neoliberal and Postfeminist Times." *Subjectivity*, 25, 432–445.
Grant, John. 2000. "Gulliver Unravels: Generic Fantasy and the Loss of Subversion." *Extrapolation*, 41 (1), 21–27.
Haase, Donald (ed.). 2004. *Fairy Tales and Feminism: New Approaches*. Detroit: Wayne State University Press.
Halberstam, Judith. 1995. *Skin Shows: Gothic Horror and the Technology of Monsters*. Durham: Duke University Press.
_____. 1998. *Female Masculinity*. Durham: Duke University Press.
_____. 2005. *In a Queer Time and Place: Transgender Bodies, Subcultural Lives*. New York: New York University Press.
Haldane, Michael. 2006a. "The Translation of the Unseen Self: Fortunatus, Mercury and the Wishing-Hat." *Folklore*, 117 (August 2006), 171–189.
_____. 2006b. "From Plato to Pullman — The Circle of Invisibility and Parallel Worlds: Fortunatus, Mercury, and the Wishing-Hat, Part II." *Folklore*, 117 (December 2006), 261–278.
Halifax, Joan. 1980. *Shamanic Voices: A Survey of Visionary Narratives*. Harmondsworth: Penguin.
Hall, Linda. 2001. "'Time No Longer': History, Enchantment and the Classic Time-slip Story." In F.M. Collins and J. Graham (eds.), *Historical Fiction for Children: Capturing the Past*. London: David Fulton, 43–53.
Haraway, Donna J. 1991. *Simians, Cyborgs, and Women: The Reinvention of Nature*. London: Free Association Books.
Harvey, Youngsook Kim. 1979. *Six Korean Women: The Socialization of Shamans*. St. Paul: West Publishing.
Heiland, Donna. 2004. *Gothic and Gender: An Introduction*. Oxford: Blackwell Publishing.
Heilbrun, Carolyn G. 1982. *Toward a Recognition of Androgyny*. New York: W.W. Norton.
Herman, David. 2004. *Story Logic: Problems and Possibilities of Narrative*. Lincoln: University of Nebraska Press.

Hoeveler, Diane Long. 1998. *Gothic Feminism: The Professionalization of Gender from Charlotte Smith to the Brontës*. University Park: Penn State University Press.
Hopkinson, Nalo. 2002. "Looking for Clues: A Guest of Honor Speech, WisCon 26, May 24–27, 2002." Retrieved from http://www.wiscon.info/downloads/hopkinson.pdf.
Hughes, Felicity A. 1990. "Children's Literature: Theory and Practice." In P. Hunt (ed.), *Children's Literature: The Development of Criticism*. London: Routledge, 71–89.
Hume, Kathryn. 1984. *Fantasy and Mimesis: Responses to Reality in Western Literature*. New York: Methuen.
Hunt, Peter. 1990. Introduction. In P. Hunt (ed.), *Children's Literature: The Development of Criticism*, London: Routledge, 1–13.
_____. 2001. *Children's Literature*. Oxford: Blackwell.
_____, and Millicent Lenz. 2001. *Alternative Worlds in Fantasy Fiction*. London: Continuum.
Hutcheon, Linda. 1989. *The Politics of Postmodernism*. London: Routledge.
Jackson, Anna. 2008. "Uncanny Hauntings, Canny Children." In A. Jackson, K. Coats, and R. McGillis (eds.), *The Gothic in Children's Literature: Haunting the Borders*. New York: Routledge, 157–176.
Jackson, Carolyn, and Penny Tinkler. 2007. "'Ladettes' and 'Modern Girls': 'Troublesome' Young Femininities." *The Sociological Review*, 55 (2), 251–272.
Jackson, Rosemary. 1981. *Fantasy: The Literature of Subversion*. London: Routledge.
James, Allison, and Adrian C. James. 2004. *Constructing Childhood: Theory, Policy and Social Practice*. Basingstoke: Palgrave Macmillan.
Jenks, Chris. 1996. *Childhood*. New York: Routledge.
Kaplan, D. 2010. "Disrupted Expectations: Young/Old Protagonists in Diana Wynne Jones's Novels." *Journal of the Fantastic in the Arts*, 21 (2), 197–209.
Kinder, Marsha. 2000. "From Mutation to Morphing: Cultural Transformations from Greek Myth to Children's Media Culture." In V. Sobchack (ed.), *Meta-morphing: Visual Transformation and the Culture of Quick-Change*. Minneapolis: University of Minnesota Press, 59–82.
Krasniewicz, Louise. 2000. Magical Transformations: Morphing and Metamorphosis in Two Cultures. In V. Sobchack (ed.), *Meta-morphing: Visual Transformation and the Culture of Quick-Change*, Minneapolis: University of Minnesota Press, 41–58.
Kristeva, Julia. 1974 (1986). *About Chinese Women*. London: Marion Boyars.
Kuznets, Lois R. 1994. *When Toys Come Alive: Narratives of Animation, Metamorphosis, and Development*. New Haven: Yale University Press.
Larbalestier, Justine. 2002. *The Battle of the Sexes in Science Fiction*. Middletown: Wesleyan University Press.
Lassén-Seger, Maria. 2006. *Adventures into Otherness: Child Metamorphs in Twentieth-century Children's Literature*. Åbo: Åbo Akademi.
Lee, Judith. 1996. "'We Are All Kin': Relatedness, Mortality, and the Paradox of Human Immortality." George Slusser, Gary Westfahl, and Eric S. Rabkin (eds.). *Immortal Engines: Life Extension and Immortality in Science Fiction and Fantasy*. Athens: University of Georgia Press, 170–182.
Lee, Linda J. 2008. "Guilty Pleasures: Reading Romance Novels as Reworked Fairy Tales." *Marvels and Tales: Journal of Fairy-Tale Studies*, 22 (1), 52–66.
Lefanu, Sarah. 1988. *In the Chinks of the World Machine: Feminism and Science Fiction*. London: Women's Press.
Lehtonen, Sanna. 2008. "Invisible Girls: Discourses of Femininity and Power in Children's Fantasy." *International Research in Children's Literature*, 1 (2), 213–226.
_____. 2009. "What Has That One-woman Force of Chaos Done to These Spells? A Girl's Metamorphosis, Voice and Agency in Diana Wynne Jones's *Howl's Moving Castle*." In B. Drillsma-Milgrom and L. Kirstinä (eds.), *Metamorphoses in Children's Literature and Culture*. Turku: Enostone, 261–269.
_____, and Piia Varis. 2009. "Examining Gender in an Autobiography and a Children's Novel: Possibilities and Challenges of Applying Feminist CDA." In J. De Bres, J. Holmes, and M. Marra (ed.), *Proceedings of the 5th International Gender and Language Association Conference IGALA 5*. Wellington: Victoria University of Wellington, 1–12.

_____. 2010a. "If You Thought This Story Sour, Sweeten It with Your Own Telling: Cross-cultural Intertextuality and a Feminist Poetics of Rewriting in Susan Price's *Ghost Dance*." *Barnboken—Journal of Children's Literature Research*, 33 (1), 5–16.
_____. 2010b. "Coal-tinged Realism Meets Female Gothic: Gender, Class and Desire in *The Ghost Wife* by Susan Price." *The Journal of Children's Literature Studies*, 7 (3), 1–18.
_____. 2011. "Shifting Back to and Away From Girlhood: Magic Changes in Age in Children's Fantasy Novels by Diana Wynne Jones." *Papers: Explorations into Children's Literature*, 21 (1), 19–32.
Löw, Martina. 2006. "The Social Construction of Space and Gender." *European Journal of Women's Studies*, 13 (2), 119–133.
Lundquist, Lynne. 1996. "Living Dolls: Images of Immortality in Children's Literature." In George Slusser, Gary Westfahl, and Eric S. Rabkin (eds.), *Immortal Engines: Life Extension and Immortality in Science Fiction and Fantasy*. Athens: University of Georgia Press, 201–210.
Lurie, Alison. 1990. *Don't Tell the Grown-Ups: The Subversive Power of Children's Literature*. Boston: Little, Brown.
Mack-Canty, Colleen. 2004. "Third-Wave Feminism and the Need to Reweave the Nature/Culture Duality." *NWSA Journal*, 16 (3), 154–179.
Mallan, Kerry. 2009. *Gender Dilemmas in Children's Fiction*. Basingstoke: Palgrave Macmillan.
Manlove, Colin N. 1999. *The Fantasy Literature of England*. Basingstoke: Macmillan Press.
_____. 2003. *From Alice to Harry Potter: Children's Fantasy in England*. Christchurch: Cyberedtions.
Marcus, Sharon. 2007. *Between Women: Friendship, Desire and Marriage in Victorian England*. Princeton: Princeton University Press.
Marshall, Elizabeth. 2004. "Stripping for the Wolf: Rethinking Representations of Gender in Children's Literature." *Reading Research Quarterly*, 39 (3), 256–270.
McCallum, Robyn. 1999. *Ideologies of Identity in Adolescent Fiction: The Dialogic Construction of Subjectivity*. New York: Garland.
McHale, Brian. 1992. *Constructing Postmodernism*. London: Routledge.
McNay, Lois. 2000. *Gender and Agency: Reconfiguring the Subject in Feminist and Social Theory*. Cambridge: Polity Press.
_____. 2008. *Against Recognition*. Cambridge: Polity Press.
McRobbie, Angela. 2009. *The Aftermath of Feminism: Gender, Culture and Social Change*. London: Sage.
Mendlesohn, Farah. 2005. *Diana Wynne Jones: The Fantastic Tradition and Children's Literature*. London: Routledge.
_____. 2008. *Rhetorics of Fantasy*. Middletown, CT: Wesleyan University Press.
Mikkonen, Kai. 1997. *The Writer's Metamorphosis: Tropes of Literary Reflection and Revision*. Tampere: Tampere University Press.
Millard, Elaine, Sara Mills, and Lynne Pearce. 1996. "French Feminisms." In S. Mills and L. Pearce (eds.), *Feminist Readings/Feminists Reading*. Hemel Hempstead: Prentice Hall, 153–184.
Miller, Joseph D. 1996. "Living Forever or Dying in the Attempt: Mortality and Immortality in Science and Science Fiction." George Slusser, Gary Westfahl and Eric S. Rabkin (eds.), *Immortal Engines: Life Extension and Immortality in Science Fiction and Fantasy*. Athens: University of Georgia Press, 77–89.
Mills, Sara. 1995. *Feminist Stylistics*. London: Routledge.
_____. 1996. *Discourse*. London: Routledge.
Moore, Suzanne. 1988. "Here's Looking at You, Kid!" In L. Gamman and M. Marshment (eds.), *The Female Gaze: Women as Viewers of Popular Culture*. London: Women's Press, 44–59.
Mulvey, Laura. 1975. "Visual Pleasure and Narrative Cinema." *Screen*, 16 (3), 6–18.
Myhill, Debra, and Susan Jones. 2004. "Noisy Boys and Invisible Girls?" *Literacy Today*, 41 (December 2004), 20–21.
Nadelman Lynn, Ruth. 2005. *Fantasy Literature for Children and Young Adults: A Comprehensive Guide*. Fifth edition. Westport, Conn.: Libraries Unlimited.
Nikolajeva, Maria. 1988. *The Magic Code: The Use of Magical Patterns in Fantasy for Children*. Stockholm: Almqvist and Wiksell International.

_____. 2003. "Fairy Tale and Fantasy: From Archaic to Postmodern." *Marvels and Tales: Journal of Fairy-Tale Studies*, 17 (1), 138–156.
Österlund, Maria. 2005. *Förklädda flickor: Könsöverskridning i 1980-talets svenska ungdomsroman* (*Girls in Disguise: Gender Transgression in Swedish Young Adult Fiction of the 1980s*). Åbo: Åbo Akademi.
Owens, Craig. 1985. "The Discourse of Others: Feminists and Postmodernism." In H. Foster (ed.), *Postmodern Culture*. London: Pluto Press, 57–82.
Oziewicz, Marek. 2010. "Representations of Eastern Europe in Philip Pullman's *His Dark Materials*, Jonathan Stroud's *The Bartimeus Trilogy*, and J.K. Rowling's *Harry Potter* Series." *International Research in Children's Literature* 3 (1), 1–14.
Palmer, Paulina. 1999. *Lesbian Gothic: Transgressive Fictions*. New York: Cassell.
Paul, Lissa. 1987. "Enigma Variations: What Feminist Theory Knows about Children's Literature." *Signal*, 54 (September 1987), 189–201.
_____. 2005. "Feminism Revisited." In P. Hunt (ed.), *Understanding Children's Literature*, London: Routledge, 114–127.
Pearson, Carol, and Katherine Pope. 1981. *The Female Hero in American and British Literature*. New York: R.R. Bowker.
Pennell, Beverley. 2002. "Redeeming Masculinity at the End of the Second Millennium." In J. Stephens (ed.), *Ways of Being Male: Representing Masculinities in Children's Literature and Film*. New York: Routledge, 55–77.
Phelan, Peggy. 1993. *Unmarked: The Politics of Performance*. London: Routledge.
Potvin, Liza. 2003. "Voodooism and Female Quest Patterns in Margaret Atwood's *Cat's Eye*." *Journal of Popular Culture*, 36 (3), 636–650.
Pratt, Annis. 1982. *Archetypal Patterns in Women's Fiction*. Brighton: Harvester Press.
Propp, Vladimir. 2005. *Morphology of the Folktale*. Revised second edition. Austin: University of Texas Press.
Pugh, Tison. 2008. "'There Lived in the Land of Oz Two Queerly Made Men': Queer Utopianism and Antisocial Eroticism in L. Frank Baum's Oz Series." *Marvels and Tales: Journal of Fairy-Tale Studies*, 22 (2), 217–239.
Purkiss, Diane. 1996. *The Witch in History: Early Modern and Twentieth-century Representations*. London: Routledge.
Rabinowitz, Rebecca. 2004. "Messy New Freedoms: Queer Theory and Children's Literature." In S. Chapleau (ed.), *New Voices in Children's Literature Criticism*. Lichfield: Pied Piper, 19–28.
Radway, Janice. 1987. *Reading the Romance: Women, Patriarchy and Popular Literature*. London: Verso.
Raninen, Sami. 2008. "Queer Vikings? Transgression of Gender and Same-sex Encounters in the Late Iron Age and Early Medieval Scandinavia." *SQS: Journal of Queer Studies in Finland*, 3 (2), 20–29.
Raudvere, Catharina. 1996. "Now You See Her, Now You Don't: Some Notes on the Conception of Female Shape-shifters in Scandinavian Traditions." In S. Billington and M. Green (eds.), *The Concept of the Goddess*. London: Routledge, 41–55.
Reay, Diane. 2001. "'Spice Girls,' 'Nice Girls,' 'Girlies,' and 'Tomboys': Gender Discourses, Girls' Cultures and Femininities in the Primary Classroom." *Gender and Education*, 13.2, 153–166.
Reynolds, Kimberley. 1994. *Children's Literature in the 1890s and the 1990s*. Plymouth: Northcote House.
_____. 2007. *Radical Children's Literature: Future Visions and Aesthetic Transformations in Juvenile Fiction*. Basingstoke: Palgrave Macmillan.
Roberts, Robin. 1993. *A New Species: Gender and Science in Science Fiction*. Chicago: University of Illinois Press.
Romøren, Rolf, and John Stephens. 2002. "Representing Masculinities in Norwegian and Australian Young Adult Fiction: A Comparative Study." In J. Stephens (ed.), *Ways of Being Male: Representing Masculinities in Children's Literature and Film*. New York: Routledge, 216–233.
Rosen, S.L. 1996. "Alienation as the Price of Immortality: The Tithonus Syndrome in Science Fiction and Fantasy." George Slusser, Gary Westfahl and Eric S. Rabkin (eds.), *Immortal*

Engines: Life Extension and Immortality in Science Fiction and Fantasy. Athens: University of Georgia Press, 125–134.
Ross, Anne. 1973. "The Divine Hag of the Pagan Celts." In V. Newall (ed.), *The Witch Figure*. London: Routledge and Kegan Paul, 139–164.
Rumbold, Margaret. 1997. "Taking the Subject Further." *Papers*, 7 (2), 16–28.
Russ, Joanna. 1981. "Recent Feminist Utopias." In M.S. Barr (ed.), *Future Females: A Critical Anthology*. Bowling Green: Bowling Green University Popular Press, 71–85.
Sellers, Susan. 2001. *Myth and Fairy Tale in Contemporary Women's Fiction*. New York: Palgrave.
Sempruch, Justyna. 2004. "Feminist Constructions of the 'Witch' as a Fantasmatic Other." *Body and Society*, 10 (4), 113–133.
Simpson, Jacqueline. 1973. "Olaf Tryggvason Versus the Powers of Darkness." In V. Newall (ed.), *The Witch Figure*. London: Routledge and Kegan Paul, 165–187.
Skeggs, Beverley. 1997. *Formations of Class and Gender: Becoming Respectable*. London: Sage.
Smith, Dorothy E. 1990. *Texts, Facts, and Femininity: Exploring the Relations of Ruling*. London: Routledge.
Smith, Karen Patricia. 1993. *The Fabulous Realm: A Literary Historical Approach to British Fantasy 1780–1990*. Metuchen: Scarecrow Press.
Smoak, Gregory. 2006. *Ghost Dances and Identity: Prophetic Religion and American Indian Ethnogenesis in the Nineteenth Century*. Ewing: University of California Press.
Sobchack, Vivian. 2000. Introduction. In V. Sobchack (ed.), *Meta-morphing: Visual Transformation and the Culture of Quick-change*. Minneapolis: University of Minnesota Press, xi–xxiii.
Spivack, Charlotte. 1987. *Merlin's Daughters: Contemporary Women Writers of Fantasy*. Westport, Conn.: Greenwood Press.
Stephens, John. 1992. *Language and Ideology in Children's Fiction*. London: Longman.
_____. 1996. "Gender, Genre and Children's Literature." *Signal*, 79 (January 1996), 17–30.
_____, and Robyn McCallum. 1998. *Retelling Stories, Framing Culture: Traditional Story and Metanarratives in Children's Literature*. New York: Garland.
_____. 2002. "'A Page Just Waiting to Be Written On.' Masculinity Schemata and the Dynamics of Subjective Agency in Junior Fiction." In J. Stephens (ed.), *Ways of Being Male: Representing Masculinities in Children's Literature and Film*. New York: Routledge, 38–54.
_____. 2003. "Witch-Figures in Recent Children's Fiction: The Subaltern and the Subversive." In A. Lawson Lucas (ed.), *The Presence of the Past in Children's Literature*. Westport: Praeger, 195–202.
Stewig, John Warren. 1995. "The Witch Woman: A Recurring Motif in Recent Fantasy Writing for Young Readers." *Children's Literature in Education*, 26 (2), 119–133.
Stone, Lynda. 1999. "Experience and Performance: Contrasting 'Identity' in Feminist Theorizings." *Studies in Philosophy and Education*, 18 (5), 327–337.
Sullivan, C.W. 1992. "Fantasy." In D. Butts (ed.), *Stories and Society: Children's Literature in its Social Context*. Basingstoke: Macmillan Press, 97–111.
_____. 1999. "The Influence of *The Mabinogi* on Modern Fantasy Literature." *Celtic Cultural Studies: An Interdisciplinary Online Journal*, Issue 3. Retrieved from http://www.celtic-cultural-studies.com/papers/03/sullivan-01.html.
Sunderland, Jane. 2004. "Gendered Discourses in Children's Literature." *Gender Studies*, 1 (3), 60–84.
Swinfen, Ann. 1984. *In Defence of Fantasy: A Study of the Genre in English and American Literature Since 1945*. London: Routledge and Kegan Paul.
Talbot, Mary. 1995. *Fictions at Work*. London: Longman.
_____. 2010. *Language and Gender*. Cambridge: Polity Press.
Tatar, Maria. 1992. *Off with Their Heads! Fairy Tales and The Culture of Childhood*. Princeton: Princeton University Press.
_____ (ed.). 1999. *The Classic Fairy Tales: Texts, Criticism*. New York: W.W. Norton.
Tedlock, Barbara. 2005. *The Woman in the Shaman's Body: Reclaiming the Feminine in Religion and Medicine*. New York: Bantam Dell.
Thompson, Stith. 1955. *Motif-Index of Folk-Literature: A Classification of Narrative Elements in*

Folktales, Ballads, Myths, Fables, Mediaeval Romances, Exempla, Fabliaux, Jest-Books, and Local Legends. Revised and enlarged edition. Bloomington: Indiana University Press.
Todorov, Tzvetan. 1990. *Genres in Discourse*. Cambridge: Cambridge University Press.
Trites, Roberta Seelinger. 1997. *Waking Sleeping Beauty: Feminist Voices in Children's Novels*. Iowa City: University of Iowa Press.
Turville-Petre, E.O.G. 1964. *Myth and Religion in the North: The Religion of Ancient Scandinavia*. London: Weidenfeld and Nicolson.
Vänskä, Annamari. 2005. "Why Are There No Lesbian Advertisements?" *Feminist Theory*, 6 (1), 67–85.
Vicinus, Martha. 1981. "'Helpless and Unfriended': Nineteenth-Century Domestic Melodrama." *New Literary History*, 13 (1), 127–143.
Walkerdine, Valerie. 1990. *Schoolgirl Fictions*. London: Verso.
_____, Helen Lucey, and June Melody. 2001. *Growing Up Girl: Psychosocial Explorations of Gender and Class*. Basingstoke: Palgrave.
Waller, Alison. 2009. *Constructing Adolescence in Fantastic Realism*. New York: Routledge.
Warner, Marina. 1995. *From the Beast to the Blonde: On Fairy Tales and Their Tellers*. London: Vintage.
_____. 2002. *Fantastic Metamorphoses, Other Worlds: Ways of Telling the Self*. Oxford: Oxford University Press.
_____. 2005. "Knowing Your Daemons: Metamorphosis from the Arabian Nights to Philip Pullman." In E. O'Sullivan, K. Reynolds, and R. Romøren (eds.), *Children's Literature Global and Local: Social and Aesthetic Perspectives*. Oslo: Novus Press, 25–43.
_____. 2008. *Phantasmagoria: Spirit Visions, Metaphors, and Media into the Twenty-first Century*. Oxford: Oxford University Press.
Warren, Karen J. 1994. Introduction. In K.J. Warren (ed.), *Ecological Feminism*, London: Routledge, 1–7.
Waterhouse, Ruth. 1991. "Time for a Ghostly Point of View." *Papers*, 2 (3), 135–142.
Waugh, Patricia. 1989. *Feminine Fictions: Revisiting the Postmodern*. London: Routledge.
Weedon, Chris. 1997. *Feminist Practice and Poststructuralist Theory*. Second edition. Oxford: Blackwell Publishing.
White, Donna R. 1998. *A Century of Welsh Myth in Children's Literature*. Westport, CT: Greenwood Press.
Wilkie-Stibbs, Christine. 2002. *The Feminine Subject in Children's Literature*. London: Routledge.
Williams, Linda. 1996. "When the Woman Looks." In B.K. Grant (ed.), *The Dread of Difference: Gender and the Horror Film*. Austin: University of Texas Press, 15–34.
Working Group on Girls of the NGO Committee on UNICEF and UNICEF's Voices of Youth 2006. "Youth Version of the Report of the Expert Group Meeting on the Elimination of All Forms of Discrimination and Violence Against the Girl Child." Retrieved from http://www.unicef.org/voy/takeaction/ takeaction_3295.html.
Zipes, Jack (ed.). 1986. *Don't Bet on the Prince: Contemporary Feminist Fairy Tales in North America and England*. Aldershot: Gower Publishing.
_____. 2004. Introduction. In J.M. Barrie, *Peter Pan*, edited with an Introduction and Notes by Jack Zipes. New York: Penguin Books, vii–xxvi.

Index

adolescence 28–29, 55, 166, 181, 184, 186, 200*n*9
Adventure in Istanbul 37
age-shifting: in myths and folk literature 42–45; as a narrative device 7–9, 13–14, 20, 23, 42–55, 164; in narratives for children 44–50, 52–55; and reversed aging 164–165, 183–190; *see also* body swapping; immortality; rejuvenation; time-slip narratives
agency 9, 13, 22, 47, 50, 56–57, 60, 98–99, 101–102, 140, 169, 193–195; and adulthood 29, 55, 133, 167; and age-shifting 90–92, 96–97, 125, 127, 133–134, 179, 183–190; intersubjective agency 78, 114, 121, 134, 174, 182–183; and (in)visibility 41, 78, 81–83, 86, 111, 113–114, 116–117, 120–121, 137, 145, 154, 158, 163; and voice 20, 36, 100–101, 111, 142–144, 147
aging 8–9, 13–14, 20–21, 29, 43–44, 48, 54–55, 134, 164; and longevity 43, 50–53, 171–173, 176, 179, 187; queer aging 164ff; *see also* age-shifting
Alexander, Lloyd: *The Chronicles of Prydain* 45
Almost Goodbye, Guzzler! 38
androgyny *see* transgenderism
Anstey, F.: *Vice Versa* 48–49
Archer's Goon 50

Babbitt, Natalie: *Tuck Everlasting* 52–53, 189
Barrie, James Matthew: *Peter Pan: Fantasy in Five Acts* 52
Being Invisible 200*n*40
Benton, Jim: *The Invisible Fran* 38
Beresford, Elisabeth: *Invisible Magic* 203*n*18
Berger, Thomas: *Being Invisible* 200*n*40
The Big Baby—A Little Joke 48
"Bluebeard" stories 91, 94, 97
bodily transformations 1–2, 5, 7–9, 13–14, 20, 22, 27–30, 191–193, 199*n*4
body swapping 46, 49, 99, 103, 115–126
Brontë, Charlotte: *Jane Eyre* 148

Brown, Jeff: *Invisible Stanley* 38
Brown, Judy: *Almost Goodbye, Guzzler!* 38
Browne, Anthony: *The Big Baby—A Little Joke* 48

Castle in the Air 203*n*73, 203*n*75
A Castle of Bone 47–48, 52–53
A Certain Slant of Light 42, 103–104, 136–137, 150–154, 162
The Chaos King 56, 75, 79, 82–83
characterization 18, 20
Charlie Bone and the Blue Boa 40
Chaucer, Geoffrey: "The Wife of Bath's Tale" 45
The Chronicles of Prydain 45
Cicero 32, 39, 141; *De Officiis* 32
Clements, Andrew: *Things Not Seen* 42, 86
closure 21–22, 193; and carnivalesque "time out" 83, 202*n*52; romance closure 53–55, 96–97, 125–126, 150, 178–179
Colin, Beatrice: *My Invisible Sister* 200*n*39
coming of age 8, 21, 46, 57–60, 86–90, 99–102, 113, 122–123, 129, 134–135, 149, 167, 177, 190, 205*n*5
consumer femininity 121–122, 138, 142, 145, 195; *see also* visibility and beauty
Cormier, Robert: *Fade* 40, 42
Cresswell, Helen: *Almost Goodbye, Guzzler!* 38
Cushman, Doug: *The Invisible Man* 38–39

Daughters of the Moon series 75–76
De Officiis 32
The Declaration Trilogy 53
deconstruction 21, 28, 49, 99–103, 111, 115, 118, 122, 124, 126, 129–130, 133–135, 198*n*9
dialogism *see* multivoicedness
discourse 11–15, 198*n*32
Duncan, Lois: *Locked in Time* 53

Eager, Edward: *Half Magic* 38
The Earth Witch 46, 56, 86–91, 97, 122

219

Elsewhere 55, 165, 183, 187–190
embodiment 11–13, 30, 47–48, 55, 91, 100–101, 118, 129–130, 132, 165, 184, 191
empowerment 4–5, 13, 20, 29–30, 41–42, 56–57, 59–61, 73–74, 78, 86, 90, 93, 97–98, 102, 111, 113, 117, 121–122, 133–134, 138, 147, 163, 167, 176–177, 179, 183, 193–195; *see also* agency
The Enchanted Castle 37–38, 47
The Epic of Gilgamesh 50
ethnicity 4, 9, 11, 14, 36, 60, 63, 165, 169, 171, 180, 193, 195, 206n17, 206n19
Ever 54
Ewing, Lynne: *Daughters of the Moon* series 75–76; *Goddess of the Night (Daughters of the Moon 1)* 56, 76–78

Fade 40, 42
The Fantastic Four 1
fantasy (as a genre) 22, 199n57, 199n61
Farmer, Penelope: *A Castle of Bone* 47–48, 52–53
female monstrosity 27, 45, 63–64, 66, 97, 139–140, 148–149, 150, 157–158, 161–162
feminist criticism: and children's literature 3–4, 59–60, 195; eco-feminism 58–59, 201n8; Jungian feminism 46, 58, 168, 205n5; liberal feminism 3–5, 36, 58–60, 90, 92, 105, 111, 113, 122, 125, 133–134, 144, 147, 192–193; postfeminism 4, 60, 121, 145, 194; poststructuralist feminism 4, 11, 90, 100–102, 104, 134, 138–139, 146–147, 169; psychoanalytical feminism 102, 137–140; radical feminism 58–61, 67, 74, 76, 86–91, 98, 167, 170–175, 179, 182–183, 192, 194; second-wave feminism 4, 19, 27, 36, 137, 168; third-wave feminism 4, 11, 13, 27, 36, 114, 192
feminist discourse analysis 10–11; 19–20
Field, Rachel: *Hitty: Her First Hundred Years* 52
Fire and Hemlock 50
"The Fitcher's Bird" 94
focalization 18, 20–21, 37, 54, 57, 137, 141–142, 199n52; and ghost stories 7, 103–104, 151, 163, 203n13, 203n17
Fortunatus 31, 34–35, 200n20
Frankenstein, or The Modern Prometheus 157
Freaky Friday (book) 48–50, 100, 122–126, 128
Freaky Friday (films) 203n61

Gaiman, Neil: *The Graveyard Book* 42
Gardner, Sally: *The Invisible Boy* 38
gaze 5, 33, 35, 42, 77–79, 122, 127, 136–143, 145–147; classing gaze 205n55; and female desire 150–162; imperial gaze and colonialism 69, 141
Ghost Dance 56, 61–64, 67–70, 98, 141, 179–183
The Ghost Drum 56, 61–66, 167, 173–179, 182–183
The Ghost of Thomas Kempe 103
Ghost Song 63, 201n19

ghost stories 22, 103–105, 150–151, 161, 203n13, 203n17
The Ghost Wife 42, 103–104, 136–137, 150–151, 155–162
Ghost World novels 41, 55, 73, 75, 79, 95, 164, 166–170, 173–183, 190, 193
Ghostgirl 41–42, 100, 103–104, 115–118, 136–137, 150–151, 154–155, 160, 162
Gifted series 75
Goddess of the Night (Daughters of the Moon 1) 56, 76–78
Gothic horror 3, 20, 22, 155–162, 197ch1n2, 204n52, 205n54
The Graveyard Book 42
Greenburg, Dan: *Now You See Me… Now You Don't* 38

Haddix, Margaret Peterson: *Turnabout* 55, 165, 183–190
Half Magic 38
Happy Birthday, Dear Amy (Replica 16) 48–50, 100, 122, 126–129
Harry Potter and the Philosopher's Stone 37
A Hat Full of Sky 56, 62, 70–74
heteroglossia *see* multivoicedness
heteronormativity 13, 21, 54–55, 88, 97, 127, 141, 165–166, 172, 178, 188–189
Hexwood 50, 100, 122, 129–135
His Dark Materials trilogy 41, 55–56, 61–67, 70, 164, 166–173, 190
"The History of Jack the Giant-Killer" 31
Hitty: Her First Hundred Years 52
The Hobbit or There and Back Again 37
Hoffmann, Mary: *A Vanishing Tail* 38
Honeycutt, Natalie: *Invisible Lissa* 200n30
Houghton, Eric: *Vincent the Invisible* 38
House of Many Ways 203n75
Howl's Moving Castle 46, 56, 68, 86, 91–98, 100, 122, 126, 193
humanist metaethics 29, 58, 60, 98, 102, 167, 169, 182–183, 193–195
Hurley, Tonya: *Ghostgirl* 41–42, 100, 103–104, 115–118, 136–137, 150–151, 154–155, 160, 162

I Shall Wear Midnight 73
identity 2, 7–8, 11, 27–28, 30, 35–36, 42, 47–50, 58, 75, 91–92, 100–102, 113, 115–118, 120–122, 139, 146, 164–166; and intersectionality 4, 9, 11, 14, 60, 141, 193; narrative identity 12–13, 47, 55, 99–100, 103–104, 107–114, 129–134, 186–190; *see also* embodiment; performativity; subjectivity
Immortal Beloved trilogy 54–55
immortality 8, 50–55, 159, 169, 179, 181–183
The Immortals series 54
intertextuality 8–9, 15–16, 198n34; *see also* rewriting
invisibility: cultural invisibility 8, 35–36, 41, 79–80, 100, 137, 191; in myths and folk literature 30–31; as a narrative device 5, 7–9, 20,

23, 30–42; in narratives for children 36–42; see also visibility
Invisible! 38
The Invisible Boy (Gardner) 38
The Invisible Boy (Townson) 200n30
The Invisible Day 38–39
The Invisible Fran 38
Invisible Lissa 200n30
Invisible Magic 203n18
The Invisible Man (picture book) 38–39
The Invisible Man: A Grotesque Romance 1, 34–35, 37–38, 74, 80
Invisible Stanley 38
Irving, Washington: "Rip Van Winkle" 44

Jane Eyre 148
Jansson, Tove: "Story of the Invisible Child" 200n38
Jason Bodger and the Priory Ghost 203n18
Jocelyn, Marthe: *The Invisible Day* 38–39
Johansson, Kerstin: *Som om jag inte fanns* 200n30
Jones, Diana Wynne: *Archer's Goon* 50; *Castle in the Air* 203n73, 203n75; *Fire and Hemlock* 50; *Hexwood* 50, 100, 122, 129–135; *House of Many Ways* 203n75; *Howl's Moving Castle* 46, 56, 68, 86, 91–98, 100, 122, 126, 193; *The Ogre Downstairs* 40; *The Time of the Ghost* 41–42, 50, 100, 103–115, 118, 122, 129–130, 133, 136–137, 142–147, 150–152

Kaye, Marilyn: *Gifted* series 75; *Happy Birthday, Dear Amy (Replica 16)* 48–50, 100, 122, 126–129; *Now You See Me (Gifted 5)* 100, 103, 118, 120–122; *Out of Sight Out of Mind (Gifted 1)* 41, 100, 103, 115, 118–122
Kemp, Gene: *Jason Bodger and the Priory Ghost* 203n18
Kindl, Patrice: *The Woman in the Wall* 41–42, 103–104, 136–137, 142, 147–150
"The King of the Golden Mountain" 31, 35
Kirby, Jack: *The Fantastic Four* 1

Lanagan, Margo: *Tender Morsels* 44
Lang, Andrew: *Prince Prigio* 202n66
Lawrence, Louise: *The Earth Witch* 46, 56, 86–91, 97, 122
Lee, Stan: *The Fantastic Four* 1
Let's Get Invisible (Goosebumps 6) 40
Levine, Gail Carson: *Ever* 54
Lewis, C.S.: *The Lion, the Witch and the Wardrobe* 44
Lindbergh, Anne: *The People in Pineapple Place* 52–53, 203n18
The Lion, the Witch and the Wardrobe 44
"Little Bear's Son" 44–45
"Little Snow White" 45
Lively, Penelope: *The Ghost of Thomas Kempe* 103
"The Loathly Lady" stories 1, 45–46, 91, 93, 96–97

Locked in Time 53
The Lord of the Rings (book) 34, 57, 74
The Lord of the Rings (films) 194

Malley, Gemma: *The Declaration Trilogy* 53
"The Marriage of Sir Gawain" 45
maturation 30, 46, 51–52, 55, 73, 85, 101, 123–129, 133, 165–167, 174–179, 190; see also coming of age
Meacham, Margaret: *Quiet! You're Invisible* 37
metamorphosis see bodily transformations
Meyer, Stephenie: *The Twilight Saga* 53–54
"Mr. Fox" 94
My Invisible Sister 200n39

narrative sequencing 21–22
Nesbit, Edith: *The Enchanted Castle* 37–38, 47
Neufeld, Sarah: *Visibility* 41, 56, 61, 75, 79–80
Nimmo, Jenny: *Charlie Bone and the Blue Boa* 40
Noël, Alyson: *The Immortals* series 54
Now You See Me (Gifted 5) 100, 103, 118, 120–122
Now You See Me... Now You Don't 38

The Ogre Downstairs 40
"The Old Man Made Young Again" 43
Den Osynlige 203n17
The Others (film) 203n13
Out of Sight Out of Mind (Gifted 1) 41, 100, 103, 115, 118–122

panopticon 11–12, 32–33, 79, 141, 158
paranormal romance 53–55, 194–195
Pearce, Philippa: *Tom's Midnight Garden* 203n18
The People in Pineapple Place 52–53, 203n18
performativity: and age 14, 46–50, 91–97, 123–130, 185–186; and gender 9, 11–12, 46–47, 49, 76–77, 91–97, 117–118, 121, 123–130, 138–139, 142–145, 147–150, 154, 156, 168–169; and parody 12, 49, 91, 96–97, 117; and situational irony 123–124, 143–144
Peter Pan: Fantasy in Five Acts 52
Pinto, Sara: *My Invisible Sister* 200n39
Plato 32, 34, 74, 141; *The Republic* 32
postmodernism 7, 10, 17, 62, 100–102, 114, 118, 134–135, 198n9, 202n7
Pratchett, Terry: *A Hat Full of Sky* 56, 62, 70–74; *I Shall Wear Midnight* 73; *Tiffany Aching* novels 41, 61–62, 70, 75, 91, 95; *The Wee Free Men* 71
Price, Susan: *Ghost Dance* 56, 61–64, 67–70, 98, 141, 179–183; *The Ghost Drum* 56, 61–66, 167, 173–179, 182–183; *Ghost Song* 63, 201n19; *The Ghost Wife* 42, 103–104, 136–137, 150–151, 155–162; *Ghost World* novels 41, 55, 73, 75, 79, 95, 164, 166–170, 173–183, 190, 193
Prince Prigio 202n66
Pullman, Philip: *His Dark Materials* trilogy 41, 55–56, 61–67, 70, 164, 166–173, 190; *The*

Subtle Knife (His Dark Materials 2) 42, 64–67

queer theory 4, 11–13, 36, 55, 74, 90, 98, 140–141, 145, 164–170, 194
quest narrative 10, 22, 57–58, 168, 176, 182–183, 194
Quiet! You're Invisible 37

rejuvenation 8, 42–43, 50–51, 53, 183, 185
The Republic 32
rewriting 5, 8–10, 15, 17–19, 22–23, 36, 38, 56–61, 64, 70, 74, 91, 97, 159, 167–168, 173, 191–195
"Rip Van Winkle" 44
"The Robber Bridegroom" 94
Rodgers, Mary: *Freaky Friday* 48–50, 100, 122–126, 128; *Summer Switch* 48–49
Rowling, J.K. 37, 75; *Harry Potter and the Philosopher's Stone* 37
Ruby, Laura: *The Chaos King* 56, 75, 79, 82–83; *The Wall and the Wing* 56, 75, 79–82

Say, Allen: *A Stranger in the Mirror* 48
school stories 75
The Schwa Was Here 42
science fiction 3, 22, 51, 53, 197*n*2
sexuality 11–13, 35, 42, 54, 64, 76–77, 86, 88, 92, 97, 123, 149–150, 165–166, 171–172; and gaze 42, 77, 127–128, 137–141, 145–146, 151–162; *see also* heteronormativity
shamanism 55, 61–68, 74, 98, 164–183, 190, 193
Shelley, Mary: *Frankenstein; or, The Modern Prometheus* 157
"Shingebiss" legend 206*n*40
"The Shoes That Were Danced to Pieces" 31
Shusterman, Neal: *The Schwa Was Here* 42
The Sixth Sense (film) 203*n*13
social class 4, 9, 14, 60, 151, 155–162, 165–166
Som om jag inte fanns 200*n*30
Stetson, Charlotte Perkins: "The Yellow Wallpaper" 148
Stine, R.L.: *Let's Get Invisible (Goosebumps 6)* 40
"Story of the Invisible Child" 200*n*38
A Stranger in the Mirror 48
subjectivity 2, 11–14, 28, 30, 41–42, 45–47, 50, 55, 60, 76, 84–87, 93–94, 99–102, 104–136, 139, 142, 148–150, 153–155, 162–163, 182–183, 191–194; and liminality 166–170; moral subjectivity and (in)visibility 32–33, 35, 61, 64–65, 71–75, 77; *see also* embodiment; identity; performativity
The Subtle Knife (His Dark Materials 2) 42, 64–67
Summer Switch 48–49
superhero team comics 75
Swindells, Robert: *Invisible!* 38

Tanglewreck 53
Taylor, Cora: *Adventure in Istanbul* 37

Tender Morsels 44
Things Not Seen 42, 86
Tiernan, Cate: *Immortal Beloved* trilogy 54–55
Tiffany Aching novels 41, 61–62, 70, 75, 91, 95
The Time of the Ghost 41–42, 50, 100, 103–115, 118, 122, 129–130, 133, 136–137, 142–147, 150–152
time-slip narratives 20, 21–23, 44, 46, 50, 99, 106, 109, 122, 129–135, 181, 203*n*18, 204*n*77
Tolkien, J.R.R.: *The Hobbit or There and Back Again* 37; *The Lord of the Rings* 34, 57, 74
Tom's Midnight Garden 203*n*18
Townson, Hazel: *The Invisible Boy* 200*n*30
transformations *see* bodily transformations
transgenderism 8, 14, 165, 168–169, 175–176, 179–182, 191
trauma narratives 41, 44, 100, 103–115, 133
triple goddess 45–46, 61, 87–91
Tuck Everlasting 52–53, 189
Turnabout 55, 165, 183–190
The Twilight Saga 53–54
"Tzar Saltan" 44–45

A Vanishing Tail 38
Vice Versa 48–49
Vincent the Invisible 38
visibility: and beauty 42, 60, 117–118, 121–122, 125–128, 135, 137–138, 142–145; in feminist theory 35–36, 111, 136–141, 146, 195; and moral subjectivity 32–33; 35; and recognition 85–86, 102–103, 142, 152, 154; and sexual gaze 42, 77–78, 146–147, 149–150, 154; *see also* invisibility
Visibility 41, 56, 61, 75, 79–80
voice 11, 15–18, 20–21, 100–101, 111, 142–144, 147, 162, 192; and magic as performative language use 65, 68–69, 94–95, 174, 202*n*73

Wahl, Mats: *Den Osynlige* 203*n*17
The Wall and the Wing 56, 75, 79–82
"The Water of Life" 43
The Wee Free Men 71
Wells, Herbert George: *The Invisible Man: A Grotesque Romance* 1, 34–35, 37–38, 74, 80
Whitcomb, Laura: *A Certain Slant of Light* 42, 103–104, 136–137, 150–154, 162
"The White Snake" 43
"The Wife of Bath's Tale" 45
Winterson, Jeanette: *Tanglewreck* 53
witches: and feminist rewritings 36, 56–59, 61–98, 167, 169–183; and moral subjectivity 41, 61, 64–65, 71–75, 98, 118; in myths and fairy tales 9, 35, 45–46, 56–57, 63–64, 70
The Woman in the Wall 41–42, 103–104, 136–137, 142, 147–150

"The Yellow Wall-paper" 148
Yorinks, Arthur: *The Invisible Man* 38–39

Zevin, Gabrielle: *Elsewhere* 55, 165, 183, 187–190

www.ingramcontent.com/pod-product-compliance
Lightning Source LLC
Chambersburg PA
CBHW032051300426
44116CB00007B/688